Contents

CHALLENGES AND OPPORTUNITIES ABROAD

WHITE PAPER ON FOREIGN POLICY

DEPARTMENT OF FOREIGN AFFAIRS

Published by the Stationery Office, Dublin, Ireland

Le ceannach díreach ón
Oifig Dhíolta Foilseachán Rialtais,
Teach Sun Alliance,
Sráid Theach Laighean,
Baile Átha Cliath 2,
nó tríd an bpost ó
Foilseacháin Rialtais, An Rannóg Post-Tráchta,
4–5 Bóthar Fhearchair,
Baile Átha Cliath 2
Teil: 01 661 3111 – fo-líne 4040/4045; Fax: 01 475 2760
nó trí aon díoltóir leabhar.

To be purchased directly from the
Government Publications Sale Office,
Sun Alliance House,
Molesworth Street,
Dublin 2
or by mail order from
Government Publications, Postal Trade Section,
4–5 Harcourt Road,
Dublin 2
Tel: 01 661 3111 – ext. 4040/4045; Fax: 01 475 2760
or through any bookseller.

ISBN 0 7076 2385 5

Design and artwork by Bill and Tina Murphy
Origination by Accu-Plate Ltd
Printed in Ireland by Cahill Printers Ltd

Pn. 2133

Introduction

DICK SPRING T.D.
Tánaiste and Minister for Foreign Affairs

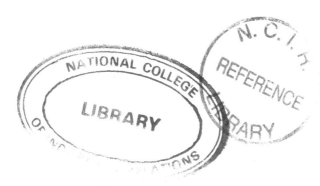

Preparation of the White Paper

A commitment to publish a White Paper on foreign policy was an important element in the policy agreement, *A Government of Renewal*, adopted by Fine Gael, the Labour Party and Democratic Left when the Government took office in December 1994. It was agreed that –

> "A White Paper on Foreign Policy will spell out the principles that underpin Ireland's commitment to peace, security, and co-operation. It will also be a central purpose of the White Paper to encourage debate about all aspects of policy, more transparency in the conduct of policy, and the maximum degree of ownership of policy by the people".

This decision confirmed an initiative I took on 6 February 1994 when, as Tánaiste and Minister for Foreign Affairs in the previous Government, I announced that work was to begin on the publication of a White Paper on foreign policy.

1. *The Tánaiste and Minister for Foreign Affairs, Mr Dick Spring T.D. addressing the 49th session of the UN General Assembly.*

Public Consultation

The decision to publish a White Paper was influenced by the rapid growth over the last few years of public interest in the formulation of foreign policy, and a desire to open this policy to greater public scrutiny. This concern was reflected in the decision to provide for a process of public consultation prior to the drafting of the White Paper. This process involved both the soliciting of written submissions and the holding of a series of public seminars.

Written Submissions

In May 1994, I wrote to over 70 non-governmental organisations (NGOs) inviting them to make written submissions on any aspect of foreign policy. I subsequently announced that it was open to any person or organisation to make such a submission. A total of 64 submissions were received. These have been lodged in the National Archives where they are available for consultation. A list of submissions received is included in the appendices.

Public Seminars

A series of seven public seminars dealing with various aspects of Ireland's foreign policy was held in Universities around the country between November 1994 and March 1995. The topics covered were: Development Cooperation, Human Rights, The European Union, Trade & International Economic Cooperation, the Common Foreign & Security Policy of the European Union, the Irish Foreign Service and the United Nations.

Participation in the seminars, which were advertised in the national press on two separate occasions, was open to all. Attendance at each of the seminars numbered between 200-250. The seminars, which brought members of the public, representatives of NGOs, public representatives and members of the diplomatic corps into direct dialogue with Ministers and civil servants on issues of foreign policy, proved a useful and stimulating innovation. Copies of seminar agendas and papers delivered by invited speakers have also been lodged in the National Archives.

I would like to place on record my gratitude to all those who forwarded written submissions and who participated in the process of public consultation. Both the written submissions and the seminars have provided an important input into the preparation of the White Paper.

Scope and Format of the White Paper

In presenting this White Paper, we have sought as a Government to provide as comprehensive a survey of our foreign policy as possible within a single volume format. It has not been possible to cover each and every issue of foreign policy in a document of this scale, although an effort has been made to present the broad range of Government policy and to address as many as possible of the issues raised at the public seminars and in written submissions.

The White Paper examines foreign policy from a number of perspectives. Most of the Chapters follow a thematic approach. Others, such as those on the *European Union* and *the United Nations*, focus on particular institutions. This approach reflects the reality of foreign policy, where issues overlap and are interconnected.

There is no such thing, for instance, as a self-contained policy on Development Cooperation or Human Rights. The approach adopted by the Government in these areas must, if it is to be effective, inform the full range of Government policy, including our bilateral relations with other states and the positions adopted within international organisations.

I have decided not to include a section on Anglo-Irish Relations and Northern Ireland in the White Paper. This decision was not taken lightly, since these areas of policy are the principal preoccupation, not only of my own day-to-day work, but of a number of senior members of the Government, including of course the Taoiseach. Northern Ireland is the fundamental priority of Irish foreign policy, and it has been since the foundation of the State.

At the time of writing, the situation brought about by the cease-fires with all its challenges and opportunities, is gravely imperilled. The golden

3

opportunity to build a new political order on the island and to improve the material well-being of all Irish people, North and South, is in danger of being lost due to a resumption of violence. It is the absolute resolve of the Government to pursue every avenue through which peace might be restored and to move the peace process speedily towards the goal of all-Party negotiations.

In the context of this White Paper, however, I do think it is appropriate to say two things about Northern Ireland. Since 1969, the engagement of our diplomatic resources in all aspects of this issue has been particularly pronounced and intensive. Public servants, many of them anonymous, have played a major part, a part it is almost impossible to measure, in developing a coherent policy approach under successive Governments.

Through them, Governments have sought to monitor the situation in Northern Ireland, to develop the most constructive dialogue possible with all the protagonists there, and to promote enhanced cooperation in economic, social and other spheres between North and South. The role of the diplomatic service has been of course particularly significant in negotiating the various agreements between the Irish and British Governments, and in mobilising support for them internationally.

Secondly, a lasting settlement of the problem would, without question, open new horizons of potential for relations between Ireland and Britain. It would resolve the last source of contention remaining from the sometimes troubled historical relationship between the two islands. In such circumstances, in the words of the Joint Framework Document, the Governments hope that the relationship between the traditions in Northern Ireland could become a positive bond of further understanding, cooperation and amity, rather than a source of contention, between the wider British and Irish democracies. This goal remains firmly before our eyes.

As stated in the White Paper, Ireland's foreign policy is about much more than self-interest. For many of us it is a statement of the kind of people we are. Irish people are genuinely committed to the principles set out in Article 29 of the Constitution for the conduct of international relations: — the ideal of peace and friendly cooperation amongst nations founded on international justice and morality; the principle of the pacific settlement of international disputes by international arbitration or judicial determination; and the principles of international law as our rule of conduct in our relations with other states.

Throughout our history as a state, Irish foreign policy has been given effect by our nurses, doctors, teachers, aid workers, soldiers and Gardaí — working at the fore-front of human tragedies and keeping the peace around the world. The high standing of our country abroad is a tribute and a testament to them, and I would like to dedicate this White Paper to them.

Irish foreign policy on a day-to-day basis is, of course, the work of many dedicated men and women in the Department of Foreign Affairs. They work in Iveagh House and in the Department's other offices in Dublin and in our missions around the world. Their contribution to the overall quality of Irish life, and to the way in which Ireland is perceived internationally, has never been fully recognised. I would like to take this opportunity to pay tribute to them. Ireland's foreign service is one of the smallest, per capita, in the western world, and one of the most effective. That would not be so without people of real quality dedicating themselves to years of service to the public.

Finally and above all, I want this White Paper to contribute to a sense of ownership of Ireland's foreign policy by all the people of Ireland.

DICK SPRING T.D.
Tánaiste and Minister for Foreign Affairs

Agenda for Irish Foreign Policy

(Paragraph numbers correspond to the point at which elements in the Agenda appear in the White Paper, and the Agenda can be seen as an executive summary of the document.)

Values in Ireland's Foreign Policy

1.   Ireland's foreign policy is about much more than self-interest. For many of us it is a statement of the kind of people we are. Irish people are committed to the principles set out in Article 29 of the Constitution for the conduct of international relations: — the ideal of peace and friendly cooperation amongst nations founded on international justice and morality; the principle of the pacific settlement of international disputes by international arbitration or judicial determination; and the principles of international law as our rule of conduct in our relations with other states. *(Paragraph 2.40)*

2.   Ireland is small and hugely dependent on external trade for its well-being. We do not have a sufficiently large domestic market or adequate natural resources to enable our economy to thrive in isolation. As we depend for our survival on a regulated international environment in which the rights and interests of even the smallest are protected, our interests require us to pursue an active policy of external engagement. *(2.37)*

7

2. Irish One World Quilt. *Made by women's groups and community groups throughout Ireland as part of an international project, the* *quilt expresses some of the central interests and concerns of Irish people regarding the world at large.*

3.   In order to prosper and to ensure our
security, Ireland must engage with other nations in a common effort to
maintain a stable framework for international relations, within which the
rights of small nations are given equal weight to the interests of the strong,
and disputes are settled through arbitration and by reference to
international law, rather than by military might. *(2.38)*

4.   Our membership of the United
Nations, the European Union and other international organisations affords
us the opportunity, despite our size, to speak on equal terms with many
larger countries. By world standards, we are relatively wealthy and can
devote more of our time and resources to promoting our interests and
concerns than can those whose daily life is dominated by the struggle to
exist. *(2.39)*

Ireland and Europe

5.   Ireland has been a full participant in
the process of European integration for a generation. We have benefited
enormously from membership of the European Union, and have at the
same time contributed constructively to the Union's development. Irish
people increasingly see the European Union not simply as an organisation
to which Ireland belongs, but as an integral part of our future. We see
ourselves, increasingly, as Europeans. *(3.8)*

6.   Ireland's membership of the Union
has always been about more than free trade and financial transfers,
important as these may be. The period of our membership of the Union has
coincided with an increase in national self-confidence, a strengthening of
our identity and an increase in our international profile. *(3.11)*

7.   The European Union faces *five major challenges* as it moves towards the 21st century.

First, the Union must ensure its balanced economic development and realise the full potential of the Single Market. It must see to it that the advantages of the richest market in the world flow fully and equitably to all its regions and all its citizens and ensure that the current high levels of unemployment, social exclusion and poverty are substantially and permanently reduced.

Secondly, it must ensure that it functions in a transparent way, that its processes and decisions are explained and understood, and that its policies are designed to respond — and are perceived to respond — to real public concerns including, for example, the fight against drugs and international crime.

Thirdly, it must equip itself to play a role commensurate with its responsibilities on the European continent and in the wider family of nations in pursuit of its essential interests and in the furtherance of its most fundamental values.

Fourthly, it must seize the historic challenge and opportunity of the further enlargement of the European Union to include the other democratic European nations which wish to become members.

Fifthly, it must continue the process of ever closer Union among the peoples of Europe so as to ensure that the enormous achievements of the Union in terms of peace and prosperity are consolidated for future generations. *(3.21)*

8.   The European Union cannot pick and choose as to which of these challenges it wishes to address. The future well-being of the Union depends on responding successfully to each of them. *(3.22)* These challenges are enormous but so is the determination to meet them, both here in Ireland and amongst our partners in Europe. If met successfully, they can be transformed into opportunities for deepening and extending the process of European integration. *(3.23)*

9.   Ireland will assume the Presidency of the European Union from 1 July to 31 December, 1996, at a crucial time in the development of the European Union. The successful conduct of the Presidency in the interests of the Union as a whole represents a significant challenge and a major priority for the Government. *(3.14)*

10.   The enlargement of the Union to the east and south, incorporating countries with considerable development needs, will be a new challenge for the principle of cohesion and convergence. *(3.52)* However, the principle of economic and social cohesion which is firmly established in the EC Treaty must be fully maintained and implemented. The enlargement of the Union to include in particular the countries of central and eastern Europe, which will bring many benefits in terms of both stability and economic opportunities, should not undermine the application of cohesion policies to existing member states. *(3.53)*

11.   The Government welcome the prospect of the EU's enlargement. At the same time, they will enter the enlargement negotiations determined to negotiate entry terms which will protect our agricultural and other interests and allow the agriculture sector sufficient time to adapt to the challenges of an enlarged Union. Agriculture within the European Union will remain a central policy area for Ireland in the years ahead. The food industry, together with forestry, have been targeted as growth areas with significant opportunities for additional employment. *(3.74–3.75)*

12.   The promotion and safeguarding of peace and prosperity on the continent of Europe demands that the European Union and its member states maintain an open and generous attitude to their European neighbours who seek membership and who fulfil the necessary conditions. The re-creation or tolerance of continental divisions, akin to those which arose in Europe earlier this century and have only recently been overcome, is no longer an option. Conditions which must be met by candidate countries include the achievement of stable democracy, the rule of law, human rights and the protection of minorities; the existence of a functioning market economy; and the capacity to cope with competitive pressure and market forces within the Union. *(3.134–3.135)*

13.   The Government would not however accept an enlargement process which altered the essential character of the Union to that of an expanded free trade area. The Union's unique supranational nature, characterised by the development of the common policies, must be maintained and strengthened as enlargement proceeds. *(3.150)*

14.   The Government support the aim of encouraging a high level of employment while progressively improving the conditions of those at work and the rights of all European citizens. They particularly welcome the fact that the Commission's White Paper on Social Policy recognises the primacy of job creation. *(3.59)*

15.   The aims of a strong social policy and
improving competitiveness are both important and are, in many ways,
complementary. On the one hand, social harmony and social dialogue
contribute to the efficiency of the economy; on the other hand, a high level
of social protection cannot be maintained unless the European economy
maintains and improves its competitiveness and achieves a high level of
employment. *(3.60)*

16.   Ireland has always supported EU
action in the area of *social exclusion.* Ireland will use its forthcoming
Presidency to explore new approaches to the issue at EU level. *(3.63)*

17.   In the context of the EU
Intergovernmental Conference, the Government will seek to identify
Treaty amendments in this area, with a view to initiating a Treaty change in
the course of the IGC. The purpose of such a Treaty change would be to
reflect in an appropriate way the rights and needs of people with a
disability. *(3.209)*

18.   The Government believe that
effective coordinated action by the Union in respect of crime and drugs is
essential. In particular they believe that the fight against drugs should
remain a central element of the work of the Union, including its work in
the area of Justice and Home Affairs. *(3.95)*

19.   Government policy has been aimed, and will continue to be aimed, at qualifying for the final stage of European Economic and Monetary Union (EMU). This involves continued sound management of the public finances and pursuing exchange rate and monetary policies based on price stability, that is the maintenance of low inflation. We meet the convergence criteria and are committed to continuing to meet them. Ireland has a good inflation record in recent years, our interest rates are well within the reference limits provided for under the Treaty and the Irish Pound trades comfortably within the Exchange Rate Mechanism of the European Monetary System. *(3.164)*

20.   It would clearly be preferable from Ireland's point of view if the UK were to enter EMU at the same time as Ireland. The UK Government have said that the UK will decide about joining EMU in 1999, closer to the date. If the UK were to remain outside EMU in 1999 it could, of course, decide to join at a later time. The key priority for Ireland is to keep meeting the qualifying conditions to enable us to join and to continue to prepare the economy for participation in EMU. Failure to meet the conditions would exclude Ireland from EMU in all circumstances. The policy requirements in these respects, of course, constitute necessary prescriptions for sustained economic and employment growth in their own right. *(3.168–3.169)*

21.   The Intergovernmental Conference (IGC), due to open on 29 March 1996, will offer an important opportunity for the Union to take stock of developments in the Union and to examine the options for future progress. While this IGC will by no means be the last such opportunity for the Union to equip itself to deal with its future challenges, a successful outcome will be of the very greatest importance to the European Union and to Ireland in terms of addressing the challenges of a new century. *(3.170)* Ireland, which has always sought to play a constructive role in the process of European integration, will be open to proposals which will advance that process, in particular by improving the functioning of the Union, equipping it to address more effectively the direct concerns of citizens, encouraging greater transparency, and enabling it to address the challenges posed by enlargement. *(3.177)*

22.   The further enlargement of the Union must not be used as an excuse — and the IGC must not be used as an occasion — to call into question the delicate institutional balances which represent the Union's most important achievement and resource. Ireland's foremost long-term interest in the Union, as indicated above, is to ensure the continued success and effectiveness of the Union which in turn depends largely on ensuring that its unique institutional arrangements can continue to function effectively. The Government will pursue this interest with the utmost vigour at the IGC. *(3.185)* Ireland could not, for example, countenance losing the right to nominate a full member of the European Commission. *(3.188)*

23.   The Government will be amongst those taking a lead in ensuring both the transparency of the IGC process itself and that the decisions taken at the IGC result in a significant improvement in the transparency of the European Union for the future. *(3.191)*

24.   The Government share the view that member states can exercise a more effective influence for the development of a stable, just and peaceful international system by acting in concert than they could accomplish individually. An effective Common Foreign and Security Policy is therefore in Ireland's interest and at the IGC the Government will be working for practicable and sustainable ways of improving its functioning. *(3.198)*

25.   More effective means are required at Union level to undertake the research and analysis which should underpin policy initiation and development on international issues. To meet this need, the Government have advocated the development of a planning and analysis capacity within the Council Secretariat of the European Union. A central planning and analysis capacity, which would be at the service of the Presidency and the Council, would facilitate the identification of the common Union interest in relation to international issues and the formulation of effective responses by the Union to these challenges. *(3.201–3.202)*

26.   Ireland will be actively involved in seeking constructive changes to the Treaty to strengthen the Union's response to unemployment and to challenges to the environment. *(3.209)*

International Security

27.   The majority of the Irish people have always cherished Ireland's military neutrality, and recognise the positive values that inspire it, in peace-time as well as time of war. Neutrality has been the policy of the State in the event of armed conflict and has provided the basis for Ireland's wider efforts to promote international peace and security. *(4.4)*

28.   An intention to remain neutral in the
event of conflict is not sufficient on its own to maintain conditions of
peace, stability and justice in Europe and beyond. Ireland has therefore
sought to promote a range of policies, directed at preventing, containing
and resolving conflict and at promoting greater equity and justice in
international affairs. *(4.6)*

The values that underlie Ireland's policy of neutrality have therefore
informed almost every aspect of Ireland's foreign policy. *(4.7)*

29.   Ireland's policy of military neutrality
has served Ireland well. Our international reputation for impartiality has
enabled us to play a meaningful role in the preservation of peace in the
world. As stated in the Programme for a Government of Renewal, that
policy will not be changed unless the people of Ireland decide otherwise in
a referendum. All steps taken by the Government to enhance our
contribution to international security will be carried out within the scope
of this undertaking. *(4.9)*

30.   Irish people have always believed that
we must make the biggest contribution that we can towards solving
problems of injustice, oppression, or want. In a world that remains troubled
and uncertain, Ireland remains willing to play a full role in contributing to
the security of Europe and the world. *(4.13)*

31.   Ireland's policy will be to strengthen
the Organisation for Security and Cooperation in Europe — OSCE — as
a permanent Organisation for European security cooperation and to further
develop the Organisation's capacity for preventive diplomacy and
peacekeeping. The Government intend to increase the level of participation
in OSCE missions. *(4.21–4.31)*

32.   The Government have already indicated that they are giving consideration to whether the cooperative security initiative known as *Partnership for Peace* is one to which Ireland could contribute. The overall objectives of PFP are consistent with Ireland's approach to international peace and European security, and participation in the Partnership could have several important advantages. Objectively speaking, participation on appropriate terms would not affect in any way Ireland's policy of neutrality nor would it prejudice or pre-empt Ireland's approach to discussions in the European Union on a common defence policy. *(4.48–4.52)*

33.   The Government have decided to explore further the benefits that Ireland might derive from participation in Partnership for Peace, and to determine the contribution that Ireland might make to the Partnership. A decision on participation in PFP will only be taken by the Government in the light of consultations, including with the relevant committees of the Oireachtas, and such a decision will be subject to a motion on the terms and scope of any participation by Ireland being approved by the Houses of the Oireachtas. *(4.53)*

34.   The Government have decided to discuss with the WEU the possibility of Ireland's taking part, on a case-by-case basis, in humanitarian and rescue tasks, and peacekeeping tasks under the *Petersberg Declaration* (the "Petersberg tasks" are humanitarian and rescue tasks; peacekeeping tasks; tasks of combat forces in crisis management, including peacemaking). They will consider such changes as may be necessary to the Defence and Garda Síochána Acts to enable Ireland's Defence Forces and Gardaí to take part in such operations. The Government do not intend that Ireland will be involved in tasks of combat forces in crisis management. *(4.80–4.88)*

35.   In discussion with the WEU of
involvement in the "Petersberg tasks" and in contributing to discussion of
overall defence policy for the Union, the Government will be guided by the
principles set out in this White Paper, and especially in paragraph *4.114.*

36.   The Government have undertaken to
put the outcome of any future negotiations that would involve Ireland's
participation in a common defence policy to the people in a referendum.
This will ensure that Ireland's policy of military neutrality remains
unchanged, unless the people themselves decide otherwise. The
Government will not be proposing that Ireland should seek membership of
NATO or the Western European Union, or the assumption of their mutual
defence guarantees. *(4.115)*

The United Nations

37   The United Nations has been a
cornerstone of Irish foreign policy since we joined the Organisation on 14
December 1955. As a nation, we take seriously our obligations under the
Charter, and our foreign policy has been framed with these obligations in
mind. Support for effective international action in areas such as
disarmament, peacekeeping, development and human rights continues to
define Irish priorities within the UN system. The building of a strong and
effective United Nations continues to form a key objective of Irish foreign
policy. *(5.7–5.9)*

38.   Ireland believes that the UN must
take account of what the Secretary- General has referred to as the "deepest
causes of conflict" — economic despair, social injustice and political
oppression. In supporting a renewed emphasis on conflict prevention, our
efforts will focus, in particular, on seeking to achieve progress in the
following areas: ensuring early consideration of disputes likely to lead to
conflict; developing the mediation capacity of the UN; utilising the
potential of the International Court of Justice. *(5.30–5.31)*

39.   Ireland will work to develop Article
65 of the Charter to enable the UN's *Economic and Social Council
(ECOSOC)* to identify and report to the Security Council on pressing
economic and social factors which have a serious potential to threaten
international peace and security. We will seek the support of other countries
for the establishment of a properly-resourced Mediation Body to which the
General Assembly or the Security Council may refer difficult issues. The
Government are giving urgent consideration to the acceptance of the
compulsory jurisdiction of the International Court of Justice, and have
initiated a review of the legal implications for Ireland of such a move.
(5.33–5.38)

40.   Ireland will support proposals which
seek to increase the interaction between the General Assembly and other
permanent bodies of the United Nations Organisation, especially the
Security Council and ECOSOC. *(5.47)*

41.   The Government will ensure that
Ireland continues to play an active role in seeking to secure a more
representative Security Council and one more responsive to the concerns of
the general membership. Ireland will seek election to the Council in the
year 2000. *(5.50–5.52)*

42.   Ireland will work vigorously to ensure that the United Nations system, at all levels, plays an increasingly active and effective role in the field of international economic and social development involving the highest possible standards of coordination and accountability. We will play our full part in promoting a new level of commitment by the international community in addressing the just needs of the developing countries and in building a new and more equitable relationship between developed and developing countries. *(5.57–5.58)*

43.   The Government have decided to establish an Interdepartmental Liaison Group to ensure a more focused national position in the various UN bodies. The Liaison Group will meet regularly to discuss issues which are relevant to the UN system as a whole. A long-term strategy will be developed regarding elections to UN bodies, executive boards and expert committees which reflect Ireland's particular concerns. The Liaison Group will be able to make recommendations in this regard. *(5.63)*

44.   To ensure greater transparency in our policy at the UN, the Minister for Foreign Affairs will publish annually a report on issues at the United Nations and on Ireland's voting record on these issues. *(5.65)*

Disarmament

45.   The Government intend to make full use of the increased opportunities afforded by the new review arrangements in the Non-Proliferation Treaty. These include the new yardstick for the measurement of the performance of states party to the Treaty provided by the set of principles and objectives for nuclear non-proliferation and disarmament which was adopted by the NPT Review Conference. They will seek to ensure that the Review Conference in 2000 addresses these issues in a comprehensive and effective manner. *(6.21)*

46.   The Government intend to ensure that the environmental, health and safety issues associated with the nuclear industry are effectively addressed in all the relevant fora. They will also seek determined action to address and resolve the health, safety and environmental issues associated with the nuclear industry. *(6.39)*

47.   In order to enhance the effectiveness of Ireland's contribution to the work of international disarmament and arms control fora, the Government will –

- ensure that Ireland uses to the full the opportunities provided by the Common Foreign and Security Policy of the EU to advance the Government's disarmament objectives;

- in this connection, ensure that the Irish Presidency of the European Union gives appropriate priority to disarmament issues;

- seek to achieve membership for Ireland of the Conference on Disarmament in Geneva in the context of enlargement of membership of that body;

- be represented at a high level at the forthcoming United Nations Review Conference on the Biological and Toxin Weapons Convention. *(6.91)*

48.   The Government are determined to
pursue the elimination of all weapons of mass destruction. In this context,
the Government will –

- continue to promote the abolition of nuclear weapons;

- work to strengthen further the international nuclear non-
  proliferation regime, using to the full the enhanced arrangements for
  review adopted in May 1995;

- press for a permanent end to nuclear testing and, in this context, for
  the conclusion in 1996 of a Comprehensive Test Ban Treaty;

- urge an immediate start to, and early conclusion of, negotiations on
  a treaty banning production of plutonium for weapons purposes,
  with appropriate attention being given to the problem of existing
  stocks;

- give priority to ratification by Ireland of the Chemical Weapons
  Convention at the earliest possible date;

- encourage effective adherence to export control guidelines designed
  to prevent the proliferation of materials and technology for making
  weapons of mass destruction. *(6.92)*

49.   The Government will endeavour to focus international attention on the problems caused by the excessive accumulation of conventional arms in many parts of the world. They are committed to promoting restraint in transfers of conventional weapons and to further prohibitions and restrictions on the use of inhumane weapons. Accordingly, the Government will –

- pursue at the United Nations Ireland's proposal for a code of conduct for conventional arms transfers;

- promote the uniform and strictest application of the EU's common criteria for conventional arms exports;

- seek support for a total ban on anti-personnel landmines;

- seek, in the context of the review of the Inhumane Weapons Convention, the broadening, to the maximum extent achievable, of the prohibitions and restrictions on landmines contained in Protocol II to the Convention;

- support the establishment of a new multilateral export control arrangement to cover arms and sensitive dual-use items. *(6.93)*

50.   In view of our traditional policy of advocating comprehensive multilateral disarmament measures, Ireland has been a strong supporter of the principles underlying the Chemical Weapons Convention since negotiations on it first began. The Government intend, therefore, that Ireland should be a party to the Convention as soon as it enters into force. Although Ireland has never possessed chemical weapons or facilities for their production, we will have mandatory obligations under the Convention in the area of monitoring production and use of toxic chemicals by the Irish chemical industry. The Government are taking the steps necessary to enable Ireland to ratify at the earliest possible date. *(6.49–6.50)*

51.   The Government are strongly opposed to the continued manufacture, transfer, export, sale and use of anti-personnel landmines and are seeking support for a total ban on these weapons. The Government will encourage the adoption of moratoria on mine exports and the broadening, to the maximum extent possible, of the prohibitions and restrictions on landmines contained in Protocol II of the Inhumane Weapons Convention. *(6.83)*

Peacekeeping

52.   The Government are committed to sustaining the overall level of Ireland's contribution to peacekeeping. However, in view of the number, size and complexity of current peacekeeping operations it will be necessary to develop a selective response to future requests from the United Nations. The factors which will inform the Government's consideration of such requests will include –

- an assessment of whether a peacekeeping operation is the most appropriate response to the situation;

- consideration of how the proposed mission relates to the priorities of Irish foreign policy;

- the degree of risk involved for UN personnel;

- the extent to which the particular skills or characteristics required relate to Irish capabilities;

- the existence of realistic objectives and a clear mandate which has the potential to contribute to a political solution;

- whether the operation is adequately resourced;

- the level of existing commitments to peacekeeping operations. *(7.12–7.13)*

53.   In order to increase further the effectiveness and coherence of policy in this area, the Government have decided to establish a Standing Interdepartmental Committee on Peacekeeping which will consider issues relating to Irish involvement in peacekeeping operations. In addition, the appointment of a military adviser to serve in the Permanent Mission to the United Nations in New York is envisaged. *(7.14)*

54.   The Government will support efforts to ensure that the UN Secretariat is provided with the additional resources which may be required for executive direction and management of peacekeeping operations needs to be strengthened further. *(7.16)*

55.   Ireland co-sponsored the resolution to establish a Convention on the Safety of United Nations and Associated Personnel. The Convention provides that each state party should make it a crime under its national law to attack UN personnel. The Government intend to sign and ratify the Convention at an early date. *(7.18)*

56.   Ireland will support efforts to ensure that mandates of peacekeeping missions take human rights considerations into account including, whenever appropriate, specific provisions which would require personnel to report on any human rights violations which they witness. *(7.19)*

57.   The Government will seek to make use of Ireland's expertise in peacekeeping, to assist other countries endeavouring to develop their own training facilities. *(7.21)*

58.   The Government believe that there is scope for considering what more can be done to provide stand by units of military and police for use by the United Nations in sudden conflicts and humanitarian emergencies. A number of proposals have been advanced for such rapid standby units and standby UN military headquarters staff and the Government believe that they merit full consideration by member states. *(7.28)*

59.   The Government's approach to participation in future peace *enforcement* operations will be guided by the following criteria –

- that the operation derives its legitimacy from decisions of the Security Council;

- that the objectives are clear and unambiguous and of sufficient urgency and importance to justify the use of force;

- that all other reasonable means of achieving the objectives have been tried and failed;

- that the duration of the operation be the minimum necessary to achieve the stated objectives;

- that diplomatic efforts to resolve the underlying disputes should be resumed at the earliest possible moment;

- that the command and control arrangements for the operation are in conformity with the relevant decisions of the Security Council, and that the Security Council is kept fully informed of the implementation of its decisions. *(7.31)*

60.   In response to the trend towards greater cooperation between the UN and regional organisations, the Government are considering such changes as may be necessary to the Defence and Garda Síochána Acts to enable Ireland to be in a position to respond to requests to participate in such missions. *(7.35)*

Human Rights

61.   As a reflection of its concern for human rights, the Government have decided to take a number of measures, including the allocation of additional resources, to ensure a continuing strong profile for human rights issues in Irish foreign policy. Within Ireland, these measures include the establishment of a Human Rights Unit within the Department of Foreign Affairs and the creation of structures to link this Unit to other actors in the human rights field. Externally, the Government intend to place a strong emphasis on human rights issues during the Irish Presidency of the EU, and to initiate a campaign to seek membership of the UN Commission on Human Rights. In addition, the focus on human rights and democratisation in the Irish Aid programme will be strengthened. *(8.2–8.4)*

62.   Ireland's first national report under the Convention on the Rights of the Child will be presented within the next few months to the monitoring committee established under that Convention. Our first national report under the Covenant on Economic, Social and Cultural Rights is in preparation. *(8.14-8.15)*

63.   The Government believe that there is need urgently to address the wider issue of establishing an *International Criminal Court* to ensure that human rights violators are made to answer for their crimes against the dignity of the human person. The Government also recognise the importance of measures which would give early warning of potential situations of human rights abuse. They consider that the UN High Commissioner for Human Rights, supported by human rights monitors, has a crucial role to play in this regard. *(8.43)*

64.   The violation of women's rights constitutes a major obstacle to development. The challenge is to empower women so that they become the agents as well as the beneficiaries of development. The Government will therefore give particular attention in the overall Irish Aid programme to gender-specific approaches and to countering violence against women. *(8.54)*

65.   The Government will provide support through Irish Aid for the following –

- human rights NGOs in the developing countries;

- assistance in the training of the judiciary, the police and the mass media;

- human rights education for police and military personnel, drawing on the expertise of the Garda Síochána and the Defence Forces. *(8.58)*

Development Co-operation

66.   Irish   Aid   and   Development
Cooperation is a practical expression of Ireland's foreign policy
commitment to peace and justice in the world.

Since the inception of the Irish Aid programme in 1974 virtually every
Irish family has had an involvement with Ireland's overall aid effort, either
by way of a family member working in the developing world or by
contributing financially to the work of one of the many Irish humanitarian
NGOs particularly in crises such as Ethiopia, Rwanda and Somalia.
(9.1–9.2)

67.   Since 1982, the Government have
spent almost £612m on Official Development Assistance. In 1996, Ireland
will spend almost £106m — the highest ever Irish contribution to the
developing world. The Government aim to make further significant
increases in ODA in the years ahead so as to put Ireland's performance on
a par with that of our European Union partners and with the ultimate aim
of meeting the UN target of 0.7% of GNP. *(9.5)*

68.   A critical objective of Irish policy is to
ensure that ODA funding is used effectively to promote the development,
health, education and welfare of those who are most deprived. Africa and
particularly Sub-Saharan Africa, containing as it does some of the least
developed countries in the world, will continue to be the main focus of
Irish Aid.

Currently the Irish Aid programme works directly in 6 priority countries
— Tanzania, Lesotho, Zambia, Sudan, Uganda and Ethiopia on a
government to government basis in areas such as health, education, water
supplies and sanitation.

Central to the Irish bilateral programme is respect by partner
governments for human rights. In that context, aid to Sudan will remain
focused on community level programmes pending a significant
improvement in the human rights situation in that country. As resources
increase, the number of priority countries will be increased and will include
Mozambique in 1996. Significant resources will be committed to the
rehabilitation of Rwanda and to post apartheid South Africa. *(9.6–9.14)*

69.   The cornerstone of Irish Aid will
continue to be long-term development. At the same time the number of
crises emerging require the Government to place a renewed focus in its
development policies on –

•   prevention of violent conflict and the promotion of human rights
       and the rule of law;

•   improving the effectiveness of aid response to humanitarian crises
       and natural disasters;

•   assisting war-ravaged societies to recover from the effects of war;

•   responding to the growing number of refugees and displaced people.
       (9.18)

70.   Recognising that much of the positive work of development is completely negated by armed conflict and the extensive availability of arms, Ireland will continue as part of its development strategy to press for arms reductions and arms controls and for the total elimination, in particular, of weapons such as landmines. *(9.15–9.20)*

71.   The Government are committed to allocating significant aid funding for the peaceful and constructive resolution of conflicts over the coming years. Such resources will also support longer-term preventive measures, e.g. support for institutions of civil society, which have a key role in conflict-prevention. *(9.20)*

72.   The Government will establish a *humanitarian liaison group* to ensure that the response of all relevant Irish Government departments and agencies is as fully coordinated as possible. The humanitarian liaison group will work to identify personnel from the public service and elsewhere who would be available for speedy deployment for emergency relief activities in response to requests received from the UN and the ICRC, and willing to have their names and skills added to a Register with a view to maximising Ireland's capacity to respond to humanitarian crises. The aim will be to establish a *"Rapid Response Register"* of personnel drawn from all aspects of the caring services. Individuals working in the private sector who wish to be placed on the Register will be encouraged and facilitated. The existence of this Register, of people willing and able to be deployed on an emergency basis wherever needed, will seek to ensure that Ireland's response, official and voluntary, to such emergencies takes into account all possible contributions and skills. Persons whose names are on the Register may be expected to participate in occasional training and orientation programmes. *(9.27–9.29)*

73.   The Bilateral Aid Programme will focus particularly in the coming years on –

• Poverty Reduction

• Self-reliant Development

• Partnership

• Sustainability

• Human Resources and Technical Cooperation

• Gender

• Food Security

(9.37–9.39).

74.   Ireland will continue to partner and financially assist the Irish NGOs in humanitarian emergencies and long-term development work. Provision has been made for the funding of basic needs projects initiated by smaller NGOs such as Irish missionaries, many working in remote areas without access to other sources of funding. *(9.64–9.65)*

75.   Ireland will play a constructive role in the debate on the evolution of a single comprehensive and coherent EU policy on development cooperation with all partner countries and a renewed emphasis on the poorest countries and populations. *(9.70–9.73)*

76.   Irish Aid will continue to contribute
to and work with UN agencies particularly UNICEF, UNHCR and
UNDP. We will actively encourage the reform process in the UN family of
agencies with a view to making these agencies more responsive to basic
needs in the developing countries. Our close relationship with these bodies
will be strengthened. Ireland will serve terms on the Boards of UNICEF
and the UNDP during the coming years. We are also seeking membership
of the Executive Committee of UNHCR. *(9.74–9.79)*

77.   Ireland will use its membership of the
UN and of the EU to promote a coherent international strategy on
development issues and will seek to address in those fora the related issues
of debt and trade. *(9.80–9.86)*

78.   Public support for development
cooperation policy is high in Ireland. It is desirable that a wide range of
citizens and organisations continue to engage in debate about aid and
development. The Government will continue to facilitate such dialogue,
for example through the NGO Forum organised annually by the Irish Aid
Advisory Committee which has been set up to advise the Government on
development issues. The National Council for Development Education
and Irish Aid will promote public knowledge and understanding of
development issues and of the Irish Aid programme, through, respectively,
development education in schools and community bodies and through
public debates and publications. *(9.92)*

The Irish Abroad

79.   In the past year significant improvements have been made in the service provided by the Passport Office. In 1995 'Passport Express' was introduced in cooperation with the An Post and the Passport Office in Cork was upgraded. The Government will keep the overall development of the passport service under review so as to ensure a high level of service to the public. *(12.21–12.24)*

80.   The welfare of Irish citizens abroad is an area of high priority for the Government. In this context the network of honorary consuls will be expanded in areas of the world where Ireland is under-represented and where there is a clear need to provide a consular service. *(12.13–12.14)*

81.   Special attention will continue to be paid to the welfare of Irish prisoners abroad. The recent ratification of the European Convention on the Transfer of Sentenced Persons will, with the agreement of the authorities of the countries concerned, enable Irish prisoners abroad who wish to do so to complete their sentences in Ireland. *(12.45–12.46)*

Public interest in foreign policy

82.   The Minister for Foreign Affairs has decided, following the success of the public seminars which were organised to prepare this White Paper, to hold similar seminars in the future. These seminars will focus on different aspects of Ireland's foreign policy and, as with the White Paper seminars, they will be fully open to the public. *(16.46)*

83.   As part of the Government's desire to
encourage a greater interest in Irish foreign policy, it has been agreed that
the Department of Foreign Affairs, in association with the Royal Irish
Academy, will publish a series of foreign policy documents of historic
interest. It is hoped that this initiative will encourage and assist greater
academic interest in the study of Irish foreign policy. *(16.48)*

Chapter 1

CHALLENGES AND
OPPORTUNITIES ABROAD

Why a White Paper on Foreign Policy?

1.1   This is the first time the Irish
Government have published a White Paper on foreign policy. A number of
White Papers have been issued in the past dealing with the specific question
of Ireland's policy towards the European Communities, but never before
have the Irish Government sought to explain the full range of their foreign
policy to the people through the medium of a White Paper. So why now?

1.2   A number of developments have
served to convince the Government that this is an appropriate moment at
which to assess the *challenges and opportunities* which Ireland must confront
in its foreign policy formulation in the years ahead, and to seek to shape a
coherent policy response. While many of these developments raise issues
which can be effectively addressed only at a global or regional level, Ireland
must play its full part if it is to reflect both the commitments to
international cooperation enshrined in the Constitution and the will of its
people.

37

*3. Medieval wood-cut illustrating the
Navigatio Brendani, the ninth century
allegorical tale of St. Brendan and his followers
who set sail in quest of 'the land of promise' and
met both wonder and danger along the way.*

1.3   Among the more significant developments of recent times which raise issues for our foreign policy are several which might be grouped together under the general heading of *global developments.* These include the following –

- **The increasing globalization of human activity**

  A rapid and unprecedented internationalisation of many areas of human activity has taken place within the last decade or so. Many areas of activity are in the process of moving onto a global level, beyond the control of individual states acting in isolation. This is increasingly the case in respect of trade, finance and communications. In many instances, this trend towards globalization has been encouraged by national governments and international organisations which have identified considerable advantages in this process.

  There are other areas where the impact of increased cross-border activity has been less welcome. This is certainly true in relation to environmental pollution and organised crime, especially drugs-trafficking.

  The challenge for the international community is to ensure that the opportunities presented by increased globalization are exploited in the interest of the common good, rather than to the exclusive advantage of a few.

- **The ever-growing gap between the world of the rich and well-fed and that of the poor and hungry**

  Despite the resources devoted to securing a more just and equal world, the gap between the North and the South, the rich and the poor, the well-fed and the hungry continues to grow. Falling commodity prices, the rising burden of debt and increased military expenditure are combining to reduce standards of living in many Third World countries, while the Developed World enjoys a steady increase in prosperity.

  This growing and destabilising gap between the haves and the have-nots presents a challenge to the entire international community.

- **The global impact of the ending of the Cold War**

  The ending of the Cold War has offered the international community the first opportunity in half a century to establish a world order built upon justice, freedom and peaceful cooperation. This would be in stark contrast to a system driven by the threat of mutual destruction; a threat which simultaneously fuelled and fed on a wasteful contest to devise ever more potent weapons of mass destruction.

  The international community faces the challenge of ensuring that this opportunity is not scorned and that real progress is made towards global disarmament. This would release resources which could be devoted to improving the quality of life of people across the globe.

- **The upsurge in regional and intra-state conflicts**

  The past few years have witnessed an upsurge of armed conflict. There continues to be an unacceptably high incidence of inter-state violence, frequently arising from disputes over territory. At the same time, there has been a worrying increase in violence within states, arising from regional or ethnic tensions.

  In many cases the outbreak of armed conflict within states has been marked by acts of appalling, and sometimes organised, savagery. Famine has been a regular accompaniment to such conflicts.

  The wider availability of sophisticated weapons and the indiscriminate use of land mines has meant that conflict has become increasingly destructive. Inevitably, this has led to greater suffering among non-combatants — mainly women and children — especially in conflict situations fed by racial or ethnic hatred, where distinctions between combatant and non-combatant are often deliberately ignored.

  The challenges confronting the international community include the development of effective systems of conflict prevention, peacekeeping and conflict control, the restriction of the availability of arms and, as a last resort, the propagation of, and respect for, agreed norms for the conduct of warfare.

- **The need to strengthen global and regional structures for international cooperation**

  The challenges presented by the new global situation require that

39

the framework for assuring international cooperation be reinforced, rationalised and made more efficient.

This applies particularly to those organisations whose primary functions are to encourage conflict prevention and to provide inclusive security, either at a global or regional level; organisations such as the United Nations and the Organisation for Security and Cooperation in Europe (OSCE).

1.4 Among other developments are those with a more European perspective, including –

- **The establishment of the Common Foreign and Security Policy of the European Union**

  The Common Foreign and Security Policy (CFSP) has been in operation since the entry into force of the Treaty on European Union (also known as the Maastricht Treaty) in November 1993. The structures established for the implementation of the CFSP, and the obligations on member states to consult and cooperate in the formulation of policy, enable the European Union to present a more coherent and effective external profile.

  Participation in the CFSP offers Ireland the opportunity to make a direct input into the policy of an institution of world importance. The challenge for Ireland is to ensure that Irish interests and concerns are reflected in EU policy and that participation in the CFSP enhances our traditional concerns in areas such as disarmament, human rights, racism etc.

- **The new security environment in Europe**

  The end of the Cold War and the collapse of the Warsaw Pact has brought about a new security environment in Europe. This presents challenges and opportunities for European institutions active in the security area such as the OSCE, NATO, WEU and the EU.

  It also raises questions for individual states, including Ireland, concerning the nature and extent of the threat to their security and their response to that threat.

  It is appropriate, therefore, that Ireland, like other European states, should examine and assess its national security policy. We need to ensure that our policy continues to meet our national security requirements, while allowing us to contribute to the Common Foreign and Security Policy of the European Union and to the development of collective security.

- **The challenge of bringing the countries of central and eastern Europe into the process of European integration**
  Prior to the collapse of the Iron Curtain, those European countries which found themselves under Soviet domination at the end of the Second World War were excluded from the process of European integration.

  They are now demanding their rightful place in this process which will involve their membership of the European Union and the right to opt for full involvement in security structures such as WEU and NATO.

  The opportunity is now open to build a Europe which will be united in peace and prosperity. The achievement of this goal poses challenges for all concerned and, in the case of Ireland, will render us a relatively middle-income rather than a low-income member state.

- **The Intergovernmental Conference (IGC) to review the European Union Treaties**
  In addition to considering the institutional changes required for an enlarged Union to function effectively, the IGC will examine a number of issues, including the future development of the Union's Common Foreign and Security Policy.

- **Other European Issues**
  In the period ahead we will also be faced by a range of other crucial issues, in particular with regard to Economic and Monetary Union, and the future financing of the Union. All of these issues demand the fullest participation by the people.

1.5   Finally, there have been developments within Ireland that form an integral part of the background against which this White Paper has been prepared. They include –

41

- **The growing public interest in foreign policy formulation**

  The level of public interest in foreign policy matters has increased significantly in this country over recent years. This is evident from the large number of NGOs which have been established, including aid agencies, human rights bodies and groups seeking to generate solidarity with a particular country. This increased level of public interest means that Irish Governments must demonstrate greater openness in the elaboration of foreign policy.

- **The Government's commitment to bringing greater openness, transparency and accountability to the way in which Ireland is governed**

  In its programme, the Government made clear its intention to introduce greater openness, transparency and accountability into the way Ireland is governed. It also expressed its determination to encourage debate about all aspects of foreign policy, and to nurture a sense of public ownership of that policy.

- **The rapid expansion of Ireland's Bilateral Aid Programme**

  Ireland's official Overseas Aid Programme has more than doubled over the past four years, rising from £40.3 million in 1992 to £106 million in 1996. It is the Government's intention that this programme will be increased each year, so as to make steady progress towards achieving the UN goal of 0.07% of GNP. Most of the increase in funding will be channelled through the Bilateral Aid Programme, which has already increased from £15.2 million in 1992 to £65 million in 1996.

  The Government will continue to ensure that the Bilateral Aid Programme is fully situated within the framework of Ireland's overall foreign policy.

- **The prospect of lasting peace on the island of Ireland**

  The ceasefires announced by the paramilitary organisations in autumn 1994 and the publication of the Framework Document by the Irish and British Governments in February 1995 opened up enormous opportunities for the people of this island. A lasting peace is now in prospect. An agreed political settlement will be based on consent and will cover relations within Northern Ireland, on the island of Ireland and between Ireland and Britain

In the new climate introduced by the ceasefires, the people of Ireland could look forward, for the first time in twenty five years, to exploiting both individually and in concert the collective trade, tourism and investment potential of the entire island. The prospect of establishing a new relationship with the United Kingdom was also opened up; a relationship relieved of past tensions, and of pursuing a foreign policy free from concerns relating to divisions in Northern Ireland.

At the time of writing, however, as indicated by the Tánaiste in his foreword to this White Paper, the situation brought about by the ceasefires, with all its challenges and opportunities, is gravely imperilled. The Government are resolved to pursue every avenue through which peace might be restored and to move the peace process speedily towards the goal of all-Party negotiations.

The Government's Response

1.6   This brief summary of recent developments which have an impact on the formulation of Ireland's foreign policy is far from comprehensive. Even so, it highlights a number of significant challenges and opportunities abroad which we, as a people, must face over the next decade. The Government are determined that our role in confronting these challenges and opportunities should be one of active engagement, based on forward-looking and proactive policies. The Government are equally determined that these policies should reflect the interests and concerns of the Irish people and have their support.

1.7   If public debate on foreign policy issues is to be fully informed, then Government have an obligation to ensure that the people are as fully briefed as possible. This White Paper, which seeks to examine the broad range of issues on Ireland's foreign policy agenda and to set out the Government's proposed response, is intended to contribute to this briefing process.

Chapter 2

BACKGROUND TO IRISH FOREIGN POLICY

2.1   This chapter is intended to provide a
brief description of the setting in which Ireland conducts its foreign policy
and introduces some of the central relationships, issues and themes which
are discussed later.

What is Foreign Policy?

2.2   While there is no universally agreed
definition of 'foreign policy', a working definition would be the pursuit by
a state of its interests, concerns, and values in the external environment.

2.3   In its broadest sense, this definition
could be taken to mean that foreign policy includes all policy having an
external dimension. In practice there is often a considerable overlap between
the foreign and domestic aspects of a country's policies, and it is not always
easy to distinguish between the two. It can be argued that all foreign policy
objectives are ultimately domestic in nature, since all such objectives in some
way reflect interests or concerns internal to the country pursuing them.

45

4 (top) "We Serve Neither King nor Kaiser
— But Ireland" — *banner of the pre-
independence Irish Citizen Army;*

*5 (bottom) 22 January 1972, the then
Taoiseach Jack Lynch and Minister for Foreign
Affairs Dr PJ Hillery sign the Treaty of
Accession to the European Community.*

2.4 There is, therefore, no absolute dividing line between foreign policy and domestic policy. The pursuit and implementation of foreign policy involves many different areas of government activity. Foreign policy is often implemented both by external and internal action. For instance, an external act, such as accession to an international organisation, can sometimes require the incorporation into national law of obligations arising from membership of that organisation.

2.5 Nevertheless, the organisation of government in most countries draws practical distinctions between different aspects of what can, in the broad sense, be described as foreign policy.

What might loosely be called "traditional diplomacy", covering essentially the political elements of external relations, is normally the responsibility of a Minister for Foreign Affairs, whereas other aspects of foreign relations, such as trade policy, are sometimes placed under the charge of other Ministers.

2.6 This is the case in Ireland where, subject to the overall direction of the Government, the Minister for Foreign Affairs has responsibility for external political affairs, the coordination of policy in the EU, policy with regard to the UN and in other international organisations, development cooperation matters, consular affairs including the issuing of passports, cultural relations, and the operation of the foreign service.

The Minister for Foreign Affairs also has day-to-day responsibility for policy in relation to Northern Ireland.

2.7 However, other Ministers also have responsibilities in relation to important aspects of the Government's external policy; for example, the Minister for Tourism and Trade in relation to external trade, the Minister for Enterprise and Employment in respect of policy on foreign investment, and the Minister for Finance in the field of external financial policy.

2.8   The primary focus of this White Paper is on those areas of policy which are the responsibility of the Minister for Foreign Affairs. Other aspects of foreign policy are also covered, particularly in the context of our membership of the European Union, but are generally dealt with in lesser detail. Government policy in relation to Northern Ireland is not covered in depth, and is dealt with largely in the context of the impact of the Northern Ireland situation on relations outside the island of Ireland.

The External Environment

2.9   International diplomacy is primarily, but not exclusively, the preserve of states. The growing number of recognised sovereign states and the increasing influence of international organisations, sub-national authorities operating at regional or local level, multinational companies, and interest groups have all served to make the foreign policy environment significantly more complex today than it was in the past.

The Nation State

2.10   Notwithstanding this development we continue to live in a world of nation states; that is, states which were either founded upon a sense of national identity among a substantial majority of their people, or which have striven, with varying degrees of success, to engender such an identity in order to lend legitimacy to their existence.

2.11   The nation state has provided a framework within which a people can establish its common identity, regulate its affairs, develop a sense of political and social cohesion, and through which it can channel its collective energies in the pursuit of mutual prosperity. It has also afforded structures through which different peoples have been able to communicate and cooperate with each other. It is likely to remain the essential building block of the international order for some time to come.

2.12   At the same time, for all the advantages of the concept, the limitations of the nation state are clearly seen in the difficulties which arise from attempting to define the human or territorial borders of a nation. The identification of a specific territory with a particular nation does not necessarily lead to peace and stability. Much conflict has resulted from the lack of distinct boundaries between nationalities, from efforts to incorporate into a nation state people who do not identify with that state, and from attempts to create an artificial nation state where none exists.

2.13   Twice in this century, terrible global wars have been fuelled by competing national claims and by state-sponsored ideologies. The multiplicity of regional conflicts arising from territorial disputes continues to place a permanent strain on international relations. Millions of people have been murdered in campaigns driven by the urge to establish the ethnic purity of states.

2.14   These events have highlighted the instability of an international order made up of competing nation states. Furthermore, the increasing globalization of human activity, together with changes in the pattern of economic activity and the evolving nature of the risks to security, including from organised crime, have clearly exposed the limited capacity of individual nation states to deal with modern-day challenges.

2.15   The nation state, for all its benefits and its likely durability, cannot on its own provide the prosperous, just, and civilised global society to which people aspire. If the nation state is to serve as a basis for peaceful and prosperous co-existence, it must operate on democratic principles, be accompanied by arrangements for the recognition and accommodation of internal diversity, and be situated within a framework providing for dialogue, consultation and cooperation between states.

2.16   While the nation state remains the basic unit of the world order, even in regions where a sense of national identity has historically been weak, there is a growing trend towards the pooling of national sovereignty in pursuit of regional integration. The European Union, in which institutions such as the European Commission and the European Parliament exercise power and influence decisions independently of the control of the member states, is the most significant example of this.

International Organisations

2.17   The dangers of inter-state rivalry, as manifested in two World Wars, have provided the impetus for half a century of increasingly intensive international cooperation aimed at ensuring the stability of the international order. During that time, the United Nations system has provided the universal framework within which states can cooperate in pursuit of peace and prosperity.

2.18   Organisations such as the *United Nations* can hardly be said to have a foreign policy in the strict sense. Nevertheless, they do act as major diplomatic players and pursue policies which impact on individual states.

The UN Security Council, for instance, has the power to take decisions concerning the maintenance of international peace and security which are binding on all UN member states, whether or not they happen to be on the Security Council at the time. If a state acts in violation of the UN Charter, it may become subject to corrective action by the UN.

2.19   International organisations increasingly provide a framework for the expression of national policies and, through the formulation of common policies, are more than ever becoming foreign policy actors in their own right.

2.20   Europe has led the way in terms of international cooperation at a regional level. The *European Union* has been the most successful example of regional integration, particularly in terms of the voluntary pooling of national sovereignty to common institutions established to oversee common policies in many areas of activity.

On another level, the *Organisation for Security and Cooperation in Europe (OSCE)*, which covers Europe, North America and the central Asian states of the former Soviet Union, has established mechanisms aimed at ensuring the stability of its member states through the accommodation of their internal diversity.

Europe's oldest political organisation, the *Council of Europe*, works through intergovernmental cooperation to strengthen pluralist democracy, protect human rights, seek solutions to social problems and promote awareness of a European cultural identity among its thirty-nine member states.

2.21 Regional entities such as the European Union have the potential to develop their own foreign policies in relation to other regions or non-member states. The EU, for example, has exercised a common commercial policy and provided a framework for cooperation on foreign policy and development cooperation policy for many years.

Since 1993, it has operated a Common Foreign and Security Policy (CFSP).

Other foreign policy players

2.22 The increasing complexity in the field of foreign policy is also seen in the tendency for some states, especially those with a federal structure, to allow their regional authorities to establish an external profile. This is particularly the case where such bodies have the right to conclude trade, commercial, cultural or other agreements with other states or regions.

2.23 At a non-governmental level, *religious and charitable movements* wield considerable influence in international relations. *Multinational corporations* have developed enormous power and influence while the role and influence of *international interest groups* have increased substantially, particularly in areas such as environmental protection, human rights and development cooperation.

2.24   A further factor is *organised crime, in particular drugs trafficking*, which has exploited the relaxation of border controls on the movement of goods, capital and services and now poses a challenge of such magnitude that it can only be met by concerted and resolute inter-governmental cooperation.

Geographical and historical context

2.25   Our history has, to a substantial extent, been determined by geography. Ireland's peripheral location relative to the continent of Europe has had a significant influence on the evolution of our foreign policy. This was an important factor in enabling us to sustain a policy of neutrality during the Second World War.

Neutrality

2.26   Since the Second World War neutrality, expressed in peace-time through Ireland's decision to abstain from membership of military alliances, has taken on a significance for Irish people over and above the essentially practical considerations on which it was originally based. Many have come to regard neutrality as a touchstone of our entire approach to international relations, eventhough, in reality, much of our policy is not dependent on our non-membership of a military alliance.

2.27   For the Irish people neutrality has never been a statement of isolationism or indifference as to the outcome of international issues. After the Second World War Ireland was fully involved in the many initiatives aimed at international cooperation and at the securing of global peace and security. During the negotiations which led to our membership of the European Communities in 1973, and on several occasions since, successive Governments have indicated that Ireland would be prepared to enter into discussion with other member states on the development of common arrangements in relation to security and defence matters.

The European Union

2.28   The Maastricht Treaty on European Union which was ratified by Ireland following the 1992 referendum, established a Common Foreign and Security Policy which includes provision for the discussion of "all questions related to the defence of the Union, including the eventual framing of a common defence policy, which might in time lead to a common defence". It also provided for the security provisions of the Treaty to be the subject of a review in the course of 1996.

2.29   Participation in the process of European integration has been crucial to Ireland's development. Through our involvement in this process and, in particular, through our membership of the European Union, Ireland is now in the mainstream of European decision-making.

Amongst other things, this White Paper will illustrate the extent to which Ireland, together with its fellow member states, has come to express its foreign policy through the medium of the European Union.

Great Britain

2.30   Relations between Ireland and Great Britain are in many respects extremely close and are of the utmost importance to both countries. We have a strong trade relationship; Great Britain takes approximately one quarter of our total exports of goods and services, while Ireland is Britain's seventh largest export market. We are bound by a shared history and by strong personal, cultural and social ties. As fellow members of the European Union, Ireland and the United Kingdom are committed to the process of creating an ever-closer union among the peoples of Europe, based upon the pooling of sovereignty in many areas of Government activity. Ireland and Great Britain also operate a highly developed system of bilateral arrangements and as recently as December 1995 the two Governments adopted further measures to intensify cooperation across a range of activities.

2.31   The long and complex history of our relationship with Great Britain has influenced many key aspects of our foreign policy While this is not the place to recount in detail the history of that relationship, an awareness of its impact is crucial to an understanding of Ireland's foreign policy and the concerns which underlie it.

2.32   Most significantly, our historical relationship with Great Britain is central to the division of the island of Ireland, the still unresolved question of Northern Ireland, and forms the background to the immense diplomatic efforts mounted by successive Irish Governments in search of a lasting political settlement involving relationships on the island of Ireland, and between Ireland and Great Britain.

The Irish Diaspora

2.33   The origins of our special relationships with the United States, with which there are particularly close links arising from extensive family ties, and with Canada, Australia and New Zealand cannot be disentangled from the older relationship with our neighbouring island, although these relationships have long since taken on a vibrant and independent life of their own. The flood of Irish emigrants who settled in these countries and who laid the foundation for our particularly close modern-day bilateral relationships, included a great many who travelled as political and economic refugees, deportees, and members of the colonial administration. The renewed emigration of more recent times has reinforced long-standing traditional links with countries with large communities of Irish origin; it is also an important influence on our foreign policy in its own right.

The Developing World

2.34   The missionary movement of the early and middle years of this century witnessed an enormous human and material contribution to the education and welfare of the people of many developing countries. Even though the numbers involved in missionary activity have since declined, the level of Irish commitment has been maintained by the flow of lay volunteers who have travelled to developing countries to assist in development or relief operations.

2.35   It would be a mistake to present Irish people as having a concern for the Third World which marks us out from others. In terms of official development assistance, we have only recently begun to bring the level of our official assistance up to that of many of our European partners. However, there is an especially strong non-governmental tradition in Ireland of citizens working in the Third World and of contributing to the funding of that work.

2.36   The high number of people involved relative to the population has meant that there is an informed public interest in Ireland in Third World issues. This is reflected in the level of support for the activities of the non-governmental aid agencies, and has a significant impact on the focus of our foreign policy.

The importance of foreign policy for Ireland

2.37   One factor of geography which might be expected to influence Ireland's foreign policy is our small size in area and population.

It is precisely because Ireland is small and hugely dependent on external trade for its well-being that we need an active foreign policy. Ireland does not have the luxury of deciding whether or not to pursue a policy of external engagement. We do not have a sufficiently large domestic market or adequate natural resources to enable our economy to thrive in isolation. We depend for our survival on a regulated international environment in which the rights and interests of even the smallest are guaranteed and protected.

2.38   What is more, Ireland is situated on the edge of what is possibly the most constantly fought-over territory on the globe and has itself suffered from the effects of invasion and occupation for much of its history. In order to prosper and to ensure its security, Ireland must engage with other nations in a common effort to develop and maintain a stable framework for international relations, within which the rights of small nations are given equal weight to the interests of the strong, and disputes are settled through arbitration and by reference to international law, rather than by military might.

2.39   Our membership of the European Union and of the United Nations and other international organisations affords us the opportunity, despite our size, to speak on equal terms with many larger countries. Our voice in world affairs is strengthened by the fact that we are a democracy. The particular nature of our democratic institutions allows our people an influence on policy that, while not unique, is greater than that enjoyed by the citizens of most of the world's states. The extent of our influence also reflects the reality that, by world standards, we are relatively wealthy and can devote more of our time and resources to promoting our interests and concerns than can those whose daily life is dominated by the struggle to exist.

2.40   Ireland's foreign policy is about much more than self-interest. For many of us it is a statement of the kind of people we are. Irish people are committed to the principles set out in the Constitution for the conduct of international relations –

- the ideal of peace and friendly cooperation amongst nations founded on international justice and morality;

- the principle of the pacific settlement of international disputes by international arbitration or judicial determination; and

- the principles of international law as our rule of conduct in our relations with other states.

Chapter 3

THE EUROPEAN UNION AND
THE NEW EUROPE

3.1   The European Union and the
Communities which came before it have brought peace and prosperity to
a large part of the continent of Europe.[1] The benefits of the European
Union in terms of stability and economic development extend well beyond
its borders.

3.2   Although the creation of a single
market, in which the barriers to trade between the member states have
been removed, lies at the heart of the integration process, the European
Union is and always has been about more than economics. It was born
from a desire to replace the age-old rivalries and bloody conflicts which
have repeatedly devastated our continent with an ever closer union
between the peoples of Europe. Moreover, as its cohesion and social
policies in particular demonstrate, it is a union which seeks to cherish the
interests of all its regions and people. The Union has begun to generate a
loyalty to a political vision of Europe based on pluralism and common
traditions.

57

6. (top) The European Parliament, Strasbourg;

7. Ireland's 1996 Presidency logo;

8. (bottom) The European Commission,
headed by Commission President Jacques Santer.

3.3   The Union was not founded as an end in itself, but as a means towards the continued and greater well-being of the people of Europe. European integration is not and should not be expected to be a panacea for all ills. Rather it must be seen as a logical, practical, imaginative and unprecedented response to the daunting challenges which face the people of Europe and which we can face most effectively together.

3.4   The success of the Union depends ultimately not on directives from Brussels but on harnessing, where appropriate within a common framework, the commitment and abilities of each and every one of our citizens. That's why the success of the Union depends on the full inclusion of all its people.

3.5   Europe is not a melting pot in which national identities are destined to be submerged or lost. On the contrary, it is intended to be a place where variety is a strength rather than an encumbrance, where differences are not denied but understood and accommodated.

3.6   In an increasingly interdependent world, the role of international organizations and cooperation will continue to grow and, of course, is of particular importance to small countries. Participation in such organizations, provided it is on equitable terms, need not dilute a country's independence, but can instead offer it an opportunity to influence decisions on a larger scale. This approach has always been part of Ireland's participation in the European Union.

Ireland and the European Union

3.7   Two fundamental considerations underlay Ireland's original application to join the European Communities.

First, it was believed that membership would provide the conditions in which Ireland could best pursue its economic and social development and would offer the best prospect for the protection and promotion of living standards in this country.

Secondly, it was felt that membership would enable us to participate fully with other democratic and like-minded countries in the movement towards European unity, based on ideals and objectives to which Ireland as a nation could readily subscribe.

This view was endorsed by the Irish people who voted in a referendum on 10 May 1972 that Ireland should accede to the European Communities.

3.8 Ireland has now been a full participant in the process of European integration for a generation. We have benefitted enormously from membership of the European Union, and have at the same time contributed constructively to the Union's development. Irish people increasingly see the European Union not simply as an organisation to which Ireland belongs, but as an integral part of our future. We see ourselves, increasingly, as Europeans.

3.9 In recent years, the Irish economy has been characterised by strong growth. Employment has been growing strongly in comparison to low and even negative rates of growth in other EU states. Net job creation in the period April 1993 — April 1995 amounted to 85,000 (7.4 per cent). Private sector, non-agricultural employment rose by 60,000 (8.6 per cent) in the same period. At the same time the annual budget deficit has been brought under control and the debt/GDP ratio reduced.

It is difficult to estimate the precise impact of membership, but it seems certain that without membership and access to EU markets for our goods and services it would not have been possible to achieve the rate of growth and the level of surplus in the balance of payments which have been seen in recent years. The strong growth of the economy is also generating substantial growth in employment.

3.10 The benefits of membership in terms of financial transfers alone have been considerable. By the end of 1995, total net transfers to Ireland, since accession, amounted to IR£18.45 billion. The bulk of these have come from the Common Agricultural Policy and the Structural Funds.

3.11 However, Ireland's membership of the Union has always been about more than free trade and financial transfers, important as these may be. The period of our membership of the Union has coincided with an increase in national self-confidence, a strengthening of our identity and an increase in our international profile.

3.12 The process of European integration has also had a positive impact on developments in Northern Ireland. The communities in Northern Ireland have worked together on some matters in pursuit of their common interests in Europe. The very significant financial support from the Structural Funds has played a key role in economic development in Northern Ireland as well as in the South. The *INTERREG* programmes are making a significant contribution to practical cross-border cooperation. The additional package of financial measures in support of the peace process showed the commitment of partners in Europe to that process. Moreover, the entire process of European integration bears witness to the fact that peace and cooperation can supplant age-old rivalries.

3.13 The Government's policy programme *A Government of Renewal* emphasises that in the next century Ireland will develop a deeper and more complex relationship with Europe. This chapter explores how Ireland might respond in the years ahead to some of the challenges posed by that relationship.

Ireland's Presidency of the European Union

3.14 Ireland will hold the Presidency of the European Union from 1 July to 31 December 1996, at a crucial time in the development of the European Union. The successful conduct of the Presidency in the interests of the Union as a whole represents a significant challenge and a major priority for the Government.

3.15 The main obligation for any Presidency is to ensure that the European Union's business is discharged in an efficient, effective and impartial manner. Planning has been underway throughout the Irish administration since early 1994 to prepare for the challenge of the Presidency. During the six month period of the Presidency Irish Ministers will chair approximately forty Council of Ministers meetings and will supervise the work of approximately 200 working groups chaired by Irish personnel at official level. In carrying out their Presidency duties Ministers will endeavour to ensure that the political, economic and social agenda is advanced in a manner that will benefit the European Union. (A list of Ministers responsible for different areas of activity is included in the appendices).

3.16 The main focus of a Presidency is the European Council held near the end of each Presidency. The European Council is chaired by the Presidency and comprises Heads of State or Government and the President of the Commission, and is assisted by Ministers for Foreign Affairs. During Ireland's Presidency it is proposed to hold the European Council in Dublin Castle in December, 1996.

3.17 Areas which will feature on the agenda of the European Council and which are likely to be the main focus for the European Union during Ireland's Presidency include –

— the Intergovernmental Conference to review aspects of the EU Treaties,

— preparations for the third stage of Economic and Monetary Union,

— growth, competitiveness, employment and social inclusion,

— agreement on the draft Union Budget for 1997,

— Third Pillar issues such as drugs, immigration, extradition and organised crime,

— implementation of the Common Foreign and Security Policy,

— further developing relations between the EU and the applicant countries in preparation for future enlargement of the Union, and

— the continuing development of relations with other countries and regions outside the Union.

61

The State of the Union and the Challenges and Opportunities ahead

3.18   Since Ireland's accession on 1 January 1973, the Communities have continued to develop to meet growing and constantly shifting challenges. The last twenty-three years have seen further enlargement, significant institutional development and new common policies. A detailed account of those developments is provided in the six-monthly reports on developments in the European Union which the Government present to the Oireachtas. However, it is worth recalling briefly some of the most significant ways in which the Union has evolved.

3.19   A Community consisting originally of six member states expanded, on our accession together with the United Kingdom and Denmark, to a Community of nine member states. Through successive further enlargements it has grown to be a European Union of fifteen member states, the largest single market in the world, and a focus for stability on the European continent. The expansion of the Union has been parallelled by the development of closer trade and other relations with Europe's immediate neighbours and in the wider world.

3.20   At the same time, the Union has equipped itself with the Treaty provisions and institutions necessary to ensure that the successive enlargements have gone hand in hand with the continued process of closer integration.

The *Single European Act*, which entered into force in 1987, provided the necessary means for completion of the Single Market as well as an explicit Treaty basis for the development of accompanying policies, most notably the policy of economic and social cohesion.

The *Treaty on European Union*, which was signed at Maastricht and entered into force on 1 November 1993, provided the basis for achieving full Economic and Monetary Union and for the development of a Common Foreign and Security Policy.

Framework provisions for cooperation in the area of Justice and Home Affairs were brought within the Treaty and the role of the European Parliament, which has been directly elected since 1979, was further enhanced. The further progress towards European integration reflected in these Treaties has been clearly endorsed by the Irish people in two referenda.

3.21   The European Union faces *five major challenges* as it moves towards the 21st century.

First, the Union must ensure its balanced economic development and realise the full potential of the Single Market. It must see to it that the advantages of the richest market in the world flow fully and equitably to all its regions and all its citizens and ensure that the current high levels of unemployment, social exclusion and poverty are substantially and permanently reduced.

Secondly, it must ensure that it functions in a transparent way, that its processes and decisions are explained clearly to the people and understood by them, and that its policies are designed to respond — and are perceived to respond — to real public concerns including, for example, the fight against drugs and international crime.

Thirdly, it must equip itself to play a role commensurate with its responsibilities on the European continent and in the wider family of nations in pursuit of its essential interests and in the furtherance of its most fundamental values.

Fourthly, it must seize the historic challenge and opportunity of further enlargement to include the other democratic European nations which wish to become members.

Fifthly, it must continue the process of ever-closer Union among the peoples of Europe so as to ensure that the enormous achievements of the Union in terms of peace and prosperity are consolidated for future generations.

3.22   The European Union cannot pick and choose as to which of these challenges it wishes to address. The future well-being of the Union depends on responding successfully to each of them. If, for example, further enlargement were to disrupt the process of closer European integration it would serve the interests of no one, least of all the long-term interests of future applicants for membership. If, on the other hand, the European Union were to pursue closer integration without regard to the importance of being open to further enlargement, or if closer integration is not accompanied by an ability and willingness to play a constructive role in the wider world, the Union would be failing not only its neighbours but itself.

3.23 These challenges are enormous but so is the determination to meet them, both here in Ireland and amongst our partners in Europe. If met successfully, they can be transformed into opportunities for deepening and extending the process of European integration.

3.24 The Intergovernmental Conference (IGC) to review aspects of EU Treaties which is due to open on 29 March this year, has an important role to play in ensuring that the Union is able to adopt a coherent response to these challenges.

The First Challenge: Balanced Economic Development and Realising the Potential of the Single Market

3.25 The *first* challenge for the European Union is to ensure its balanced economic development and the realization of the full potential of the Single Market in a manner which fully respects the principle of environmental sustainability. (Community policy in relation to the environment is dealt with in Chapter 13).

3.26 A *Single Market* consisting of 370 million people is now very largely in place. The market has brought great benefits, especially to a small export-dependent economy such as our own.

3.27 Ireland exports some two-thirds of what it produces in comparison with an average in the European Union of just over one quarter. 72% of Ireland's exports go to the enlarged European Union market. The United Kingdom remains our largest single market but our dependence on that market has decreased significantly, from 54% in

1973 to 27.5% in 1994. Ireland has a significant trade surplus with its European partners.

Employment

3.28   The central current economic challenge for the Union and its member states is to address the unacceptable level of unemployment. Unemployment in the Union is much higher than in the US or Japan and has become a serious problem in most European countries, even in those which historically have had a very low level of unemployment. Unemployment blights people's lives and hopes, and wastes our most precious resource, our people's skills and abilities.

3.29   Ireland has pressed for a specific recognition of the priority of this problem for some time. Since 1992 it has been put at the top of the agenda by European Councils and by successive Presidencies. It must remain a foremost priority. It has been recognised and acknowledged that economic recovery in Europe cannot of itself resolve the problem of unemployment. The EU and, in the wider area, the OECD, recognise that, while the economic recovery now in progress is expected to reduce unemployment in Europe, it will not eliminate it.

3.30   The Commission's *White Paper on Growth, Competitiveness and Employment,* presented in December 1993, recognised that economic growth is a necessary condition for tackling unemployment, but not a sufficient one. It indicated that if significant inroads were to be made into the structural unemployment which is now a feature of the economies of most of the member states, active measures would have to be taken that would make businesses more competitive and create an economic structure more favourable to jobs.

3.31   The Commission's White Paper covered measures necessary at the level of member states as well as at European Union level. It included measures necessary to make sustained recovery and economic growth possible, as well as the kind of policies necessary to translate growth into jobs.

65

3.32   The Essen European Council in
December 1994 gave further focus to the need to combat unemployment.
It called on member states to develop multi-annual programmes in relation
to five key areas of labour market policy: increasing investment in vocational
training, improving the employment intensiveness of growth, reducing non-
wage labour costs, improving the effectiveness of labour market policy (by
avoiding practices which are detrimental to readiness to work and by
moving from a passive to an active approach) and improving measures to
help groups which are particularly hard hit by unemployment.

3.33   These multi-annual programmes
formed the basis of a first Annual Report on Employment which was
approved by the European Council at Madrid in December 1995. The
approach agreed at Essen was consolidated and more precise priorities for
action were established, with special emphasis on youth and long-term
unemployment and on unemployed women. The second Annual Report on
Employment will be presented to the Dublin European Council in
December 1996.

3.34   Citizens of the Union face major and
increasingly universal changes in the living and working environment in
which they live. In addition to the actions which are possible under the
Structural Funds, the Union is pursuing a number of programmes designed
specifically to address the challenges posed by these changes. The *Leonardo*
programme, for example, is designed to assist young people to learn the
requisite skills for gaining employment and adapting to change. The *Socrates*
Action Programme focuses on cooperation in education, on developing
quality education and on promoting awareness of cultures within Europe.

3.35   The Government will seek to ensure
that the Council of Ministers, and indeed all the institutions of the Union,
continue to give priority to the issue of employment. It will continue to
emphasise the central importance of education and training, of action to
help the long-term unemployed and of active labour market policies. The
Government will also maintain Ireland's demand for greater attention to be

given to the potential for creating employment through non-traditional working arrangements and local initiatives. (This year the Irish Presidency will host a Conference on local development in the European Union at which the opportunities for job creation in that context will be explored). The Government will highlight the need for both sides of industry to be involved in combatting unemployment. It will support efforts to promote labour market adaptability to facilitate the creation of jobs.

Making Europe More Competitive

3.36 The Government will work with our partners to make the European economy more productive, to meet the challenge of increasing world-wide competition, as well as to restructure the economy so that it is more conducive to job creation.

3.37 It is necessary to ensure the full implementation of the *Single Market*. In particular, there must be continued strict implementation of the policies of the Union which ensure fair competition by, for example, preventing the granting of illegal state aids and preventing monopoly situations developing. This is essential both for the successful functioning of the Single Market and for success of the cohesion policies.

3.38 The Government support efforts to reduce the administrative burden on firms, in particular on small and medium-sized enterprises. The Commission has been examining the question of simplification of regulations with the aid of a group of high-level independent experts drawn from all member states. The quest for simplification of rules must be a continuing process in the European Union and in the member states, but must not be used as a pretext for the dismantling of the Single Market or delaying its completion.

3.39 Rapidity, ease and coherence of communication are crucial to competitiveness. Europe's transport, energy and telecommunications systems are fragmented into national networks. For this reason the establishment of high-quality *Trans European Networks*

(TENs) covering the whole of the European Union is an important objective. The Treaty emphasises in particular the importance of the role TENs can play in relation to peripheral and island areas. Network development will take place in three sectors –

- Transport (road, rail, air, sea, combined)

- Energy (electricity and gas distribution)

- Information technology.

3.40 The development of *Trans-European Networks* will require major investment. Public finance is necessary to mobilise private finance in areas such as transport networks. Progress has already been made towards reaching agreement on financing the networks. Ireland's view is that, in principle, the existing financial instruments of the Union should be used for this purpose. However, we regard the development of the networks as of such importance that new instruments should not be ruled out, if they prove necessary in particular cases.

3.41 There is a growing realisation of the contribution which science, technology and innovation can make to international competitiveness, especially when they can be harnessed in a way which converts knowledge into products and processes. For a number of years, the EU has operated a series of *Framework Programmes for Research and Technological Development* covering all of the main science and technology disciplines, and in which institutes and industry throughout the member states may participate and collaborate.

3.42 The Fourth Framework Programme, covering the period 1994–1999 with a budget of 12.3 BECU, is the most significant effort thus far in cooperation between the EU member states in this area. However, the Programme is equivalent to less than 6% of the total national budgets of the EU member states for science and technology. Recognising the benefits of pooled action and on foot of the obligations in the Maastricht Treaty, the Commission is beginning to institute steps to develop greater coordination of the national science and technology policies of the EU member states.

3.43   Ireland's approach to *Research and Development* is coordinated by the Office of Science and Technology (OST) at the Department of Enterprise and Employment. The evolution of the EU Framework Programmes has generated valuable opportunities for Irish researchers to participate in European Programmes. Under the Third Framework Programme, 750 contracts were awarded to Irish researchers, worth approximately £80 million.

3.44   It will be important to ensure that Irish researchers and industry derive maximum advantage from the current Fourth Framework Programme and that the results of EU research are disseminated throughout the Union so that the disadvantages which firms in peripheral regions suffer in this regard are reduced.

Economic and Social Cohesion

3.45   The principle of reducing over time the disparities between the richer and poorer regions of the Community was implicit in the Treaties from the beginning. It was successively strengthened by the setting up of the European Regional Development Fund in 1975, by the introduction of a specific title on economic and social cohesion in the Single European Act, and by the reform and increase of the Structural Funds which followed it, including an overall doubling of the funds for the least prosperous (Objective 1) regions, including Ireland.

3.46   The Treaty on European Union further enhanced the Treaty provisions on cohesion and a new fund, the Cohesion Fund, additional to the existing Structural Funds, was introduced for the four member states with a per capita GNP lower than 90% of the Community average (Ireland, Greece, Portugal and Spain).

3.47   The Treaty now provides that the formulation as well as the implementation of Community policies and actions shall take into account the cohesion objective and contribute towards achieving it. The financial package for the years up to 1999 again increased significantly the overall budgetary allocations to cohesion policies.

3.48   Ireland has benefitted considerably from transfers under the Union's cohesion policy and will receive approximately £1 billion per year in funding under the Structural Funds and Cohesion Fund each year up to 1999. In recent years Ireland has been closing the gap significantly with the more prosperous regions of the Union. From a per capita GDP of 62% of the EC average in 1980 (on the basis of a Community of Twelve), the figure had moved to about 82% on the same basis in 1994 and is forecast to rise to around 89% in 1996.[2]

3.49   The Union faces a two-fold challenge in the context of cohesion. First, it must ensure that the very significant resources available under the present round of funding are spent to good effect and, secondly, it must address how the policy of cohesion can be strengthened for the future and developed in the light of further enlargement.

3.50   The level of the Structural and Cohesion Funds in the European Union is agreed up to and including 1999. The Structural Fund regulations have been streamlined and every effort has been and is being made to make the Funds more effective. The Commission is due to bring forward a tri-annual report on progress towards greater economic and social cohesion in the course of 1996. This will require an assessment of the results being achieved by the funds in each of the member states. The Commission intends that all operational programmes will be subject to mid-term review in 1997.

3.51   The consideration of structural funding beyond the year 2000 will take place in the context of the prospect, as we approach the end of the century, of accession by a series of countries which have much lower per capita incomes than Ireland.

3.52 The enlargement of the Union to the east and south, incorporating countries with considerable development needs, will be a new challenge for the principle of cohesion and convergence.

3.53 However, the principle of economic and social cohesion which is firmly established in the EC Treaty must be fully maintained and implemented. The enlargement of the Union to include in particular the countries of central and eastern Europe, which will bring many benefits in terms of both stability and economic opportunities, should not undermine the application of cohesion policies to existing member states. The conclusions of the Essen European Council in December 1994 that "the Union's capacity to absorb new members, while maintaining the momentum of European integration and respecting its internal cohesion and fundamental principles, is also an important consideration" should continue to underpin all further discussion of enlargement.

3.54 It is essential that Ireland should use the present funding well. The Community Support Framework for Ireland is, therefore, designed precisely to have a dynamic long-term impact on the Irish economy through improved infrastructure, a more highly qualified workforce and a more widespread participation in employment, particularly by the long-term unemployed and other marginalised groups. The Government will continue to ensure that the funds are spent as effectively as possible. This is important not only for Ireland but for the contribution it can make to the economic development of the Union as a whole and for the continued success of the cohesion policy.

Social Policy

3.55 Recent years have seen considerable development of the *social dimension* of the Union. In 1989, to give an additional impetus to work in the social policy area, eleven member states (the then membership less the UK) adopted the *Community Charter of Fundamental Social Rights for Workers*. Austria, Finland and Sweden have

71

since acceded to the Charter. This "*Social Charter*" was a political statement of intent rather than a legally binding text. To give effect to the Charter, the Commission drew up in 1989 an *Action Programme* of almost fifty measures over the full range of social policy.

3.56   Twenty-four of the thirty-one legal instruments proposed by the Commission under the Charter have now been adopted by the Council, all but one (Directive on information and consultation in European-scale undertakings) applying to the UK.

3.57   In 1992 the member states other than the UK adopted an Agreement on Social Policy between themselves, which is annexed as a Protocol to the Maastricht Treaty. The role of the social partners is significantly enhanced under the Agreement. The Commission published a White Paper entitled `European Social Policy — a way forward for the Union' in July 1994 which sets out a framework for action to meet the challenges facing the Union. The rolling Social Action Programme of April 1995 lists the Commission's current policy intentions to 1999.

3.58   The social policy of the European Union covers action in a wide range of areas –

—   minimum standards regarding the working environment and the health and safety of workers;

—   the ability of people to transfer benefits from one member state to another in the Single Market;

—   the reduction of the difference in social standards between member states, so as to reduce distortions of competition;

—   equality of treatment of men and women (to which the Government attach particular importance); and

—   the European Social Fund, one of the three Structural Funds.

3.59   The Government support the aim of encouraging a high level of employment while progressively improving the conditions of those at work and the rights of all European citizens. It particularly welcomes the fact that the Commission's White Paper on Social Policy recognises the primacy of job creation.

3.60 The aims of a strong social policy and improving competitiveness are both important and are, in many ways, complementary.

On the one hand, social harmony and social dialogue contribute to the efficiency of the economy. On the other hand, a high level of social protection and social welfare systems cannot be maintained unless the economy maintains and improves its competitiveness and achieves a high level of employment.

3.61 In a Union with complete freedom of movement of goods and services, there is a concern to ensure that fair conditions of competition are maintained and that some do not gain unfair advantage by having lower social standards.

The process of harmonisation of social standards must, however, recognise the different levels of economic development of different parts of the Union, and the different factors needed to maintain the competitiveness of the less developed or more peripheral parts.

3.62 The absence of the UK from the Agreement on Social Policy annexed to the Maastricht Treaty is a matter of concern for the Union as a whole, but particularly for Ireland, because of the close links between the two economies. It would clearly be in the interests of the Union as a whole, including Ireland, if Britain were to join the Agreement on Social Policy at an early date. In the meantime Ireland will pay particular attention to the implications for competitiveness and employment of proposals which are being developed under the Agreement.

3.63 Ireland has always supported EU action in the area of social exclusion. The EU *'Poverty Three'* Programme ended in June 1994 and will not be replaced. Ireland will use its forthcoming Presidency to explore new approaches to the issue at EU level.

3.64   A particular aspect of social policy which the European Commission has indicated it will move forward is that of *social dialogue*. Ireland is well advanced as regards the level and extent of social dialogue at national level.

3.65   Europe as a whole is exposed to the economic realities of globalized competition. Ireland is among the most exposed countries, since we depend so much on trade.

3.66   In European discussions on social policy the Government will give high priority to measures that improve competitiveness and the prospect of preserving and creating jobs while at the same time encouraging the progressive improvement of the conditions of those at work and the rights of citizens. This policy is fully compatible with a balanced European social policy.

Agriculture, Food and Forestry

3.67   Right from the beginning of the European Economic Community, agriculture was included amongst the areas dealt with at European level. The *Common Agricultural Policy (CAP)* has been of crucial importance to Ireland. Agriculture remains Ireland's largest single industry. It accounts for 9% of GDP and 12% of employment. When the food processing sector is included, these figures rise to 15% and 15.3% respectively. Irish food production is heavily export-oriented.

3.68   Our membership of the European Community since 1973 has been a major factor in the growth of the agricultural and food industries and the enhancement of farm incomes. The CAP provides access to a single market of 370 million consumers, as well as direct aid to farmers and mechanisms to facilitate exports to third countries.

3.69   The benefits of the CAP to Irish agriculture should not be measured in terms of budgetary receipts alone. Access to European markets at European prices must also be considered. However, CAP transfers[3] to Ireland continue to be of major significance. It is estimated that in 1995 they will have amounted to approximately IR£1,200 million out of estimated total gross receipts of IR£2,400 million.

3.70   In May 1992, a major reform of the CAP was agreed against the background of surplus production and the increasing impact of those surpluses on budget costs and world trade. The reform reduced the emphasis on price support and increased the element of direct aid to farmers, while at the same time retaining the essential principle of common prices, financial solidarity and Community preference.

3.71   Reform in 1992 marked a new phase in the CAP. The new arrangements were primarily designed to align agricultural production more closely with market demands, while at the same time protecting the income of farmers. In addition, the reform included a range of other measures relating to early retirement for farmers, forestry and agri-environment. Farmers now receive income support within a predictable framework.

3.72   The reform of the CAP has allowed the EU and Ireland to approach changes in GATT (General Agreement on Tariffs and Trade) rules in a positive way.

The GATT Agreement on Agriculture will be reviewed at the end of the decade when it is expected that there will be pressure on the Union to reduce export support further and to grant increased access to Union markets.

While the Union will probably be able to absorb current GATT commitments without undue difficulty, further commitments would be likely to necessitate a review of the existing CAP.

3.73   The enlargement of the Union eastwards will also pose fundamental questions for the CAP. The prospective entrants have huge potential as producers of agricultural products. There are also, however, opportunities for Irish agriculture and food in the form of new markets.

3.74   The Government welcome the prospect of the EU's enlargement. At the same time, they will enter the enlargement negotiations determined to ensure terms which will protect our agricultural and other interests and allow the agriculture sector sufficient time to adapt to the challenges of an enlarged Union.

3.75   Agriculture within the European Union will remain a central policy area for Ireland in the years ahead. The food industry has been targeted as a growth area with significant opportunities for additional employment.

Among areas for further development, the Government have identified forestry as an indigenous resource which can provide additional sustainable employment, both directly and in associated industries.

The Government intend to develop the agriculture, food and forestry sectors in a manner which will maximize their contribution to employment and wealth creation while ensuring that the environment is protected and enhanced.

Fisheries

3.76   The *Common Fisheries Policy (CFP)*, introduced in 1975, requires full access by all member states to Community markets and reflects the principle of equal access for all EU fishermen to the 200 mile fishing zones of the member states, subject to certain qualifications aimed at ensuring that fishing is carried out in a balanced and sustainable way. There are also restrictions on fishing by vessels of other member states within national 12-mile coastal zones.

3.77   The main instrument of the CFP is the system of *Total Allowable Catches (TACs)*, which limits catches of certain fish stocks for management and conservation purposes. The TACs are divided among the member states. The shares or quotas for member states are based on the principle of maintaining the 'relative stability' of their respective levels of fishing activity. In general terms, the quotas therefore reflect the 'historic' performance of member states in fishing the stocks concerned.

3.78   The Irish fishing industry was under-developed in 1975. As a result, the base for allocating quotas to Ireland was very low. Although Ireland was, uniquely, allowed to double its catch between 1975-1979 and to use the 1979 figure as the basis for calculating its future quota shares, this increase was from a low base. This means that the quotas available to Irish fishermen have placed a restriction on the development of the fishing industry.

3.79   Because of decreasing stocks of many species and the consequent need to protect them from overfishing, TACs for many important species and the quotas available to all member states have been very restrictive. In such a situation, any increase in the quotas for Ireland would mean not only a relative but an absolute reduction for other member states. This makes it very difficult to negotiate increased quota shares for Ireland.

3.80   Nevertheless, the Government's Programme of Renewal includes the following objectives with regard to marine resources —

- to continue to pursue an equitable share of the EU fish quota, based on our geographical position rather than on our fishing catches in the past;

- to introduce strict conservation and resource management measures for in-shore areas (these will include an integrated approach to the exploitation of in-shore resources by all sectors — fishing, aquaculture and tourism);

- to improve working conditions and safety by reducing the age of off-shore and in-shore fleets.

3.81   In view of the large proportion of the EU area accounted for by Irish waters and the vital need, in the interests of conservation and efficient management of stocks, to ensure respect for the fishing regimes laid down for those waters, the Government have pursued, as a matter of equity, the question of EU aid for fisheries protection and surveillance. The Government accordingly welcome the agreement reached by the Council of Fisheries Ministers in October 1995 to continue and to increase that support over the next five years. In the case of Ireland, this assistance will cover operational as well as capital costs.

3.82 The *Operational Programme for Fisheries* provides financial help for the development and adaptation of the fishing industry, including fleet modernisation, fish processing and aquaculture. Ireland has benefitted and will continue to benefit substantially from this.

3.83 The long-term preservation and improvement of fishing stocks is vital. The problems of stock management extend beyond EU waters. For example, overfishing has greatly depleted many important species in the Atlantic. In many cases the species migrate from one area to another, so that overfishing in other areas can directly affect EU waters. Ireland will continue to participate in a positive way with the EU in international bodies such as the North Atlantic Fisheries Organisation or the UN to ensure the proper management of stocks.

The Second Challenge: Europe and the Citizen

3.84 The *second* challenge for the Union is to ensure that it remains close to the citizen and functions in a transparent way, so that its processes and decisions are explained and understood clearly by the people, and that its policies are designed and respond — and are perceived to respond — to real public concerns.

3.85 The Maastricht Treaty included a number of initiatives designed to emphasise the human face of the European Union, including the concept of a citizenship of the Union to which is attached both rights and duties. However, it was unable to redress a widespread perception that a gap had opened between the Union and the people. It became clear from the public debate in some member states on the ratification of Maastricht that many citizens were not convinced that the further development of European integration envisaged by the Treaty was in their interest.

3.86 The low turnout for the elections to the European Parliament in June 1994, and the tone and content of much of the public debate in the member states during the elections, also seemed to confirm the view of many citizens that the Union and its institutions were remote. If the Union is to retain the allegiance of its citizens and public support for further European integration, it must listen closely to the concerns of the public and be seen to act effectively to address those concerns.

3.87 It is essential for the future success of the Union that its institutions, which may seem remote, its decision-making procedures which may seem opaque, and its language which seems laden with jargon, are made transparent and comprehensible to ordinary people. *Demonstrating* that the Union is relevant will be just as important as *making* it relevant. Greater openness in the conduct of Union business is not an optional extra.

3.88 The Government fully support present moves within the European Union towards the introduction of greater *transparency and openness* in the institutions and business of the Union. This reflects the importance which the Government attach to greater openness at the national level as well as the particular importance — if the momentum of European integration is to be maintained — of ensuring that its inevitable complexities are understood by the public.

3.89 The Government have taken a positive view of the progress towards greater openness which has already been made at Union level under the existing Treaties and will continue to support further improvements. At the national level the present White Paper represents an important step in the process of encouraging public interest in, and debate about, the issues arising in the European Union.

The public seminars which played a key role in the preparation of the White Paper demonstrated a high level of public interest in debating European issues. The useful contributions which were made underlined the important role which can and should be played by the public in developing the national position on those issues. The Government's *Communicating Europe* initiative is designed to present information about EU affairs to the public more effectively and in a more user-friendly way. The establishment of the Joint Oireachtas Committee on European Affairs reflects the importance the Government attach to encouraging public and political discussion about European issues.

Justice and Home Affairs

3.90   In parallel with greater openness, it will be essential to develop policies of direct and immediate concern to ordinary citizens. Progress in the Justice and Home Affairs area could play a very important role in this regard. Before the coming into effect of the Treaty on European Union, cooperation between the member states in such areas as the fight against drugs, immigration, customs, police cooperation and judicial matters took place mainly outside the framework of the Treaties. The Treaty on European Union creates in Title VI a Treaty basis for common action in these areas. The procedures in this area of the Treaty (known as the *"third pillar"*) differ in some respects from the classical Community model.

3.91   A certain amount of progress has recently been made in the Union in these areas. A convention has been signed providing for the establishment of Europol, which will assist in combatting various forms of transnational crime, in particular drugs offences. Conventions have also been signed on simplified extradition procedures, on the Customs Information System and on fraud against the Community budget. A number of joint actions (including one on the Europol drugs unit) and recommendations have been adopted. Nonetheless this is one important area where there is a public perception that the Union is not adequately addressing the concerns of ordinary citizens.

3.92   In addition to action by the Union as a whole, seven member states have entered into the Schengen Agreement, which came into effect (but not fully into operation) on 26 March, 1995. The Agreement provides for the elimination of all border checks on travellers between the participating states.

Ireland and the UK have historically constituted a single travel zone without passport requirements. The UK has remained outside Schengen. Because approximately 70 per cent of journeys out of Ireland are to Britain, and because of traffic to and from Northern Ireland, Ireland has not acceded to the Agreement.

3.93   The Commission recently brought forward proposals in relation to the free movement of persons in the European Union as a whole. These proposals, if and when agreed, would extend many of the features of the Schengen agreement to the whole Union.

3.94   It is recognised that many of the aspects covered by the third pillar are sensitive and in many cases touch closely on matters of national sovereignty. Such issues are at the same time of immediate relevance to ordinary citizens, for example, the prevention of terrorism, of drug smuggling and of international organised crime.

3.95   The Government believe that effective coordinated action by the Union in these areas is essential. In particular they believe that the fight against drugs should remain a central element of the work of the Union, including its work in the area of Justice and Home Affairs. They will press for more rapid progress in this area.

3.96   Experience in using the Treaty provisions on Justice and Home Affairs is recent and is developing. Nonetheless it is clear that there is a need to have a thorough examination of the provisions of the existing Treaty covering Justice and Home Affairs to ensure that progress in areas such as the fight against drugs and international crime is facilitated.

3.97   The Government believe that there is considerable room for improving the functioning of the Treaty in this area by, for example, reducing the number of layers of decision-making.

The Third Challenge: Europe's Role in the World

3.98   The *third* challenge is for the European Union to play a role on the European continent and in the wider world commensurate with its responsibilities.

3.99   The Maastricht Treaty laid the foundation for the development of the Union's external profile through the establishment of a Common Foreign and Security Policy, based on Title V of the Treaty; the consolidation of the provisions governing the Union's external trade and economic relations; and the provision of an explicit legal base for the Union's Development Cooperation Policy (this latter policy is covered in Chapter Nine — Development Cooperation).

The Common Foreign and Security Policy (CFSP)

3.100   When Ireland joined the European Communities in 1973, we also became fully involved in the procedures then in operation between member states for consultation and coordination on matters of foreign policy. This process, known as European Political Cooperation (EPC) was codified and rendered into Treaty form in the Single European Act which entered into force in 1987.

3.101   The provisions on the Common Foreign and Security Policy (CFSP) in the Maastricht Treaty represented a further development in the efforts of the European Union to coordinate its positions, to develop common policies and to act jointly in international affairs.

3.102   In particular, they set the formulation of Union foreign and security policy in the framework of specific objectives, including –

— the preservation of peace and international security,

— the promotion of international cooperation,

— the development and consolidation of democracy,

— the rule of law and respect for human rights.

3.103   The Treaty endows the Union with a greater capacity for action through the definition of common positions on international issues and the formulation of joint actions in which member states pool resources in the implementation of specific tasks.

3.104   There has been a significant intensification of the foreign policy activity of the Union under the new arrangements with a particular focus on the major contemporary issues including the former Yugoslavia, the Middle East Peace Process, Rwanda and Burundi.

A range of common positions and joint actions have been adopted through which the Union has contributed to initiatives on conflict prevention and resolution, democratisation and respect for human rights, economic development and humanitarian aid.

3.105   New and innovative mechanisms have been created in this context. For example, the Stability Pact in Europe, an initiative of the Union, provides a framework for the development of good-neighbourly relations and cooperation in central and eastern Europe.

3.106   The Union's efforts to find a peaceful solution in the former Yugoslavia have involved it in –

constitution-building through the work of the International Conference on Former Yugoslavia;

peace-brokering through the efforts of the International Mediators and the Contact Group;

cease-fire-monitoring through the Union's Monitoring Mission; and the *civil administration* of the city of Mostar.

83

3.107   Although the EU has become increasingly active on the international scene, there is nonetheless a sense that it has not been sufficiently effective in that role. This perception stems partly from difficulties it encountered in promoting a peaceful settlement in the former Yugoslavia. However, the Peace Agreement which was concluded for Bosnia-Herzegovina was based upon the approach developed by the European Union.

3.108   Criticisms of the performance of the CFSP have tended to focus on its decision-making and management procedures. Doubts have also been expressed as to whether the present institutional structure of CFSP would be a sustainable basis for effective decision-making in an enlarged Union of twenty or more member states.

3.109   On the other hand, the fact that the CFSP has been in operation for little more than two years has to be taken into account. Inevitably, it has taken time to develop and acquire experience in using the new mechanisms offered by the Maastricht Treaty.

3.110   The current international environment, in particular the emergence of new risks arising from complex internal ethnic conflicts and tensions within states, poses difficult challenges for the entire international system.

3.111   The 1996 Intergovernmental Conference will review the functioning of the CFSP and consider whether and to what extent Treaty amendments may be required to achieve the improvements desired by member states. The Government's approach to the review is set out later, in the section on the Intergovernmental Conference.

Transatlantic Relations

3.112   Relations between the European Union and the United States of America are of central importance to both partners. Their economies are the two biggest in the world, with the highest two-way trade flow. The scale of EU-US investment flows is equally impressive.

3.113   Underpinning this relationship is the commitment shared on both sides of the Atlantic to civil society, democratic values, the rule of law and human rights. There also exists a broad measure of agreement between the EU and the US on the main challenges facing the international community. Active and substantive cooperation between the EU and the US can lead to the achievement of real progress on a global scale, as was evident in the successful conclusion of the Uruguay Round of multilateral trade liberalisation negotiations.

3.114   For Ireland, the transatlantic relationship involves two of the major strands of foreign policy: our active participation in the process of European integration and our extensive human and economic ties with the United States. It is no coincidence that the current institutional framework within which EU-US relations are conducted, the Transatlantic Declaration of November, 1990, arose out of an initiative taken by the Irish EC Presidency in that year.

3.115   EU-US relations which are of such bilateral and world significance must not, however, be taken for granted by either party on the basis of old certainties or allowed to be overshadowed by occasional disagreements between them. Nor should the importance of the relationship be minimised by the development by each side of new continental or regional perspectives.

The ties that bind North America and Europe must be open to development and capable of growth so as to respond to the changing needs of both parties and the demands of the future. In this respect, the EU and the US embarked on a joint exercise designed to enhance and strengthen their relationship in areas of practical significance for both parties and for the wider world. This work led to the adoption by the EU and the US in December 1995, at the highest political level, of a detailed action plan for co-operation over the period ahead. The plan will be geared towards promoting international peace and stability, responding to global challenges, contributing to the expansion of world trade and expanding bilateral economic and other co-operation.

3.116   The transatlantic relationship has always had many strands and this is reflected in many shared values and concerns on issues of foreign policy and security. For a number of countries, there is also a military dimension to this relationship based on alliance commitments. Recognising this multi-faceted relationship the EU and the United States solemnly stated at Madrid in December 1995 that "increasingly, our common security is further enhanced by strengthening and reaffirming the ties between the European Union and the United States within the existing network of relationships which join us together". In this regard, priority has been given by the EU and the US to the promotion of peace and stability, democracy and development around the world.

3.117   Ireland, as an EU member state, played its full part in developing this initiative for the New Transatlantic Agenda and the EU-US Action Plan and will exercise a key role during its EU Presidency regarding its effective implementation and follow up. At the same time we will be mindful of the importance of developing and strengthening the EU's relations with its other North American partners, Canada and Mexico.

The Union's Relations with its Neighbours

3.118   The Union has devoted considerable energy to developing its relations with those immediate neighbours to the east and south which are potential members of the EU. The rapid and substantial evolution in relations with those countries aspiring to accession to the Union are examined in later paragraphs, but significant developments have also occurred in the Union's relations with the countries of the former Soviet Union, the countries which border the Mediterranean, and those western European countries which are not members of the Union. In the latter connection, the creation of the European Economic Area (EEA) was an ambitious undertaking in the area of intra-European economic and political relations.

Former Soviet Union

3.119	Ireland and the other member states of the European Union fully support the economic and political reforms being undertaken by Russia and by other countries of the former Soviet Union.

Following the latter's collapse, the Union undertook to negotiate *Partnership and Cooperation Agreements (PCAs)* with Russia and each of the newly independent states. To date, PCAs have been negotiated with Russia, Ukraine, Moldova, Kazakhstan, the Kyrgyz Republic and with Belarus but have not yet entered into force pending completion of ratification procedures by all of the parties concerned. These agreements are comprehensive and wide-ranging in scope and cover such areas as trade and economic relations, political dialogue and cultural relations, with the specific provisions of each determined by the situation in each country. The PCAs contain important measures regarding respect for human rights.

3.120	Partnership between the EU and the countries of the former Soviet Union presupposes the implementation of the important programmes of political and economic reform in these countries. Close cooperation between the region and the EU is an essential element in ensuring peace and stability in Europe and the world. Consequently, Ireland, together with its EU partners, has a clear interest in continuing its support for the consolidation of democracy, economic reform and the strengthening of political and economic freedoms in Russia and in the other members of the CIS (Commonwealth of Independent States).

3.121	The negotiation by the EU of Partnership and Cooperation Agreements with the countries of the former Soviet Union is an important plank in the European Union's support for the policy of economic and political reform in the region. The PCAs' trade and economic provisions underpin the continued progress by the countries concerned towards a market economy. The Union and its member states are also the major financial contributors to the international effort to aid the reform process, having contributed over two-thirds of total assistance to date.

Russia

3.122 Ireland, in common with its EU partners, recognises that the process of change in Russia over the past decade has been fundamental. It is essential that the reform process should continue to receive our support. This consideration is central to the Union's political approach to its future relations with Russia.

3.123 Underlying our policy is the recognition that Russia should not feel marginalised by the West, and that relations with Russia should be built on partnership, not confrontation — there must be no new divisions in Europe. The Government also believe that Russian membership of the Council of Europe will strengthen the reform process in Russia and contribute to stability on the continent.

3.124 Ireland and its EU partners have repeatedly made clear that the development of relations with Russia should be based on respect for human rights and the principles of the United Nations and the Organisation for Security and Cooperation in Europe. This is particularly the case in relation to the situation in Chechnya. The Government continue to work through the OSCE to help promote a lasting political solution to the conflict.

Ukraine

3.125 The EU has also been developing its relations with Ukraine and assisting the programme of reform and democratisation there. In that regard, the EU adopted on 28 November 1994, under Article J.2 of the Maastricht Treaty, a Common Position on Ukraine, with the objective of developing a strong political relationship with that country and increasing cooperation with it. This involves, amongst other things, support for democratic development and economic stabilisation and reform. Through the EU's assistance towards the reform of the economic and energy sectors of the former Soviet Union, Ireland seeks the highest levels of safety in the nuclear sector and the closure of Chernobyl, as well as other unsafe reactors in the region.

A New EU-Mediterranean Partnership

3.126   The EU has recently developed a major initiative which establishes a new multilateral framework between Europe and the Mediterranean region, with a view to ensuring that the latter can become an area of trade and dialogue guaranteeing peace, stability and prosperity. At the heart of the new Euro-Mediterranean partnership, launched at a special Conference in Barcelona on 27-28 November 1995, is a commitment by the EU to become more actively involved in the socio-economic development of the Mediterranean partner countries.

This reflects the Union's perception, set down in the conclusions of the 1992 Lisbon European Council, that the peace and stability of this region are of the highest priority for Europe. The new initiative, which embraces both the southern and eastern Mediterranean region, is intended to have a wider scope than the conflict-resolution mandate of the Middle East Peace Process, although it is recognised that the objectives of the Peace Process will be complemented by the EU Mediterranean policy.

3.127   The Government support the new Mediterranean initiative as set out in the Barcelona Declaration as a timely recognition of the interdependence of the two regions. This interdependence notably includes such areas as environment, energy, migration, as well as the links forged by geography and by history. In the Union's preparatory work for the Euro-Mediterranean Conference, and at the Barcelona Conference itself, the Government took the position that the new partnership must be based on codes of conduct, both within participating states, and in relations between states, that are generally recognised by the international community.

EU Relations with Other Regions

3.128   Traditionally, the EU conducts its relations with many Asian countries in the framework of bilateral trade and cooperation agreements. The Union also has a structured political dialogue with most of its Asian partners. In the years ahead the Union will need to strengthen these relations in order to maintain its leading role in the world

89

economy and to contribute to stability in the region by promoting international cooperation and understanding. The Summit meeting in March 1996 with key Asian partners was an important step in this process.

Similarly, the growing importance of Latin America in the world economy is recognised by the Union and its member states. An interregional framework agreement covering economic and trade cooperation was recently negotiated with *Mercosur* (the Southern Cone Common Market comprising Argentina, Brazil, Uruguay and Paraguay). Ireland supports the development of relations with this and other regions of Latin America.

The Fourth Challenge: Future Enlargement of the Union

3.129   The *fourth* challenge facing the Union is to seize the historic opportunity of further enlargement to include the other democratic nations of Europe which wish to become members.

The Countries of Central and Eastern Europe

3.130   The countries of central and eastern Europe are involved in a difficult political and economic transition after decades of totalitarianism and enforced isolation. They see membership of the Union as the key to consolidating the results of democratic reform and accelerating their economic development and most importantly as enhancing their security and confirming their place in Europe.

3.131   All of the countries of central and eastern Europe, together with the Baltic States, aspire to eventual membership of the European Union. Hungary, Poland, Romania, the Slovak Republic, Latvia, Estonia, Lithuania, Bulgaria and the Czech Republic have submitted applications for membership.

3.132   The timing of accession by these countries will depend on a number of factors, most notably –

- the date of completion of the Intergovernmental Conference;

- the pace and complexity of enlargement negotiations;

- the capacity of the applicants to assume the demands of membership.

3.133　　　　　　　　　　At this stage, it would be impossible to specify a date for accession, but it is likely that some applicants will be members of the Union early in the next decade.

3.134　　　　　　　　　　The promotion and safeguarding of peace and prosperity on the continent of Europe demands that the European Union and its member states maintain an open and generous attitude to their European neighbours who seek membership and who fulfil the necessary conditions. The re-creation or tolerance of continental divisions, akin to those which arose in Europe earlier this century and have only recently been overcome, is no longer an option.

3.135　　　　　　　　　　Conditions which must be met by candidate countries include the achievement of stable democracy, the rule of law, human rights and the protection of minorities; the existence of a functioning market economy; and the capacity to cope with competitive pressure and market forces within the Union.

3.136　　　　　　　　　　The challenges facing the countries of central and eastern Europe in meeting these conditions, particularly insofar as they necessitate fundamental economic transformation and modernisation, are enormous. In recognition of this, the European Union has developed a comprehensive approach designed to deepen relations with the countries concerned by means of Association Agreements (sometimes known as *Europe Agreements*) and to assist them on the road to membership by means of a detailed pre-accession strategy.

3.137　　　　　　　　　　The potential of these agreements must be fully exploited if the aspirations of the associated countries of central and eastern Europe to eventual Union membership are to be realised. In this regard, primary responsibility lies with the aspirants themselves. It is most unlikely that all of the countries concerned will accede to the Union at the same time. Each application for membership will be considered on its

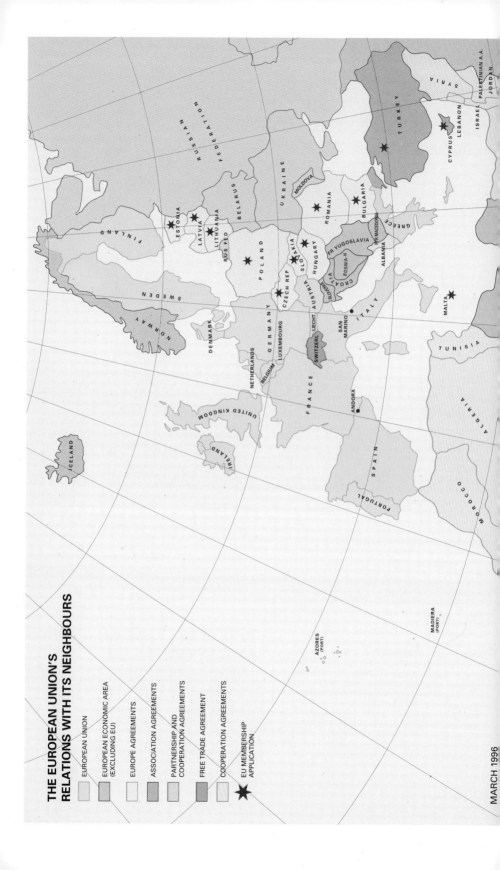

THE EUROPEAN UNION'S RELATIONS WITH ITS NEIGHBOURS

EUROPEAN UNION

EUROPEAN ECONOMIC AREA
(EXCLUDING EU)

EUROPE AGREEMENTS

ASSOCIATION AGREEMENTS

PARTNERSHIP AND
COOPERATION AGREEMENTS

FREE TRADE AGREEMENT

COOPERATION AGREEMENTS

EU MEMBERSHIP
APPLICATION

MARCH 1996

ICELAND

NORWAY

SWEDEN

FINLAND

RUSSIAN FEDERATION

ESTONIA

LATVIA

LITHUANIA

RUS FED

BELARUS

POLAND

UKRAINE

MOLDOVA

ROMANIA

BULGARIA

DENMARK

UNITED KINGDOM

IRELAND

NETHERLANDS

BELGIUM

LUXEMBOURG

GERMANY

CZECH REP

SLOVAKIA

AUSTRIA

HUNGARY

LIECHT.

SWITZERL.

FRANCE

ANDORRA

SAN MARINO

ITALY

SLOVENIA

CROATIA

BOSNIA-H

FR YUGOSLAVIA

FYR MACEDONIA

ALBANIA

GREECE

TURKEY

SYRIA

PALESTINIAN A.A.

JORDAN

ISRAEL

LEBANON

CYPRUS

MALTA

TUNISIA

ALGERIA

MOROCCO

SPAIN

PORTUGAL

AZORES
(PORT)

MADIERA
(PORT)

merits. In this connection, the required Commission opinions on the applications for EU membership will be made available to the European Council as soon as possible after the conclusion of the Intergovernmental Conference. The Commission will also prepare a composite paper on enlargement. This procedure will ensure that the applicant countries are treated on an equal basis.

Cyprus and Malta

3.138　　　　　　　　　　Applications for European Union membership have also been lodged by Cyprus and Malta and are already the subject of favourable Commission Opinions. The Essen European Council, in December 1994, confirmed that the next phase of enlargement will involve Cyprus and Malta. In the context of a decision on a Customs Union with Turkey (see below), the European Union agreed to begin accession negotiations with Cyprus six months after the completion of the IGC and in the light of its results. A similar timescale was later agreed for Malta.

3.139　　　　　　　　　　With regard to Cyprus, it is hoped that the prospect of accession, and the closer relations with Turkey which the Customs Union will bring, will facilitate the UN Secretary General's efforts to make progress towards an agreed political settlement on the island. Such a settlement would be based on the concept of bi-zonal and bi-communal federation which would respect the sovereignty and territorial integrity of Cyprus.

Turkey

3.140　　　　　　　　　　Turkey has also lodged a membership application. Turkey's application was the subject of a Commission Opinion in 1989 which concluded that it would not be useful to open accession negotiations straight away but that relations with Turkey should be intensified. In line with this approach, the final phase of a Customs Union with Turkey entered into force on 31 December 1995.

3.141　　　　　　　　　　The Government welcome the Customs Union which is a central element in the European Union's strategy to support the democratisation process and promote improvements in the human rights situation in Turkey. The Customs Union should strengthen the framework for economic development in Turkey and thereby help to foster a more favourable climate for acceleration of the internal reform process.

In agreeing to the Customs Union, Ireland and its partners in the European Union stressed that the observance of a state of law and basic liberties will continue to be the basis for the development of our relations with Turkey. While recognising the difficulties posed for the Turkish authorities by a sustained campaign of violence, the fight against terrorism must be conducted within the law and with full respect for human rights. The process of completion of the Customs Union has already given significant impetus to reform in Turkey. A series of constitutional amendments and changes to the anti-terror law have been adopted. The Government will continue to urge Turkey to adopt and implement the further reforms necessary to ensure full respect for human rights.

The Challenges of Enlargement

3.142 The issues raised by the future enlargement of the European Union are clearly of a different order of magnitude to those raised by the four previous rounds of enlargement, not only because of the nature of the economic problems facing the Union's eastern neighbours but also because of the challenges which enlargement will present to the European Union itself. These challenges are unprecedented.

3.143 The *institutional arrangements* necessary to ensure the proper functioning of a Union of 25 or more member states must be put in place in advance of any future enlargement in order to safeguard the efficiency and effectiveness of Union decision-making.

The Conclusions of the European Council at Corfu in June 1994 stated that the institutional conditions for ensuring the proper functioning of the Union must be created at the 1996 Intergovernmental Conference, which for that reason must take place before accession negotiations begin.

Equally importantly, the accession of central and eastern European countries whose economic development lags substantially behind the present Community average, poses important questions, especially as regards the future of the Union Budget, the Union's cohesion policies and the Common Agricultural Policy. The European Council meeting in Madrid in December 1995 called upon the Commission to take its recent evaluation of the effects of enlargement on community policies further, particularly with regard to agricultural and structural policies.

3.144 The Edinburgh European Council (December 1992) adopted the *budgetary framework* for the Union's finances for the period up to 1999. This sets down the maximum income and expenditure parameters. For the period to 1999, transfers from the developed to the less-developed regions of the European Union have already been agreed, with increased aid to central and eastern Europe to assist its reconstruction being found within the external actions part of the Union's budget.

Beyond 1999, however, there could well be reluctance on the part of the wealthier member states to increase substantially contributions to the EU budget and corresponding pressure to divert funds towards support for the continued reconstruction and development of central and eastern Europe in the perspective of enlargement.

At this stage, however, a forecast of the financial implications of enlargement for the EU budget would be hazardous, given the number of unknown or uncertain factors, including the timing of accessions, the conditions of accession and the state of economic development of the countries concerned at that time. The Commission will undertake a detailed analysis as soon as possible of the Union's financing system in order to submit, immediately after the conclusion of the Intergovernmental Conference, a communication on the EU's future financial framework from the year 2000, having regard to the prospect of enlargement.

3.145 *Agriculture*, though currently relatively undeveloped, is important in most of the economies of the associated countries of central and eastern Europe. The sector has enormous potential for development and, in the main, produces the same range of products as the Union, including meat, milk and cereals which are of particular interest to Ireland.

The challenge facing the Union is how to promote these countries' integration into its agriculture trading system, without disrupting Union markets or putting excessive pressure on the CAP budget. In a recent study, the European Commission expressed itself in favour of developing the 1992 CAP reform approach, allied to a range of pre-accession measures in favour of central and eastern European agriculture.

The Commission's views provide a starting point for an in-depth analysis and debate within the institutions of the European Union and in the member states in relation to the effects of enlargement on each agricultural sector with a view to ascertaining what problems may lie ahead. Satisfactory solutions for these problems will have to be found and agreed.

Ireland's Approach to Enlargement

3.146 The Government's attitude to enlargement is open and positive. It considers that enlargement will enhance European stability and confidence and, in the case of central and eastern Europe, open up new markets with significant potential. In this regard we have already seen considerable growth in our exports, notably in manufactured goods and foodstuffs, to central and eastern Europe.

3.147 The development and analysis of preliminary studies undertaken by the European Commission of the effects of enlargement for the Union's current policies, including agriculture, and their further development will have an important bearing on the detailed position to be adopted by Ireland in preparing for enlargement negotiations.

3.148 At this stage, the Government consider that it is already possible to identify a number of key concerns which should be uppermost in the approach of both Ireland and the Union as a whole.

3.149 Enlargement must take place in the context of the deepening of European integration and the maintenance of the Union's key policies, notably in the areas of agriculture and economic and social cohesion.

3.150 The Government would not accept an enlargement process which altered the essential character of the Union to that of an expanded free trade area. The Union's unique supranational nature, characterised by the development of the common policies, must be maintained and strengthened as enlargement proceeds. Its achievements in areas of vital importance to the Union must not be put at risk.

3.151 The Government will seek to ensure that the unique features of enlargement towards the east are fully acknowledged and that the Union's determination to grasp the historic opportunities presented is matched by the necessary resources. Enlargement will clearly have implications for the EU budget which will have to be addressed. While the EU budget ceiling is set to rise from 1.20% to 1.27% of Community GDP by 1999 it remains very low.[4] The Government will seek a commitment that the overall costs of enlargement are borne in an equitable manner between the Union's developed and less-developed regions and in a way which does not prejudice the operation of the Union's existing policies.

3.152 It is clear, even now, that enlargement of the Union to include the more developed associated countries of central and eastern Europe will pose important challenges to Ireland, in particular in terms of job creation. The countries concerned enjoy low labour costs, a strategic geographical position, traditional market links with the countries of the former Soviet Union and increasingly skilled workforces. In the context of enlargement to the East, the need for Union solidarity with the less developed regions of the existing Union, through the policy of cohesion, remains undiminished.

3.153 The future of the CAP and the development of rural areas will be of vital concern to the Union. During the negotiations on accession, Ireland will aim to ensure a Union negotiating position which takes full account of Irish interests in agriculture, food processing and rural development. This involves two essential elements. First, enlargement must not be used as a pretext to change the essential nature of the CAP. The principle of common financing of the Common Agricultural Policy must be fully respected. Secondly, the arrangements for membership must, as in the case of those negotiated at the time of Ireland's entry, be such as to permit a gradual adaptation by agriculture in central and eastern Europe to the CAP regime. Derogations from certain Union requirements may be necessary but these will have to be temporary. The transitional periods — in effect the timescale for derogations — may vary as between the applicant countries.

3.154 An enlarged Union will include countries of widely varying levels of economic and social development. Some degree of flexibility in the process of integration may be necessary in order to ensure that the new member states can be absorbed without hindering the continued development of the Union. However the Government would be firmly opposed to proposals leading to the creation of an exclusive hard core of member states which would result in the fragmentation of the Union and work to the detriment of its coherence.

The Fifth Challenge: An Ever Closer Union among the People of Europe

3.155 The *fifth* broad challenge facing the Union is to continue the process of European integration so that the achievements of the Union in terms of peace and prosperity are consolidated for future generations. The main tasks facing the Union in this context are on the one hand the completion of *Economic and Monetary Union (EMU)*, for which the arrangements have been laid down in the Maastricht Treaty, and on the other hand the Intergovernmental Conference, due to begin in 1996.

Economic and Monetary Union

3.156 The achievement of EMU will mark an important further step in the process of European integration. It will involve not only the creation of a single currency and monetary policy to underpin the single market but also closer coordination of participating member states' economic and fiscal policies. The Maastricht Treaty provides for transition to full Economic and Monetary Union and a single currency in three stages, although the first stage had already begun in July 1990, before the Treaty was signed. This first stage involved, for example, the liberalisation of capital movements and the adoption by member states of programmes of economic convergence.

3.157　　　　　　　　The second stage began in January 1994 and involved intensifying co-ordination of member states' economic and monetary policies. The Treaty constraints on the budget deficits of member states as set out in the excessive deficits procedure came into force in January 1994. The European Monetary Institute (EMI), the forerunner of the European Central Bank, was established at the start of stage two to foster closer co-ordination of the monetary policies of the member states and to prepare for the monetary aspects of stage three.

3.158　　　　　　　　The Treaty provides that if by the end of 1997 the date for the beginning of the third stage has not been set, it will start on 1 January 1999. The European Council will decide, by qualified majority, after consulting the European Parliament, which member states fulfil the conditions to join.

3.159　　　　　　　　Participation in EMU by a majority of member states is not required for EMU to proceed in 1999. The European Council at Madrid in December 1995 confirmed that 1 January 1999 will be the starting date for the third stage.

3.160　　　　　　　　The third stage will involve the irrevocable locking of the exchange rates of the currencies of the participating member states (leading to a single currency among them), the setting up of a European Central Bank (ECB) and the transfer of responsibility for monetary policy to a European System of Central Banks (ESCB) consisting of the ECB and the Central Banks of participating member states. The Madrid European Council agreed on the 'changeover scenario' under which the locking of participating currencies on 1 January 1999 will lead to the issue of single currency notes and coins within three years of that date and the subsequent withdrawal (within six months) of national currency notes and coins. It also agreed that the new currency would be called the *"Euro"*.

3.161   When the third stage begins, only those member states which fulfil the conditions will initially participate in it. Member states which do not initially qualify to join the third stage can join when they fulfil the conditions. Member states may be admitted to EMU after it has been formed if the European Council, meeting in the composition of the Heads of State or Government, after consulting the European Parliament, on a proposal from the Commission decides that they fulfil the necessary conditions.

3.162   In other words, the Treaty provisions allow for a limited number of member states proceeding first, but without excluding others from eventual membership.

3.163   EMU is to the advantage of an open economy such as ours which is heavily dependent on trade. Also, in EMU we would participate in the major monetary decisions affecting us instead of being in a situation where in practice we often must, as a small country, live with the consequences of decisions taken by others.

3.164   Irish Government policy has been aimed, and will continue to be aimed, at qualifying for the final stage of EMU. This involves continued sound management of the public finances and pursuing exchange rate and monetary policies based on price stability, that is the maintenance of low inflation. We meet the convergence criteria and are committed to continuing to meet them. Ireland has a good inflation record in recent years, our interest rates are well within the reference limits provided for under the Treaty and the Irish Pound trades comfortably within the Exchange Rate Mechanism of the European Monetary System.

3.165   In 1994, Ireland was one of only two member states, and in 1995 one of only three, adjudged by the European Commission to satisfy the budgetary performance criteria in the Treaty in respect of Government deficit and debt. These decisions were formal recognition of the substantial progress achieved by Ireland in recent years in keeping annual Government deficits consistently below 3% of GDP and reducing the debt/GDP ratio from over 117% in 1986 to under 92% at the end of 1994 and to under 87% at the end of 1995.

3.166   Government policy is to continue to meet the criteria through keeping the annual budget deficit comfortably below 3% of GDP and continuing to make satisfactory progress in reducing the debt/GDP ratio towards 60%. In addition to satisfying the convergence criteria, Government policy is also aimed at enhancing the competitiveness and flexibility of the economy.

3.167   The member states of the Union are increasingly required to frame their economic policies with the EMU objective in view. Ireland must therefore continue to meet the qualifying conditions and to prepare the economy for participation in the final stage.

3.168   A Protocol attached to the Treaty allows the United Kingdom to remain outside full EMU unless it notifies its intention to participate. Ireland in common with most other member states decided not to negotiate such an option. Nevertheless, it would clearly be preferable from Ireland's point of view if the United Kingdom were to enter EMU at the same time as Ireland. The UK Government have said that the UK will decide about joining EMU in 1999, closer to the date. If the UK were to remain outside EMU in 1999 it could, of course, decide to join at a later time.

3.169   The key priority for Ireland is to keep meeting the qualifying conditions to enable us to join and to continue to prepare the economy for participation in EMU. Failure to meet the conditions would exclude Ireland from EMU in all circumstances. The policy requirements in these respects, of course, constitute necessary prescriptions for sustained economic and employment growth in their own right.

1996 Intergovernmental Conference

3.170   The Intergovernmental Conference (IGC) will offer an important opportunity for the Union to take stock of developments in the Union and to examine the options for future progress. While this IGC will by no means be the last such opportunity for the Union to equip itself to deal with its future challenges, a successful outcome will be of the greatest importance to the European Union and to Ireland in terms of addressing the challenges of a new century. The IGC, which is convened specifically to consider possible Treaty changes, will not address issues on which the Treaty provisions have already been agreed (such as EMU) or which do not require Treaty change and will fall to be dealt with later in a different framework (such as the size and priorities of the Union's budget when the present multi-annual package comes to an end in 1999).

3.171   The Government are committed to ensuring that Ireland makes a constructive and imaginative contribution to the IGC. The chairing of the IGC in the second half of 1996 will be one of the major tasks of the Irish Presidency. When in the chair, the Government will seek to advance the work of the IGC as constructively and expeditiously as possible. The IGC will itself determine its precise agenda and its level of ambition. There has always been, and remains, a likelihood that the IGC will run into 1997.

3.172   The Treaty on European Union provides that the IGC should examine those Treaty provisions for which explicit provision is made for a review. These include security policy and the provisions of the Common Foreign and Security Policy generally; the decision-making powers of the European Parliament (extension of the co-decision procedure); the Union's legislative procedures; and the possible extension of explicit Community competence into the areas of Energy, Tourism and Civil Protection.

3.173   The Brussels European Council in December 1993 and the Informal Foreign Ministers meeting in April 1994 have subsequently added to the agenda: the weighting of the votes of the member states in the Council; the number of members of the Commission; and any measures deemed necessary to facilitate the work of the institutions of the Union and guarantee their effective operation in the perspective of future enlargement. The Council, Commission and Parliament have also agreed that certain budgetary and management matters should be considered by the IGC. Moreover, it is open to any member state or to the Commission to propose revisions to the Treaty in other areas for consideration at the IGC.

3.174   The European Council meeting in Corfu in June 1994 decided to establish a Reflection Group consisting of Personal Representatives of Foreign Ministers and of the President of the Commission as well as two representatives of the European Parliament to help to prepare the agenda of the IGC. The Minister of State for European Affairs, Gay Mitchell, T.D., was Ireland's representative on the Reflection Group. The Reflection Group was not a negotiating forum. Its role was to clarify the issues and challenges facing the European Union and where possible to identify options for consideration by the IGC. The Reflection Group, which started its work on 3 June, submitted its final report to the Madrid European Council in December 1995. The European Council considered that the guidelines which emerged from the Group's work constituted a sound basis for the work of the IGC.

3.175   The Reflection Group considered that results should be achieved by the IGC in three main areas: (i) making Europe more relevant to its citizens (including through cooperation on Justice and Home Affairs); (ii) enabling the Union to work better and preparing it for enlargement; and (iii) giving the Union greater capacity for external action.

3.176   It would not be possible or indeed appropriate to attempt to set out in detail in advance of negotiations the Government's approach to all the issues which may arise at the IGC. It is only in the negotiations themselves that each member state can and should set out its detailed negotiating approach.

3.177   However, it is entirely appropriate to set out here some of the broad considerations which will influence the Government's approach to the Conference. These include the following –

- Like every member state, Ireland will pursue its interests at the IGC. Foremost amongst Ireland's long-term interests are the success and effectiveness of the European Union itself and Ireland's continued involvement at the heart of the Union.

- Ireland, which has always sought to play a constructive role in the process of European integration, will be open to proposals which will advance that process, in particular by improving the functioning of the Union, equipping it to address more effectively the direct concerns of citizens, encouraging greater transparency, and enabling it to address the challenges posed by future enlargement. We will ourselves consider bringing forward proposals to that effect.

- One of the fundamental principles and practices of the European Union is that the views and interests of all member states are taken fully into account. Just as Ireland expects its partners to give due weight to our concerns, we must be prepared to take their concerns into account also. The outcome of an IGC requires the unanimous agreement of the member states.

- While the Government will defend and promote Ireland's interests at the IGC, the overall success of the IGC does not depend on narrow negotiating successes for one member state or another on specific agenda items but on balanced advantage for all member states and especially for the Union as a whole. This will be a central consideration when Ireland chairs the IGC in the second half of 1996.

- The European Union has had major achievements to date. Those achievements and the broad institutional arrangements which made them possible represent the foundation on which the future success of the Union must be built.

- The development of an exclusive inner core of member states should be avoided. Provision for member states to approach the same objectives at different speeds, as in the case of EMU, should be considered where necessary on a case by case basis.

- It will be essential to ensure that the IGC negotiations are, from beginning to end, an open and transparent process; that the public throughout Europe is informed about and involved in that process; and that the outcome is comprehensible and meaningful to all European citizens. It will also be important to consider whether the IGC can reach decisions which would enhance transparency in the conduct of Union business in the longer term.

3.178　　　　　　　　The Government's priority will be to ensure that, to as a great an extent as possible, the Treaty changes agreed at the IGC make the Union and its institutions more responsive to real public concerns.

3.179　　　　　　　　In this regard four concerns should be highlighted:

(i)　*The preservation of peace and stability.* The success of the Union in preserving peace and contributing to stability, not only within its own borders but beyond, is now so taken for granted that it is sometimes lost sight of. Ireland's approach to the IGC and to European integration more generally will continue to reflect this central concern.

(ii)　*The need to increase the efficiency of the Union's decision-making procedures.* This will also be a central concern in the overall Irish approach not just for its own sake but so that the Union can be more effective in addressing the concerns of its citizens. The Government are prepared to consider, for example, greater recourse to qualified majority voting for Community matters and a reduction in the number of legislative procedures. Where proposals would make a genuine contribution to improving efficiency these will be considered in a favourable light.

(iii)   *The need to improve accountability/transparency in the Union.* It is essential for the development of the Union that it should be understood by, and seen as responsive to, ordinary citizens.

(iv)   *The need to address more effectively issues of most direct concern to citizens including employment, social exclusion, the fight against international crime and the scourge of drugs in our society.* The last-mentioned is an issue which cuts across each of the three pillars of the Union. It is an area in which progress has been insufficient and falls far short of public expectations in Ireland and the Union more generally.

Institutional Reform

3.180   The institutions of the European Union and the relationship between them represent the essential backbone of the construction of the European Union. These unprecedented and uniquely innovative institutions have made it possible to transform good neighbourliness and intergovernmental cooperation into a real community of interests, states and peoples, which is without precedent anywhere in the world.

3.181   At the heart of the institutional system is the European Commission which, in its role of initiating proposals for legislation, and implementing and supervising Community law, acts as the necessary guardian of the interests of each and every member state and of the common interest.

3.182   The European Parliament, directly elected by the people of Europe, is both a symbol of the democratic Union which we are constructing together and an increasingly central actor in transforming that ideal into reality. The Council, which ensures that the views of all member states are taken into account, is unique in its provision for majority voting and in its culture of patiently seeking to accommodate the interests of all. The Court of Justice is responsible for ensuring that the law is observed in the interpretation and application of the Treaties. The Court of Auditors, which audits the correct expenditure of European monies, was raised to the status of an institution by the Maastricht Treaty.

3.183　　　　　　　　At the Intergovernmental Conference, many proposals will be considered to improve the functioning of the institutions and their relationship with each other. The Government will contribute to the debate and will view positively any proposals which would make a real contribution towards that end. It will be particularly important to ensure that the Union is equipped institutionally to accommodate, at the appropriate time, the further enlargement of the Union, and that its democratic nature is maintained and, where possible, enhanced. The Government will not favour proposals which would undermine any of the institutions in the exercise of its basic functions under the Treaty or would call into question the broad institutional framework which has served the Union well.

3.184　　　　　　　　There are many ideas which can be considered in a broadly positive light. To cite some examples, these could include –

- a reduction in the number of legislative procedures, accompanied by a simplification in the operation of those procedures;

- an extension of the co-decision procedure to strengthen the role of the European Parliament which plays a crucial part in the democratic operation of the European Union;

- an extension of the provision for qualified majority voting in the Council.

3.185　　　　　　　　At the same time, the Government are conscious that a number of the ideas likely to be put forward at the IGC under the banner of institutional improvements would not represent improvements in the process of European integration. The further enlargement of the Union must not be used as an excuse — and the IGC must not be used as an occasion — to call into question the delicate institutional balances which represent the Union's most important achievement and resource. Ireland's foremost long-term interest in the Union, as indicated above, is to ensure the continued success and effectiveness of the Union which in turn depends largely on ensuring that its unique institutional arrangements can continue to function effectively. The Government will pursue this interest with the utmost vigour at the IGC.

3.186	There are two possible approaches in particular which, even if they are presented in the guise of strengthening or democratising the decision-making process, will be resisted by the Government.

3.187	The first such approach would be to seek to make the decision-making process more intergovernmental, at the expense of the Community mechanisms which apply to the core activities of the European Community. Any attempt to undermine the role of the European Parliament or the Commission will be firmly resisted. The role of the Court of Justice should also be fully protected. The broad balance between the institutions must be preserved.

3.188	The second such approach would be to use the IGC as an occasion to alter the broad balance between the member states. This approach could arise, for example, in relation to membership of the European Commission and Parliament, the relative voting weights in Council and the rotation of the Presidency. Ireland could not, for example, countenance losing the right to nominate a full member of the European Commission.

3.189	The Government are conscious of the fact that the larger member states take the view that successive enlargements of the Union to include more and more small or medium-sized member states alter the balance unfavourably from their point of view, and may ultimately raise questions about the democratic legitimacy of the decisions taken by the Council.

The large member states must equally be conscious of the view of many of their partners that the small and medium-sized member states do not in any sense represent a grouping and do not therefore derive any specific benefit from the accession of other smaller states. The risk of Governments representing a majority of the Union's citizens being outvoted seems likely to be at most a remote possibility.

3.190 The strength of the Union is that the views of all member states are listened to and respected and this will apply fully to the issues which may arise in this area of the IGC's work. It cannot be excluded that certain adjustments will be agreed. For example, in the perspective of further enlargements it would be appropriate and reasonable that the larger member states would agree to nominate only one full member of the Commission. What is important is that in the Union as a whole the broad balance between the member states is maintained.

Openness and Transparency

3.191 The Government will be amongst those taking a lead in ensuring both the transparency of the IGC process itself and that the decisions taken at the IGC result in a significant improvement in the transparency of the European Union for the future.

3.192 It is important that public awareness and debate about the issues involved in the IGC is encouraged throughout the process. That is what the Government have been doing and will continue to do including especially during the Irish Presidency in the second half of 1996. It is also essential that the outcome of the IGC should be lucid and comprehensible.

3.193 As far as improvements for the future conduct of Union business which might be agreed by the IGC are concerned, the Government will strongly support a simplification of the Union's legislative procedures, including a reduction in their number. The Government also recognize that a greater role for national Parliaments would contribute to bringing citizens closer to the process of decision-making.

3.194   If an appropriate way could be found
of reflecting the importance of transparency in the Treaty itself the
Government will support this.

The Common Foreign and Security Policy

3.195   The Maastricht Treaty provides for a
review of the operation of the CFSP at the Intergovernmental Conference,
including the question of "the eventual framing of a common defence policy
which might in time lead to a common defence". The security and defence
policy aspects of this review are dealt with in Chapter Four — International
Security.

3.196   The IGC will consider ways of
improving the capacity of the European Union to contribute, through the
Common Foreign and Security Policy, to the promotion of international
peace and stability.

3.197   In this context, it is likely that there
will be proposals for modification of the present CFSP decision-making
process, in which major foreign policy decisions are taken by consensus,
with a view to facilitating effective EU foreign policy action, particularly in
an enlarged Union. Proposals may also be made with a view to achieving
greater continuity in the management and implementation of CFSP actions
and the conduct of relations with third countries, functions which are
currently vested mainly in the rotating Presidency. These tasks are growing
considerably as the Union's engagement in international issues intensifies.
Ways in which the international profile of the Union can be enhanced are
also likely to be considered.

3.198   Ireland will play a constructive role in
the review. The CFSP occupies a central place in the conduct of the foreign
relations of all member states including Ireland. The Government share the
view that member states can exercise a more effective influence for the
development of a stable, just and peaceful international system by acting in
concert than they could accomplish individually. An effective CFSP is

therefore in Ireland's interest and at the IGC the Government will be working for practicable and sustainable ways of improving its functioning. It is important that the review should be based on a realistic appraisal of the operation of the present system and that the aspects which may require strengthening are correctly identified.

3.199   The European Union's positions on international issues derive their authority and credibility from the backing they enjoy from the member states. Decisions on sensitive foreign policy matters, accordingly, have to be underpinned by broad support in the member states if they are to be sustainable and effective. This aspect must be taken into account in considering any proposals to adjust CFSP decision-making procedures. More use could be made of the provision in the Maastricht Treaty for qualified majority voting on decisions which implement the foreign policies decided by consensus in the Council of Ministers.

3.200   The Government believe, on the basis of the experience to date, that the key to more effective decision-making in the CFSP area lies in improving the structures for the development of common analysis and preparation of proposals on international issues. At present, there is no counterpart in CFSP to the role the Commission fulfils in policy planning in Community matters.

3.201   More effective means are required at Union level to undertake the research and analysis which should underpin policy initiation and development on international issues.

3.202   To meet this need, the Government have advocated the development of a planning and analysis capacity within the Council Secretariat of the European Union. This idea attracted broad support in the Reflection Group. A central planning and analysis capacity, which would be at the service of the Presidency and the Council, would facilitate the identification of the common Union interest in relation to international issues and the formulation of effective responses by the Union to these challenges.

3.203   It would be important to make
provision for close cooperation between a Secretariat planning and analysis
unit and the Commission in view of the latter's competence in the external
economic relations area and the need to ensure coherence between the
political and economic aspects of foreign policy.

A development of the role of the Council Secretariat would also enhance
its capacity to assist the Presidency in implementing the CFSP and
contribute to greater continuity between Presidencies in policy development
and execution.

Justice and Home Affairs

3.204   It is clear that the Treaty provisions on
Justice and Home Affairs must be discussed at the IGC and the Government
will support all efforts to ensure that those provisions are appropriately
strengthened.

3.205   For example, the Government would
consider proposals to transfer some of the issues (perhaps immigration and
asylum) dealt with under Title VI of the Treaty on European Union (which
is essentially intergovernmental in nature) into the EC Treaty to facilitate
easier decision-making and more rapid progress.

3.206   In any event the Government would
favour extending to all matters in Title VI the Commission's shared right to
bring forward proposals, could see advantage in setting clear objectives and
could consider ending the unanimity requirement for certain matters to
strengthen the effectiveness of the Union's action.

3.207   Furthermore, the Government accept
that as the issues dealt with under Title VI of the Treaty on European Union
are of such direct concern to the citizens of the member states, decisions
taken by the Council on Justice and Home Affairs must be open to
appropriate parliamentary scrutiny, whether at European or national level.

3.208   In relation to the fight against drugs,
to which Ireland attaches a high priority, the Government have established

an Interdepartmental Committee with a view to considering how progress can be made in the work of the Union. This Committee is also assisting in the preparation of a detailed national position at the IGC in relation to this issue.

Other Issues

3.209 Among the other issues which may arise at the IGC are the following –

- The IGC is likely to examine whether the Treaty provisions could be strengthened to facilitate the fight to maintain and create *employment*. Apart from what must be done at national level, the Union already, on the basis of the present Treaty, attaches the highest importance to promoting a high level of employment (and has, for example, developed a process of surveillance of employment trends and systems in the member states). Ireland will be actively involved in exploring the scope for constructive Treaty amendments.

- Another issue which is likely to be addressed at the IGC is how the *environment* provisions of the EC Treaty can be strengthened. The possibility of strengthening the *EURATOM* provisions on nuclear safety has already been raised by the Irish member of the IGC Reflection Group.

- With regard to *social policy* and the possible wish of some member states to introduce new elements into the Treaty, the Government are open to considering any such proposals. Clearly it will take full account of any possible effect on competitiveness and employment.

In particular, if new provisions were not to apply to all member states, they could aggravate the different conditions of competition between member states and work directly against the objective of providing a level playing field within the European Union.

- The issue of a *non-discrimination* clause, covering such matters as disability, is likely to be considered by the IGC. The implications of such a clause will be examined at European and national level. The

Government will seek to identify Treaty amendments in this area, with a view to initiating a Treaty change in the course of the IGC. The purpose of such a Treaty change would be to reflect in an appropriate way the rights and needs of people with a disability.

- The concept of *subsidiarity* was introduced by the Treaty on European Union to ensure that the Community will take action if and only if the objectives of the proposed action can better be achieved by the Community. The concept has proved a useful one. If any attempt is made at the IGC to define further the concept of subsidiarity it will be important broadly to maintain the present balance between Community and member state competence. Apart from the Treaty provisions on subsidiarity itself, the importance attached to subsidiarity will play a key role in relation to many of the other issues arising at the IGC.

- It is possible but at this stage unlikely that the *linguistic regime* of the European Union will fall for consideration at the IGC. There is already an authentic version of the Treaties in Irish and certain other documents are also translated into Irish. The Government would like to see an appropriate increase in the use of Irish. Progress can be achieved without a Treaty amendment, but if a suitable opportunity arises at the IGC or in the context of the subsequent enlargement negotiations to make a case for enhancing the use of Irish in the European Union, the Government will avail itself of that opportunity.

- Proposals are likely to be put forward which would increase the role of *national Parliaments* in relation to the business of the European Union. It would be appropriate for the Oireachtas and other national Parliaments to formulate their own ideas in that regard. The Government's commitment to such an increased role for the Oireachtas is reflected in the establishment of the Joint Oireachtas Committee on European Affairs. However, the Government share the view of a large majority of member states that an enhanced role for national Parliaments should not cut across the European Parliament or make procedures at European Union level more cumbersome.

- The possibility of strengthening the European *citizenship* provisions of the Treaty by, for example, incorporating certain rights or anti-discrimination provisions, is also likely to be considered. Ireland will look positively at possible improvements in this area.

3.210   The above listing of items likely to arise at the IGC is not and cannot be comprehensive at this stage. The Government will continue to review how they can make a constructive contribution to advance the process of European integration as well as Ireland's interests in that process, and will bring forward proposals as appropriate.

3.211   The Government will ensure that the Oireachtas and the public are kept fully informed of developments and of the Irish approach to the issues arising.

FOOTNOTES

1   The European Union consists of three distinct elements, referred to as pillars. The *first pillar* comprises essentially the three Communities which existed before the creation of the Union: the European Community (formerly European Economic Community), the European Coal and Steel Community and the European Atomic Energy Community. The *second pillar* concerns the Common Foreign and Security Policy. The *third pillar* concerns the area of Justice and Home Affairs. The White Paper, to simplify the terminology, refers generally to the European Union unless the context requires otherwise.

2   Ireland's Gross Domestic Product (GDP — the annual value of goods and services produced in the country) per capita is considerably higher than its Gross National Product (GNP — the annual value of goods and services produced minus the net outflow of income) per capita but the trend of closing the gap with the more prosperous regions of the Union is also evident for GNP.

3   These do not include agricultural payments that are considered to be part of the Structural Funds (see paragraph 3.46).

4. In highly developed federal systems such as Australia, Canada, Switzerland and the U.S., federal expenditure is between 5% and 10% of GNP.

Reproduced by kind permission of An Post

Chapter 4

INTERNATIONAL SECURITY

Ireland's Approach to International Security

4.1 The foundation of Ireland's approach to international peace and security is set out in Article 29.1 of the Constitution in which the State "affirms its devotion to the ideal of peace and friendly cooperation amongst nations founded on international justice and morality."

4.2 Successive Governments have sought to implement these provisions in the light of the prevailing security situation and in a way that best contributes to international peace and to Ireland's security.

4.3 The central elements of Ireland's security policy over many years comprise –

• a policy of military neutrality, embodied by non-participation in military alliances;

9. Irish postage stamps on the theme of peace.

- the promotion of the rule of international law and the peaceful settlement of disputes;

- the promotion of greater equity and justice in international affairs through efforts to eliminate the causes of conflict and to protect human rights;

- a commitment to collective security through the development of international organisations, especially the United Nations;

- a willingness to participate in peace-keeping and humanitarian operations throughout the world;

- participation in the construction of the European Union as a way of overcoming age-old rivalries in Europe;

- the promotion of an active policy of disarmament and arms control;

- a commitment to regional cooperation, especially in Europe, through the promotion of, and participation in, regional organisations such as the Organisation for Security and Cooperation in Europe, the OECD, and the Council of Europe.

Neutrality

4.4 The majority of the Irish people have always cherished Ireland's military neutrality, and recognise the positive values that inspire it, in peace-time as well as in time of war. It has embraced the policy of the State in the event of armed conflict and has provided the basis for Ireland's wider efforts to promote international peace and security.

4.5 In the strict sense of international law and practice, neutrality and its attendant rights and duties do not exist in peacetime; they arise only during a state of war. Neutrality represents an attitude of impartiality adopted by a state towards the participants in a conflict and recognised as such by the belligerents. Such an attitude creates certain rights and duties between the neutral state and the belligerents which commence at the outbreak of war and end with its cessation.

4.6   An intention to remain neutral in the event of conflict is not sufficient on its own to maintain conditions of peace, stability and justice in Europe and beyond. Ireland has therefore sought to promote a range of policies, directed at preventing, containing and resolving conflict and at promoting greater equity and justice in international affairs.

4.7   The values that underlie Ireland's policy of neutrality have therefore informed almost every aspect of our foreign policy. These values have been a principal motivation behind our involvement in the search for collective security arrangements in the United Nations, in our participation in international peacekeeping, in working together with our partners in the European Union to preserve peace in Europe and worldwide, in our work for human rights and development, and in our promotion of arms control and disarmament.

4.8   The conduct of this policy embraces many actions and activities of the State carried out bilaterally with other states and through Ireland's participation in international organisations which are described in detail in this and other Chapters of the White Paper.

4.9   Ireland's policy of military neutrality has served Ireland well. Our international reputation for impartiality has enabled us to play a meaningful role in the preservation of peace in the world. As stated in the Programme for a Government of Renewal, that policy will not be changed unless the people of Ireland decide otherwise in a referendum. All steps taken by the Government to enhance our contribution to international security will be carried out within the scope of this undertaking.

4.10   The Government will not be proposing that Ireland should seek membership of NATO or the Western European Union, or the assumption of their mutual defence guarantees.

4.11   Successive Irish Governments have taken the view that in the event of a major international or European conflict the security of the State could best be preserved by the adoption of an attitude of neutrality. Irish foreign and security policy has therefore been conducted in such a way as to preserve the option of neutrality in the event of an outbreak of hostilities that might threaten the security of the State. Ireland's decision not to participate in the two western military alliances established after the Second World War — the North Atlantic Treaty Organisation and the Western European Union — reflected this approach. Both alliances contain in their founding Treaties provisions committing the parties to collective action in the event of an armed attack against one or more of them, and membership of either would not be compatible with an intention to remain neutral.

4.12 This is also the reason the Government sought and secured in the Maastricht Treaty negotiations the inclusion in the Treaty on European Union of a provision that stipulates that the Union's security policy should not prejudice the specific character of the security and defence policy of certain member states.

4.13 None of this is to argue that Ireland can, or should, turn its back on the problems of the world. Irish people have always believed that we must make the biggest contribution that we can towards solving problems of injustice, oppression, or want. In a world that remains troubled and uncertain, Ireland remains willing to play a full role in contributing to the security of Europe and the world.

Ireland's Security Environment

4.14 The international and European security environments in which Ireland pursues these policies have changed dramatically in recent years. The democratic revolutions in central and eastern Europe and the dissolution of the Warsaw Pact that brought the Cold War to an end have greatly reduced the risk of a massive military confrontation in Europe. Ireland's security situation has improved substantially as a result.

4.15   Notwithstanding these welcome developments, risks and uncertainties remain which have a capacity to affect our interests and the welfare and prosperity of our people. Amongst the most important of these are –

• ethnic conflicts, and disputes arising out of the neglect of the rights of persons belonging to national minorities;

• border disputes that may lead to armed conflict;

• the proliferation of weapons of mass destruction and their delivery systems;

• international terrorism;

• organised crime and drugs-trafficking;

• transnational environmental risks.

4.16   These questions cannot be dealt with by any state acting alone, and cooperative action is necessary to reduce the risks involved and to overcome them. Such action may be carried out through the main international and European organisations.

United Nations and Regional Arrangements

4.17   In view of the responsibilities which it assumes under its Charter the United Nations has a key role to play in the maintenance of international peace and security, in particular through its machinery for the peaceful settlement of disputes, its activities in the field of conflict prevention, and the measures that it can take to deal with breaches of the peace and acts of aggression. The United Nations has in addition a vital role to play in the area of multilateral disarmament with regard to weapons of mass destruction and conventional armaments.

The role of the United Nations in these areas is set out in Chapters 5, 6, 7 and 8 which outline Ireland's policy with regard to the reform of the UN Organisation, disarmament and arms control, peacekeeping and human rights.

121

4.18   Since the end of the Cold War there
has been a dramatic increase in the activities of the United Nations related
to international peace and security. In a period of just over five years the
number of Security Council Resolutions has increased fourfold, the
number of disputes and conflicts in which the UN is actively involved is
three times greater, and peacekeeping operations have increased from 5 to
19.

4.19   In these circumstances it is clear that
the capacity of the United Nations to become involved in every question of
regional security is constrained, and the UN has in recent years encouraged
regional organisations to use their own potential for preventive diplomacy,
peacekeeping, peace-making, and post conflict peace-building in
accordance with Chapter VIII of the UN Charter.[1]

4.20   In addition to lightening the burden
on the UN Organisation itself it is envisaged that such an approach would
also contribute to a deeper sense of participation, consensus and
democratisation in international affairs. European organisations have been
reassessing their roles and capabilities accordingly.

The Organisation for Security and Cooperation in Europe (OSCE)

4.21   Since its beginning in Helsinki in
1973, the Conference on Security and Cooperation in Europe (since
renamed the Organisation for Security and Cooperation in Europe —
OSCE) has played a particularly valuable role in strengthening friendly
relations and cooperation amongst the states of Europe, the United States
and Canada.

4.22   Ireland has been a strong supporter of
the CSCE and was an original participant in the Helsinki Conference in
1973. The Final Act of the Conference established a comprehensive
approach to European security embracing principles for the conduct of
relations between states, confidence-building measures, economic

cooperation, and cooperation in humanitarian and other areas. During the Cold War the CSCE played an important role in providing a framework for a cooperative approach to security and it developed mechanisms for the protection of human rights.

4.23   Since the end of the Cold War a series of Summits, in Paris in 1990, Helsinki in 1992, and Budapest in 1994, have redefined the role of the OSCE in the light of the changed security situation in Europe and enhanced its capabilities, particularly in the areas of conflict prevention and the peaceful resolution of disputes.

4.24   Amongst the most important of these developments, in which Ireland has been actively involved, are –

• the development of the CSCE as a permanent Organisation with its own institutions and structures;

• a declaration that the OSCE is a regional arrangement in the sense of Chapter VIII of the UN Charter;

• the development of new mechanisms for early warning, conflict prevention and crisis management, including fact-finding and reporting missions and an OSCE peacekeeping capability;

• the development of mechanisms for the protection of human rights;

• the creation of an OSCE High Commissioner on National Minorities;

• the development of a Forum for Security Cooperation with responsibility for arms control and confidence- and security-building measures;

• the adoption of a politically binding Code of Conduct on Politico-Military Aspects of Security;

• the establishment of a Conflict Prevention Centre and an Office for Democratic Institutions and Human Rights;

- a decision to start discussions on a model of common and comprehensive security for Europe for the twenty-first century based on OSCE principles and commitments.

4.25   In line with these developments the OSCE has been increasing its involvement in potential and actual conflicts in Europe. It has undertaken a wide range of missions, both short-term and long-term, in central and eastern Europe and in the states of the former Soviet Union. While this work has received less attention than the more extensive peacekeeping operations of the United Nations, it has made a particularly useful contribution in helping to defuse tensions.

The OSCE is playing a substantial role in the implementation of the civilian, election, human rights and confidence building dimensions of the Dayton Accords on Bosnia-Herzegovina.

4.26   The work of the OSCE High Commissioner for National Minorities is another example of the positive contribution that can be made in the area of conflict prevention by the OSCE. The impartial activities of the High Commissioner have been generally recognised as having proved very effective in helping to defuse tensions arising with regard to national minorities — notably in the Baltic States, but also in other central and eastern European states and in the former Soviet Union.

4.27   The Government believe that, as the only regional organisation to which all the states of Europe and North America adhere, the OSCE is uniquely placed to develop further its existing role as a focal point for European security cooperation. The OSCE, at its Summit in Budapest in 1994, committed itself "to pursue more systematic and practical cooperation between the OSCE and European and other regional and transatlantic organisations and institutions that share its values and objectives". This commitment builds on earlier commitments from the OSCE and the other European and transatlantic organisations to mutually reinforce each others' efforts in pursuit of international peace and security.

The broad concept of security on which the work of the OSCE is based, which extends to the human dimension and to the economic and environmental aspects of security, as well as to work in support of democratic institutions, is one with which Ireland can readily identify.

Ireland's policy will be to strengthen the OSCE as a permanent Organisation for European security cooperation and to further develop the Organisation's capacity for preventive diplomacy and peacekeeping.

4.28 The Government have already taken steps to strengthen Ireland's representation to the OSCE by opening a Permanent Delegation at the Headquarters of the OSCE in Vienna staffed by diplomatic and military officers. Ireland has participated in a number of OSCE missions, notably those in the Former Yugoslav Republic of Macedonia and in Georgia. The Government intend to increase the level of participation in OSCE missions.

4.29 The next Summit of the OSCE will take place in Lisbon in late 1996 during Ireland's Presidency of the European Union. One of the objectives of Ireland's Presidency will be to ensure that the European Union plays a leading role in maximising the contribution that the OSCE can make to European security.

4.30 In this context the Government attach particular importance to the discussions that have recently commenced in the OSCE on a new security model for Europe. The Government see the discussions on the security model as providing the focal point for the debate, involving all European as well as North American countries, on the broad principles that should underlie the new European security architecture. We believe that the model should be based on the OSCE's comprehensive approach to European security and it should reflect the OSCE's concept that security is indivisible. The model should contribute to efforts to create a common space of security, stability and cooperation.

4.31 Ireland will be an active participant in the discussions on the model, with special regard to our EU Presidency responsibilities during the preparations for the Lisbon Summit

North Atlantic Treaty Organisation (NATO)

4.32   Although Ireland is not a member of the North Atlantic Treaty Organisation, NATO's strategies and policies as the principal defensive alliance in Europe have an important bearing on Ireland's security environment.

4.33   Since the end of the Cold War, NATO has been conducting a far- reaching review of its role in parallel with the review of roles being undertaken by other organisations involved in European security. At its Summit in Rome in November 1991, it announced a New Strategic Concept based on a fundamental strategic review of security developments in Europe. It concluded that the security challenges and risks which NATO faced were different in nature from what they had been in the past. NATO members no longer faced the threat of a massive attack and the risk of such an attack no longer provided the focus for NATO strategy.

4.34   The new risks were more likely to result from the adverse consequences of instabilities that might arise from serious economic, social and political difficulties, including ethnic rivalries and territorial disputes.

4.35   Alongside NATO's own review, the countries of central and eastern Europe and the Baltic States have expressed their desire to become full members of the Alliance and, in the interim, they have indicated their wish to develop their own links with NATO.

4.36   As a result of its strategic review and in response to developments in central and eastern Europe, NATO has taken a number of important decisions on its future role.

These include decisions to –

- reduce the overall size of NATO forces;

- reduce NATO's reliance on nuclear weapons and to cut substantially sub-strategic nuclear forces in Europe;

- give greater emphasis to political means of enhancing security through dialogue and cooperation and through the development of NATO's capacities for conflict prevention and crisis management;

- support the development of a European Security and Defence Identity;

- make the collective assets of NATO available for WEU operations undertaken in pursuit of the Common Foreign and Security Policy of the European Union;

- support peacekeeping and other operations under the authority of the UN Security Council or the responsibility of the OSCE, including by making available NATO resources and expertise;

- initiate a programme of examination to determine how NATO will enlarge, the principles to guide this process and the implications of membership.

4.37   As a consequence of these decisions NATO has been developing its links and cooperation with non-member states and with other organisations involved in European security in areas that do not directly involve its basic mutual defence commitment. One of the most significant of these was NATO's contribution in support of the UN's efforts in Bosnia-Herzegovina, including the provision of close air support for the UN Protection Force (UNPROFOR) in Bosnia and the use of NATO air power to protect the safe areas in accordance with UN Security Council Resolutions and arrangements worked out with the United Nations. In addition, NATO has been assisting, together with the Western European Union, in the implementation of UN Security Council sanctions through the conduct of maritime embargo enforcement operations in the Adriatic.

4.38   NATO is playing a major role in
military aspects of the implementation of the Peace Agreement for Bosnia-
Herzegovina through the multinational military Implementation Force
(IFOR). IFOR's establishment was authorised by the UN Security Council
on 15 December 1995 in Resolution 1031. IFOR comprises some 60,000
troops, 20,000 of whom are from the United States. NATO members are
contributing troops to IFOR, as are Russia, Austria, Finland, Sweden, and
a number of Islamic and central and eastern European states.

4.39   At the institutional level NATO has
instituted the North Atlantic Cooperation Council (NACC) as a forum for
consultation and cooperation with the central and eastern European
countries, the Baltic States and Russia on political and security issues.
Finland is an observer in NACC, while other neutral countries including
Ireland attend, as observers, meetings of NACC's Ad Hoc Group on
Peacekeeping — a forum for exchange of information and experience on
peacekeeping.

4.40   In addition to the creation of NACC,
the Alliance initiated at the beginning of 1994 a Partnership for Peace
programme open to all the member states of the OSCE.

The Partnership for Peace

4.41   NATO's *Partnership for Peace* was
launched at the NATO Summit in Brussels in January 1994 as a
cooperative security initiative designed to intensify political and military
cooperation in Europe, promote stability, reduce threats to the peace and
build strengthened relationships by promoting practical cooperation
amongst its participants.

4.42   Since its launch, Partnership for Peace
has attracted the support of almost all members of the OSCE, and forty-
three states now subscribe to the Partnership for Peace Framework
Document. This includes, as well as the sixteen members of NATO,

— six countries of central and eastern Europe;

— the three Baltic States;

— four European neutrals: Austria, Finland, Sweden and Malta;

— Albania, Slovenia and the Former Yugoslav Republic of Macedonia;

— Russia and all but one of the states of the former Soviet Union.

4.43 Aside from the small states of Liechtenstein, Monaco, San Marino and the Holy See, there are only seven OSCE states which have not so far joined PFP: the three states involved in the Balkan conflicts (Bosnia-Herzegovina, Croatia and the Former Republic of Yugoslavia (Serbia-Montenegro)); and Cyprus, Ireland, Switzerland and Tajikistan.

4.44 Participants in Partnership for Peace subscribe to a Framework Document which sets out the basic purposes and objectives of PFP, and, in a subsequent step, they agree with NATO a practical programme of cooperation in areas of interest to them. PFP is a flexible concept in that each participating state determines the areas of interest, and the level and extent of involvement in PFP activities. The range of countries involved illustrates the flexible and inclusive nature of PFP.

4.45 The purposes of PFP set out in the Framework Document include the protection and promotion of human rights, the safeguarding of freedom, justice and peace, the preservation of democracy, the upholding of international law, and the fulfilment of the obligations of the UN Charter and OSCE commitments. The objectives of PFP include –

• the facilitation of transparency in national defence planning and budgets;

• ensuring democratic control of defence forces;

- maintenance of the capability and readiness to contribute to operations under the authority of the UN or the responsibility of the OSCE;

- joint planning, training and exercises to strengthen states' abilities to undertake peacekeeping, search and rescue and humanitarian missions.

4.46   To meet the concerns of the central and eastern European countries NATO undertakes, under PFP, to consult bilaterally with any participant that perceives a direct threat to its territorial integrity, political independence or security.

4.47   After signature of the Framework Document a subscribing state provides NATO with a Presentation Document setting out its approach to PFP and identifying the areas in which it is interested. On the basis of this the subscribing state enters into discussions with NATO on an agreed work programme tailored to the country's needs, interests and capabilities. This may include training programmes and exercises in the areas of interest to the country concerned.

4.48   The Government have already indicated that we are giving consideration to whether this new cooperative security initiative is one to which Ireland could contribute. Some aspects of PFP such as transparency in defence planning and democratic control of defence forces are aimed at the countries of central and eastern Europe and are not of direct and immediate relevance to Ireland in the Partnership context. Nor do the Government envisage consultations with NATO on questions relating to Ireland's territorial integrity, political independence or security.

4.49   However, the overall objectives of PFP are consistent with Ireland's approach to international peace and European security, and participation in the Partnership could have several important advantages –

- we would be working together with OSCE partners on programmes of practical cooperation designed to reduce tension and promote overall security in Europe. We have consistently called for and encouraged the development of such inclusive cooperative security arrangements;

- it would enhance the capacity and readiness of our Defence Forces to participate in UN or OSCE peacekeeping operations through training and exercises with countries with which we share a peacekeeping tradition, and thus help to ensure that Ireland is in a position to continue to make an important contribution in the field of peacekeeping;

- it would enable our Defence Forces to make available to European countries which wish to develop their peacekeeping capacities the benefits and lessons of Ireland's long experience in international peacekeeping operations;

- it would enhance Ireland's capacity to carry out search-and-rescue operations off our coasts and to conduct humanitarian missions in response to national or other disasters;

- it would provide a framework for practical cooperation and planning to deal with threats to the environment and drugs-trafficking.

4.50 The focus of the PFP is on cooperation, training and joint exercises. Nothing in the PFP Framework Document entails international commitments of a treaty nature and participation in PFP programmes is entirely voluntary.

4.51 Although PFP is not a "stand-alone" organisation (as has been made clear above, the application procedure, for example, involves direct consultations with NATO), membership of PFP does not involve membership of NATO, the assumption of any mutual defence commitments, or any commitment or obligation in relation to future membership of NATO.

4.52   Objectively speaking, participation
on appropriate terms would not therefore affect in any way Ireland's policy
of neutrality nor would it prejudice or pre-empt Ireland's approach to
discussions in the European Union on a common defence policy.

4.53   The Government have decided to
explore further the benefits that Ireland might derive from participation in
PFP and to determine the contribution that Ireland might make to the
Partnership against the background of the principles set out later in this
Chapter, in paragraph 4.114. A decision on participation in PFP will only
be taken by the Government in the light of consultations, including with
the relevant committees of the Oireachtas, and such a decision will be
subject to a motion on the terms and scope of any participation by Ireland
being approved by the Houses of the Oireachtas.

European Union[2]

4.54   The European Community has
always been more than an economic grouping. From the beginning it has
rested on a particular concept of integration and solidarity, seen not only as
a means of promoting economic development but also as the way to
overcome age-old European rivalries and to contribute to world peace.

4.55   The ever-closer union among the
peoples of Europe to which the Community aspires in the preamble to the
Treaty of Rome has always had Ireland's fullest support. The 1972 White
Paper on the accession of Ireland to the European Communities made clear
that "Ireland's application for membership of the EEC was made in full
awareness of the political ideals and aims of the Treaty which inspired the
founding members of the Community" and that "as a member of the
Community, we shall participate fully in the work of shaping its future
political development".

4.56   When Ireland joined the European
Communities in 1973 we also became fully involved in the procedures then

in operation between the member states for consultation and coordination on matters of foreign policy. That process, known as European Political Cooperation (EPC), was codified and rendered into Treaty form in the Single European Act.

4.57 The provisions on the Common Foreign and Security Policy (CFSP) in the Maastricht Treaty, which replaced EPC, represented a further development in the efforts of the European Union to coordinate its positions, to develop common policies and to act jointly in international affairs.

4.58 Although questions of peace and security have always been a central concern of European foreign policy cooperation, the Maastricht Treaty sought to take that cooperation forward in several important respects.

4.59 In the first place the objectives of the CFSP gave prominence to security issues.

These were the safeguarding of the common values, fundamental interests and independence of the Union; the strengthening of the security of the Union and its member states in all ways; the preservation of peace and the strengthening of international security; the promotion of international cooperation; and the development and consolidation of democracy, the rule of law and human rights.

4.60 Secondly, the Treaty specified that the scope of CFSP shall include "all questions related to the security of the Union, including the eventual framing of a common defence policy, which might in time lead to a common defence." This was the furthest that the member states were prepared to go in the direction of a common defence policy in 1991.

4.61 The Maastricht Treaty, therefore, did not establish a common defence policy or a common defence for the Union. Decisions on the scope and content of a common defence policy and on the question of a common defence were left to a future negotiation and it was agreed that another Intergovernmental Conference would take place in 1996.

4.62   The Treaty provisions were nonetheless significant. The limitation placed by the Single European Act, which confined discussions on security to its political and economic aspects, was lifted. Henceforth the Union could discuss security questions in their broadest sense. Moreover the Treaty provided that where decisions and actions of the Union had defence implications the Union could request the Western European Union to elaborate and implement them.

4.63   Delays in the ratification process meant that the Treaty provisions on CFSP did not come into effect until November 1993 and, as a result, the experience gained in implementing its provisions in the security area has been limited. Nonetheless, the Union has carried out an initial analysis of European security interests in the new strategic context in order to develop some common security principles on which CFSP could be based. It has also examined the implications for the Union's security of developments in central and eastern Europe, the former Soviet Union and the Mediterranean area.

4.64   In these discussions Ireland has laid particular stress on the need for a comprehensive approach to security that goes beyond the purely military dimension. In particular we have emphasised the need for the policies of the Union to –

- address the social, political and economic problems that lie at the root of many conflicts;

- support economic reform and development in areas of potential conflict;

- further the rule of law and other agreed standards of behaviour;

- promote arms control and disarmament measures aimed at preventing the threat or use of force for aggressive purposes;

- strengthen regimes for preventing the proliferation of weapons of mass destruction and their delivery systems;

- encourage transparency and restraint in the field of conventional arms transfers and exports.

4.65 These points are included in the Union's analysis which has formed the basis for the definition of several common policies and joint actions in the security area, including the Union's initiative for a European Stability Pact, its position at the Nuclear Non-Proliferation Review and Extension Conference, its approach to the Conference to Review the Convention on Inhumane Weapons with particular reference to the problem of landmines, and the establishment of an EU administration for the city of Mostar in Bosnia-Herzegovina.

4.66 The Government will continue to advocate a broad and comprehensive approach to security, as outlined above, in discussions within the Union on security and defence matters.

Western European Union

4.67 Like other European organisations the Western European Union has also been engaged in a process of adaptation to take account of the changed security landscape in Europe. In particular the WEU has been –

- developing its links with the European Union and strengthening its operational role to enable it to respond to requests under the Maastricht Treaty;

- broadening and deepening its relations with the countries of central and eastern Europe and the Baltic States;

- considering the new security conditions in Europe and the formulation of a Common European Defence Policy.

4.68 In the Maastricht Treaty the members of the European Union agreed that the WEU was an integral part of the development of the European Union, and that the European Union could request the WEU to elaborate and implement decisions and actions of the Union which have defence implications.

4.69 One consequence of this was an expansion of the WEU's membership and the creation of new categories of observers and associates. In their Maastricht Declaration of 10 December 1991, issued in parallel with the agreement of the EU to the Treaty on European Union, the WEU proposed that member states of the European Union be invited to accede to the WEU, or to become observers. Simultaneously the other European states of NATO were invited to become associate members of the WEU in a way which would give them a possibility of participating fully in the activities of the WEU.

4.70 In response to this invitation Greece has become a full member of the WEU. Ireland, Denmark, and the three new members of the European Union, Austria, Finland and Sweden, have become observers. Iceland, Norway and Turkey have become associate members.

4.71 The Maastricht Declaration of the WEU also set out the objectives of WEU member states for the future development of the body. They agreed on the need to develop a European security and defence identity, a greater European responsibility on defence matters, and the development of the WEU as the defence component of the European Union. They also agreed to enhance the operational capabilities of the WEU in a way that would equip it to respond to requests from the European Union under the Maastricht Treaty.

4.72 One of the most significant developments in this area is the decision of the WEU at Petersberg, Germany, in June 1992 to become involved in tasks other than those arising from the mutual defence commitments in the NATO and WEU Treaties.

4.73 These tasks, known as the "Petersberg tasks", are identified as –

- humanitarian and rescue tasks;

- peacekeeping tasks;

- tasks of combat forces in crisis management, including peacemaking.

4.74 To help carry out these tasks the WEU has agreed that military units will be drawn from the forces of WEU members. Several WEU members have already designated military units that could be made available to the WEU — these are known as *Forces Answerable to the WEU (FAWEU)*. In this context, some WEU members have agreed to establish multinational forces — examples would be the *EUROCORPS* involving Belgium, France, Germany, Luxembourg and Spain; a UK-Netherlands Amphibious Force; a land force, *EUROFOR*, involving France, Italy, Spain and Portugal; and a maritime force known as *EUROMARFOR*, involving the same four countries.

4.75 In addition to the creation of these forces answerable to the WEU, NATO has agreed to make its collective assets available for WEU operations undertaken in pursuit of the Common Foreign and Security Policy of the European Union. This means that the WEU does not need to duplicate capabilities already available through NATO in areas such as transport, logistics and communications in order to carry out humanitarian, peacekeeping or crisis management operations.

4.76 Since signature of the Maastricht Treaty the operations of the WEU have all related to the efforts of the international community to find a peaceful solution to the conflict in former Yugoslavia. The WEU has been helping to implement UN Security Council sanctions through a police-and-customs operation on the Danube and through its contribution to a joint WEU-NATO maritime operation in the Adriatic. The WEU is also contributing a police element of 180 officers to the European Union's administration of the city of Mostar in

Bosnia. Three WEU observers — Austria, Sweden and Finland — are taking part in the Mostar operation and are making available to it officers of their police forces alongside officers from the WEU member states.

4.77 In addition to developing its operational capacities the WEU has taken steps to broaden and deepen its relations with the countries of central and eastern Europe and the Baltic States. These nine countries have become associate partners of the WEU which allows them to participate in WEU meetings and opens to them the possibility of involvement in WEU exercises and operations under the Petersberg Declaration. Foreign and Defence Ministers from these countries have attended recent Ministerial meetings of the WEU.

4.78 The expansion in the WEU's membership and the creation of the new categories of observers, associate members, and associate partners have increased the number of states participating in WEU activities to twenty-seven. As part of the WEU's preparations for the EU's Intergovernmental Conference, all twenty-seven states, including Ireland, have been involved in an extensive examination of Europe's new security conditions.

4.79 Amongst the issues under consideration are the way in which Europe can contribute to the promotion of democratic values, human rights, and a peaceful international order; the identification of the new risks that may arise in European security; Europe's security relations with the United States and Russia; and regional security questions in the Middle East, Africa, Asia and Latin America. The examination also looks at possible responses to the new security conditions, including the contribution the WEU can make.

Ireland's Participation in the WEU

4.80 As an observer Ireland may attend and speak at meetings of the WEU Ministerial Council and participate in the WEU working groups and committees. We do not however take part in decisions taken under the WEU Treaty, nor are we required to undertake any mutual defence commitments or military obligations under that Treaty.

4.81 To carry out our role as an observer the Government have established a Permanent Representation to the WEU in Brussels and our Ambassador to Belgium is accredited as Ireland's Permanent Representative to the WEU.

Since taking up observer status Ireland has attended meetings of the Ministerial Council. Officials of the Department of Foreign Affairs and the Department of Defence and officers of the Defence Forces attend WEU meetings as appropriate.

4.82 As an observer Ireland is not obliged to become involved in the operational activities of the WEU. The question arises nonetheless whether, like other observers and associates, Ireland should be prepared to participate on a voluntary basis in certain of the operations envisaged in the Petersberg Declaration such as humanitarian tasks and peacekeeping. Our Defence Forces and Garda Síochána have acquired extensive experience of humanitarian and peacekeeping operations worldwide in the service of the United Nations.

4.83 It would seem appropriate that as European states, through the WEU, develop their capacities in these areas, Ireland should make available this experience and knowledge for tasks which have as their objective the protection of life and the maintenance of peace.

4.84 Furthermore it is envisaged that such operations would be carried out at the request of the United Nations, of the OSCE, or of the European Union under its Common Foreign and Security Policy.

4.85 It is desirable and right that Ireland should be prepared to make a contribution to such requests in areas where it has a proven capacity and experience.

4.86   The Government believe that such involvement would be in keeping with Ireland's commitment to international peace; it would constitute a concrete contribution to European security; and it would be a sign of solidarity with our European partners and neighbours in the search for a more secure and stable security order in Europe.

4.87   Participation in humanitarian and peacekeeping operations through the WEU would not involve Ireland in defence commitments of any kind under the WEU Treaty and would not therefore have implications for our policy of military neutrality.

4.88   In the light of the above considerations the Government have decided to discuss with the WEU the possibility of Ireland's taking part, on a case-by-case basis, in humanitarian and rescue tasks and peacekeeping tasks under the Petersberg Declaration, and to consider such changes as may be necessary to the Defence and Garda Síochána Acts to enable Ireland's Defence Forces and Gardaí to take part in such operations. The Government do not intend that Ireland will be involved in tasks of combat forces in crisis management.

The Intergovernmental Conference: security and defence policy aspects

4.89   The provisions of the Maastricht Treaty on security and defence represented a compromise which reflected the different emphasis given by the various member states to aspects of European and transatlantic security. It was the furthest that member states were prepared collectively to go at the time. As a result the question of "the eventual framing of a common defence policy, which might in time lead to a common defence", to quote the words of the Treaty, was left to future negotiation. In line with this the Treaty provided for a review and possible revision of its security provisions at the 1996 Intergovernmental Conference, and it is expected that issues of security and defence will be important items on the Conference agenda.

4.90 Earlier parts of this Chapter have examined in some detail the major developments in European security and defence over the past few years and most of those will have a bearing on the security and defence discussions in the IGC. The conditions in which the IGC will take place will be different in several respects to the circumstances in which the Maastricht Treaty was negotiated.

4.91 One significant change is that the democratic revolutions in central and eastern Europe and in the Baltic States have been consolidated and these nine states, all of which aspire to early EU membership, have developed close security relations with the principal European organisations.

4.92 Another change is that the European Union has been enlarged to include three countries which, like Ireland, are not members of a military alliance. All three have become observers in the WEU and are willing to participate in certain WEU operations.

4.93 A third important factor is the agreement by NATO members, including the United States, to support the development of a European security and defence identity.

4.94 A fourth factor, as described above, is that significant progress has been made in developing the WEU as the potential defence component of the European Union.

4.95 Finally, the relationship between further economic and political union remains a fundamental consideration in the discussions in this, as in other areas.

Possible Issues for the Intergovernmental Conference

4.96 While precise proposals for amendments to the Treaty can be expected to emerge as the IGC progresses, the report of the Reflection Group set up to assist in preparation of the IGC is a significant pointer to the priorities of our Partners. The WEU has also offered a contribution which sets out options for the consideration of the IGC. Certain themes likely to arise in the course of the negotiations include –

- the role and contribution the European Union can make to enhancing Europe's security and defence capabilities for conflict prevention and crisis management;

- the relationship between the European Union and the WEU;

- the question of a mutual defence guarantee.

4.97 The Intergovernmental Conference is likely to discuss the ability of the European Union, including through its relationship with the WEU, to cope with the new risks in European security, with a particular focus on the acknowledged need to enhance European capabilities for conflict prevention and crisis management.

4.98 Already, as described above, the WEU has taken on the task of developing its capacities in the areas of humanitarian action, search and rescue, peacekeeping and crisis management. This work will continue although the WEU Treaty does not make explicit provision for it. A question that may arise is whether these tasks should be given a Treaty base in the Treaty on European Union or in the WEU Treaty.

4.99 A key question in this context to be addressed by the Conference is the relationship between the European Union and the Western European Union. Already the WEU is recognised in the Maastricht Treaty as "an integral part of the development of the Union", and the majority of member states of the Union have declared their intention to develop the WEU as the defence component of the Union.

4.100 The WEU Treaty was concluded for an initial period of 50 years, which expires in 1998, but the Treaty will continue beyond that date unless it is terminated. A range of options are being identified and explored with regard to future EU-WEU relations.

Some member states may favour merging the WEU into the European Union as a part of the further development of the Union's Common Foreign and Security Policy. Others have a preference for maintaining the European Union and the WEU as separate organisations, but to develop deeper cooperation between them.

4.101 It may be expected that the Intergovernmental Conference could also consider, in the context of the future relationship between the EU and the WEU, whether the Treaty on European Union should include a mutual defence commitment similar to that in Article V of the WEU Treaty and Article 5 of the NATO Treaty. Under these Articles, member states undertake to assist another member that is the object of an armed attack.

4.102 For the NATO countries, the NATO commitment and NATO capacities will remain the primary means of collective defence against an attack on their territories. Some members of the European Union may nonetheless wish to develop the concept of a European Security and Defence Identity by establishing a mutual defence guarantee as a new objective for the Union to be achieved at a future date.

4.103 This could arise as an issue in particular if proposals for the eventual merger of the European Union and the WEU are put forward in the Conference. Such a merger could have the effect of bringing the WEU's existing Article V commitment within the ambit of the Treaty on European Union, although it is likely that most of the member states would not wish to alter or undermine the current arrangement under which the fulfilment of defence obligations are carried out by NATO. Of relevance in this connection is the recent stated decision by France to move closer to the military structures of NATO and to participate actively in the reform of NATO with the objective also of developing the European pillar of that Alliance through the Western European Union.

Ireland's Approach to the Intergovernmental Conference

4.104   A discussion on security and defence along the lines indicated above would raise fundamental questions for Ireland's relationship with our European Union partners and for our foreign and security policy. Although merger of the European Union and the Western European Union seems unlikely in the short term, the discussions are expected to include the development of the EU/WEU relationship, particularly with a view to improving the EU's role and contribution in conflict prevention and crisis management. Thus a central issue for us is likely to be: what should Ireland's relationship with the WEU be?

4.105   One option would be for Ireland to become a full member of the WEU alongside other members of the Union. The principal advantage of this is that it would give Ireland full access to the WEU's decision-making and enable us to press our views on European security and defence. Membership would involve acceding to the WEU Treaty, including Article V under which member states undertake to provide all the military and other aid in their power if one of the WEU members is the object of an armed attack in Europe.

4.106   Accession to the WEU would therefore bring Ireland into a mutual defence arrangement with the other members involving reciprocal defence obligations which would not be compatible with our existing policy of neutrality. It is not clear at this stage if our partners in the European Union see WEU membership by all EU states as a necessary requirement for the Union's defence policy, or as necessarily contributing to overall European security.

4.107   Moreover, although membership of the WEU is in theory open to any member of the European Union, certain NATO members appear to take the view that it is not possible in practice to separate the mutual defence commitments in the WEU and NATO Treaties. For them membership of the WEU implies membership of NATO also.

4.108   A second option would be to maintain our status as an observer. This allows us to attend and participate in WEU meetings at Ministerial and official level. It has certain advantages, principally in ensuring that the Government are fully informed on developments in the WEU which might have a bearing on discussions in the European Union.

4.109   But it also has drawbacks — the chief one being that, although our contribution at WEU meetings may be taken into account, the WEU members are under no obligation to do so. This imposes a limit on how far and how hard we can press our views on such matters as the need for an inclusive approach to European security, our belief that security is broader than the purely military dimension, or the link between security and disarmament.

4.110   A third option would be an arrangement under which members of the European Union, including Ireland, would undertake to deepen their military cooperation in the humanitarian, peacekeeping, and crisis management areas. But they would not enter into a mutual defence commitment, which would remain a matter for full members of the WEU and NATO. Under such an approach the European Union and the WEU could develop their policies and actions in ways that take account of the varying strengths and capacities of partners.

4.111   This would allow a country like Ireland, which has a long record of service with the United Nations and extensive experience of peacekeeping, to make available its expertise for operations undertaken in conformity with the UN Charter, and to limit our involvement to that extent. This kind of arrangement may be more in keeping with the current needs of European security than the geographical extension of military alliances created in a different security situation with the aim of deterring a large-scale attack.

4.112   The end of the Cold War has created an unprecedented opportunity to build a Europe prosperous, free and at peace. The Government believe that Ireland should take a full part in the debate about European security and the efforts under way to develop new security arrangements capable of meeting the challenges ahead. Without certainty about the full range and extent of proposals that may be tabled in this sensitive area at the Intergovernmental Conference, it would be difficult, and possibly counter-productive, to pre-determine negotiating positions at this stage. At the same time, it is possible to outline the general principles that will govern our approach.

4.113 Ireland has argued that the formulation of a common defence policy should take account of the level of political and economic integration achieved by the European Union, be responsive to broader developments in European security, and reflect the varying capacities and experience of the member states.

4.114 In discussion with the WEU of involvement in the "Petersberg tasks", and in contributing to discussion of overall defence policy for the Union, the Government will be guided by the following underlying principles –

- the commitment of successive Irish Governments that when the time came Ireland would be willing to enter into negotiations on a common defence policy for the Union. In line with this Ireland should be a constructive participant in the IGC on this issue, one which wants to contribute to and influence the outcome, and one which wishes to participate in its implementation;

- the common defence policy should have as its primary objective the preservation of peace and the strengthening of international security in accordance with the UN Charter and OSCE principles;

- The Union's defence policy must be relevant to the broader role of the United Nations which has a unique legitimacy in the area of international peace and security;

- the Union's defence arrangements should form part of a comprehensive cooperative security framework in Europe. The efforts to create a security and defence policy for the Union must not lead to new divisions and further instability in Europe;

- the common defence policy must be situated in the context of a broad approach to security that recognises the crucial contribution to security that can be made by economic progress, the removal of the causes of conflict, the fight against crime and drugs and the protection of the environment;

- the defence policy must be compatible with Ireland's continued pursuit of its objectives in the areas of disarmament and arms control. We will continue to work for a reduction in armaments, for the strengthening of non-proliferation regimes, and for an end to nuclear, biological and chemical weapons.

4.115 The Government have undertaken to put the outcome of any future negotiations that would involve Ireland's participation in a common defence policy to the people in a referendum. This will ensure that Ireland's policy of military neutrality remains unchanged, unless the people themselves decide otherwise.

As stated already in this White Paper, the Government will not be proposing that Ireland should seek membership of NATO or the Western European Union, or the assumption of their mutual defence guarantees.

FOOTNOTES

1 Chapter VIII of the UN Charter enables regional arrangements or agencies to deal with such matters relating to the maintenance of international peace and security as are appropriate for regional action consistent with the Principles and Purposes of the United Nations. Activities under Chapter VIII can include the peaceful settlement of disputes, and enforcement action under the authority of the UN Security Council.

2 The material in the paragraphs that follow deals with the security and defence dimension of the European Union. A fuller examination of the operation of the Union's Common Foreign and Security Policy is given in Chapter 3 — The European Union and the New Europe.

UNITED NATION

1945-199

Chapter 5

THE UNITED NATIONS

Background

5.1   It is now half a century since the United Nations Charter was signed in San Francisco. It was the second attempt during the course of this century to create an internationally guaranteed framework for peaceful coexistence and, like the League of Nations before it, rose from the ashes of a global war.

5.2   The United Nations Organisation was created as an organisation designed to save humanity from the scourge of war; to reaffirm faith in the rights and dignity of the human person, the equal rights of men and women, and of nations; to maintain respect for international law; and to promote social progress and material prosperity.

5.3   The 51 countries which signed the Charter in June 1945 committed themselves to –

•   maintain international peace and security;

10. Commemorative poster celebrating the 50th anniversary of the UN.

- develop friendly relations amongst nations based on respect for the principle of equal rights and self-determination of peoples;

- achieve international cooperation in solving international problems of an economic, social, cultural or humanitarian character and in promoting and encouraging respect for human rights and for fundamental freedoms for all without distinction as to race, sex, language or religion.

5.4 The Charter focused on the prevention of conflict through the development of an effective system of collective security. Yet, even as it was signed, deepening East-West tensions were emerging which hampered the Organisation from developing entirely as its founders had envisaged.

5.5 Fifty years later, it is widely perceived that the UN is in crisis and its effectiveness is frequently called in question. However, the UN today, with 185 members, enjoys an almost universal membership and continues to be the only international organisation with the capacity to assert the will of the entire international community in the area of peace and security. It is imperfect, but irreplaceable.

5.6 The Government are determined to make a full contribution to the current review of the Organisation and its work.

Ireland's membership of the UN

5.7 The United Nations has been a cornerstone of Irish foreign policy since we joined the Organisation on 14 December 1955. As a nation, we take seriously our obligations under the Charter, and our foreign policy has been framed with these obligations in mind. For many years, prior to our accession to the European Community, our membership of the UN provided us with the only forum where we could express our concerns across a wide range of international issues including decolonisation, disarmament, human rights and peacekeeping. With the emergence of newly independent states in the nineteen-sixties, Ireland took up issues of development and equity in economic relations which came to assume increasing importance at the UN.

5.8 Support for effective international action in areas such as disarmament, peacekeeping, development and human rights continues to define Irish priorities within the UN system. This approach also characterises the positions Ireland adopts within the European Union, as we seek to ensure that EU positions reflect key elements of our traditional policy.

5.9 The building of a strong and effective United Nations continues to form a key objective of Irish foreign policy. In addition to ensuring that Ireland plays a full and constructive part in the debate on UN reform, the Government will seek to ensure an Irish dimension to the development of progressive EU positions on issues before the United Nations. Ireland's Presidency of the EU in the second half of 1996, which will coincide with the 51st session of the General Assembly, will provide an important opportunity in this regard.

The structure of the UN system

5.10 The UN Charter established six principal organs of the Organisation: the General Assembly, the Security Council, the Economic and Social Council (ECOSOC), the Trusteeship Council, the International Court of Justice and the Secretariat. The Organisation is also at the centre of an extensive system of subsidiary bodies, including related organs and programmes, specialised agencies and autonomous bodies, all connected in some way to the UN.

5.11 The UN family consists of a number of organs and interlocking agencies which at times can have overlapping responsibilities. As a result it is always necessary to be alert to the possibility of duplication and waste. The mere fact that the UN is supposed to be a representative world organisation means that costly administrative compromises are sometimes made and to some extent this may be inevitable. Ireland, however, will continue to support the efforts of the Secretary-General to control costs and reduce inefficiencies and overlap within the Secretariat. We will also support efforts in the governing bodies of the specialised agencies to identify efficiency savings and eliminate duplication and waste.

5.12   The Government accept that the UN system is in need of reform. Such reform must take careful account of the concerns of the entire international community. This Chapter examines Ireland's policy in relation to the UN's central aim of promoting international peace and security, with particular reference to the reform of the Security Council and the General Assembly. A number of the other aspects of the UN's activities are looked at in other Chapters, such as those on Disarmament and Arms Control, Peacekeeping, Human Rights and Development Cooperation.

The Future Role of the UN in International Peace and Security

5.13   The end of the Cold War raised expectations that a new era of international cooperation would re-invigorate the Organisation. In addition, the peace dividend was expected to release resources from military expenditure for economic development.

5.14   The disappearance of the East-West divide did introduce a new international consensus which was reflected in efforts to develop the potential of the UN in the area of international peace and security. The number of peacekeeping operations increased to 19 in 1996 with over 29,000 personnel deployed.

The fact that the Gulf War was fought under UN authority, although not by a UN force, suggested that the UN was in reality what it had always been in theory — the primary body with the authority to deter aggression.

5.15 The increased demands on the UN reflected the re-emergence of long-suppressed regional and ethnic conflicts. The major problems of the late eighties and nineties have been the problems of intra-state conflict rather than between states or the conflicts by proxy between power blocs that had characterised earlier decades. Cambodia, El Salvador, Guatemala, Mozambique, Somalia and Rwanda witnessed decisions for UN intervention in problems which might previously have been blocked on the grounds that they represented interference in the internal affairs of member states.

5.16 The instability which followed the Cold War and the breakup of the former Soviet Union has added to the dangers of nuclear proliferation. There is also growing concern at the continuing trade in conventional arms and the apparent willingness of some regimes to use chemical and biological weapons, even against civilian populations.

5.17 The effectiveness of the UN response to the challenges of recent years has been mixed, but we have to analyse both the UN's strengths and its failures if we are to ensure a more effective Organisation.

5.18 While the international community working through the UN has not fulfilled the role expected of it in Somalia, Rwanda and former Yugoslavia, there has been a tendency to overlook the UN's many successes — in facilitating national reconciliation and the emergence of democratic structures in Cambodia, Namibia, Central America, in ending the Iran/Iraq war, in asserting Lebanese sovereignty throughout a period of occupation and civil war. In Somalia and Bosnia-Herzegovina, the UN's record in delivering humanitarian relief and thereby saving many lives, was overshadowed by the continuation of these conflicts.

5.19 As the demands on the UN system have grown, it has become obvious that existing personnel, financial and logistical resources are inadequate. In some cases UN operations were given mandates which were either over-ambitious, contradictory or seriously under-resourced.

5.20   On a broader level, the concept of international security is being redefined.

In particular, there is a greater awareness of the role which economic underdevelopment can play in contributing to instability within states and tensions between states. It is now obvious that an effective international security system must take fully into account the need to ensure sustainable development.

5.21   Reflecting a growing awareness of the interdependence of economic, political and social issues, a series of United Nations Conferences, including the World Summit on Social Development in Copenhagen and the Fourth World Conference on Women in Beijing, has been addressing issues which can have a significant impact on security in its broadest sense.

5.22   The outcome of these meetings suggests the emergence of a new international consensus. However, unless this consensus is translated into the detailed work programmes of the UN and its agencies there is a danger that the consensus will remain one of aspiration rather than of action.

5.23   The role of the UN is evolving to meet changed international circumstances. The disappointment often expressed about its ability to resolve international problems may at times reflect unrealistic expectations. Member states must take responsibility for raising such expectations by giving the UN responsibility for problems which they themselves have neither the capacity, nor sometimes even the will, to resolve. The strength of the UN lies in –

- its intergovernmental nature;

- its almost universal membership;

- the willingness of the international community to respect and apply its decisions.

5.24   In brief, therefore, the UN is uniquely equipped and at its most effective in dealing with relations between states. To ignore this fact would be to undermine the consensus on which it is built. However, the Organisation has been increasingly called upon in recent years to deal with disputes within states.

5.25   The UN has increasingly been drawn into intra-state conflict both as an honest broker and as a force to deter aggression against civilian populations. In such conflicts it is not always easy to identify the aggressor, to operate with the support of the parties to the conflict or to mediate agreements. The UN at times finds itself dealing with forces which may have neither the will nor the capacity to reach or enforce agreement. Parties to a civil conflict are not necessarily amenable to international pressure, nor do they see themselves as bound by international rules.

5.26   Article 2.7 of the Charter indicates that the UN is not authorised "to intervene in matters which are essentially within the domestic jurisdiction of any state". A restrictive application of this Article would leave the UN open to the charge of indifference in the face of the often overwhelming humanitarian crises which arise from such conflicts. It would also ignore the danger which intra-state conflicts can pose to the stability of neighbouring states.

5.27   The question must be asked about the role which the UN can effectively play in conflicts of both an inter-state and intra-state character. The United Nations has developed a range of instruments for controlling and resolving conflicts between and within states including preventive diplomacy and peace-making, peacekeeping, peace-building, disarmament, sanctions and peace-enforcement.

5.28   While it is important to maintain the UN's capacity to deter aggression, including if necessary through enforcement action under Chapter VII[1] of the Charter, the Government consider that greater attention needs to be paid to developing the UN's capability in relation to conflict prevention, peacekeeping and peace-making. In relation to intra-state conflict, the Government believe that before a decision is taken by the UN to intervene in an internal conflict, the Organisation should clearly define its objectives and determine whether the will and means exist, both among the parties to the conflict and within the international community, to resolve the conflict.

5.29 The growing level of demand for UN intervention and the strain which this has placed on the Organisation has led to a re-examination of the role which the Charter assigns to regional arrangements in the maintenance of international peace and security and in the peaceful settlement of local disputes. The potential of such organisations, inhibited during the Cold War era, is being reassessed. Chapter Four considers the implications of this trend for Ireland. In some cases, international assistance will be required in order to assist regional groupings to develop their capacity in the area of the peaceful settlement of disputes and in participating in peacekeeping operations.

Conflict Prevention

5.30 In light of recent experience, greater attention is being paid to the role of the Organisation in the area of conflict prevention. The *Agenda for Peace* and the *Supplement to An Agenda for Peace*, issued by the Secretary-General, give particular prominence to the development of the UN's capacity in this area. Ireland supports this development and believes in that context that the UN must take account of what the Secretary-General has referred to as the "deepest causes of conflict" — economic despair, social injustice and political oppression.

5.31 In supporting a renewed emphasis on conflict prevention, Irish efforts will focus, in particular, on seeking to achieve progress in the following areas –

- ensuring early consideration of disputes likely to lead to conflict;

- developing the mediation capacity of the UN;

- utilising the potential of the International Court of Justice.

Early Warning

5.32 The UN system is the author and recipient of a multiplicity of reports including many on issues which may lead to conflict. However there are difficulties in prioritising matters of greatest importance and in ensuring that these are acted upon as a matter of urgency by the responsible UN body.

5.33 To address this, Ireland will work to –

(a) develop the potential of regional organisations to bring urgently to the attention of the UN issues which have the potential to threaten peace in their region; and

(b) develop Article 65 of the Charter to enable the UN's Economic and Social Council (ECOSOC) to identify and report to the Security Council on pressing economic and social factors which have a serious potential to threaten international peace and security.

Mediation Body

5.34 Despite their undoubted authority under the Charter, the Security Council and the General Assembly are not always the most suitable instruments for the direct mediation of conflict. At the 49th Session of the General Assembly in 1994 and again in 1995, Ireland proposed that existing mediation arrangements should be put on a more organised basis. At the United Nations, we will seek the support of other countries for the establishment of a properly-resourced Mediation Body to which the General Assembly or the Security Council may refer difficult issues.

5.35 The Mediation Body would be an expert body elected by the General Assembly and having available to it the services of senior personnel on a full-time basis. It would consider any issue referred to it with a view to establishing the background to the problem and the basis for a negotiated settlement, and could, with the authority of the UN, pursue options for a settlement. Any settlement achieved through its intervention would be endorsed by the appropriate UN organ. The Mediation Body would work closely with the Secretary-General and could draw on the political, economic, social and humanitarian expertise of the UN system as a whole. The Mediation Body would also work closely with relevant regional organisations.

5.36 The Government believe that a Mediation Body, drawing on the pool of personnel skilled in mediation, backed up by effective staff and properly resourced, could rapidly acquire an expertise and authority that would significantly enhance the peace-making capabilities of the UN.

International Court of Justice

5.37 The Government believe that the potential of the International Court of Justice to contribute to the peaceful resolution of disputes should be further developed. In this context it is worth noting that the Secretary General in his *Agenda for Peace* recommends that –

> "All Member States should accept the general jurisdiction of the International Court [of Justice] under Article 36 of its Statute, without any reservation, before the end of the United Nations Decade of International Law in the year 2000."

5.38 The Government are giving urgent consideration to the acceptance of the compulsory jurisdiction of the Court, and have initiated a review of the legal implications for Ireland of such a move. The Government also support both the Secretary-General's recommendation that those UN organs authorized to do so turn more frequently to the Court for advisory opinions, and his request that he be given authorization to do the same, pursuant to Article 96.2 of the Charter.

Sanctions

5.39 In those circumstances where preventive action fails, the United Nations may have to resort to enforcement action. Sanctions provide a non-violent means of seeking to secure compliance with the international rule of law. They are, however, a blunt instrument and must be designed and targeted to minimise the hardship imposed on civilian populations. Before taking a decision to impose sanctions, the Security Council should have available to it an assessment of their likely effects on third countries and should consult with such countries on the basis of Article 50 of the Charter. The Council could also request ECOSOC to propose measures to ameliorate the effects of sanctions on third countries.

5.40 In addition, UN sanctions legislation should indicate (a) that all realistic diplomatic means to resolve the dispute have been exhausted, (b) the specific objectives which sanctions are expected to achieve, © the steps which the target country must take to have sanctions lifted and (d) the application of a regular and thorough review.

Humanitarian Disaster as a Consequence of Political Failure

5.41 There will be situations, especially in the area of intra-state conflict, where deployment of UN peacekeeping may not be feasible or acceptable but where UN intervention is necessary in order to deal with major humanitarian crises, such as occurred in relation to the Kurds in Northern Iraq and following the genocide in Rwanda. In such cases the immediate need may be for the rapid mobilisation of relief measures to deal with large scale population movements in circumstances of insecurity and the virtual collapse of normal governmental and administrative structures.

5.42 It was in response to this type of emergency that the Government made troops available for service with the UN High Commissioner for Refugees in Zaire during the 1994 Rwandan refugee crisis. Drawing on this experience and on the experience of public servants who were released from their official duties at home to work in the refugee camps, Chapter 9 of this White Paper sets out proposals for the establishment of a national emergency relief mechanism. This would take the form of a humanitarian liaison group, and would be available to respond to requests from the UN, the International Committee of the Red Cross (ICRC) or regional organisations operating under a UN mandate in such emergency situations. It is proposed that this mechanism would be distinct from our UN peacekeeping involvement, but would draw on the expertise of the Defence Forces, the Garda Síochána, the public sector and other sectors of Irish life.

Reform of UN Organs

5.43   Given its almost universal membership, the breadth of its mandate and the level of political and popular support which the UN commands, the Organisation must remain at the centre of international cooperation. However, there is a widely accepted need to adapt the structures of the Organisation to take account of the changes which have taken place in the past fifty years. In the Government's view, the UN should operate more clearly as an instrument of effective international consensus, with greater transparency and with greater coherence in relation to its political, security and developmental goals. It also requires a more realistic assessment of its capacity and its limitations.

General Assembly

5.44   The entire membership of the UN is represented at the General Assembly. The General Assembly receives reports from the other organs of the UN. It also has the right to consider any issue relating to the Charter, or to the action of the organs established under the Charter. It can make recommendations on such issues to both members of the UN and to the Security Council.

However, the General Assembly cannot issue a recommendation in respect of any dispute or situation on which the Security Council is in the process of exercising its functions under the Charter, except at the invitation of the Security Council. Decisions on important issues, as defined in the Charter, require a two-thirds majority, while other matters are decided by a simple majority of members.

5.45 The General Assembly elects the ten non-permanent members of the Security Council, the 54 members of the Economic and Social Council, and some members of the Trusteeship Council. Together with the Security Council, it elects the members of the International Court of Justice. It appoints the Secretary-General on the recommendation of the Security Council.

5.46 During the years of the Cold War, debate in the General Assembly was marked by a strong tendency to rehearse well-worn positions without necessarily advancing realistic proposals for dealing with issues of concern. The Government wish to see the General Assembly accord greater relevance to current international issues. The deliberations of the General Assembly should give expression to the widest possible range of views with the objective of securing widespread agreement on the elements for effective international action.

5.47 The General Assembly has a valuable role to play in identifying key issues, in seeking through preventive diplomacy to avert or contain conflict, and in building an international consensus for action across the political, economic and social spectrum. Ireland will support proposals which seek to increase the interaction between the General Assembly and other permanent bodies of the United Nations Organisation, especially the Security Council and ECOSOC.

Security Council

5.48 Under the Charter, member states of the United Nations confer on the Security Council primary responsibility for international peace and security, and agree that in carrying out its duties the Council acts on their behalf.

5.49   Membership of the Security Council comprises five permanent members (the United States, the Russian Federation, China, France and the United Kingdom) and ten non-permanent members selected on the basis of regional constituencies. It is clear that the composition of the Council does not adequately represent today's realities.

However, given the competing interests of a number of countries, it has not yet been possible to reach agreement on the scale and scope of an enlargement. Any decision on this issue will require an amendment to the UN Charter.

5.50   The Government will ensure that Ireland continues to play an active role in seeking to secure a more representative Security Council and one more responsive to the concerns of the general membership.

The Government's position, which contains a number of elements, is founded on the following principles –

- the Council must be in a position to deal effectively with issues of international peace and security;

- since the Council acts on behalf of all member states, it should broadly reflect the concerns and interests of the membership as a whole;

- the Council should be broadly representative of the general membership in both its permanent and non-permanent membership — in this context the issue of the under-representation of developing countries must be redressed;

- all member states have responsibilities in relation to the maintenance of international peace and security, and any change in the composition of the Council should not lessen the possibilities for smaller countries to serve on it;

- as with any executive authority, the Council should operate with maximum transparency and accountability.

5.51   The main elements of the Government's position are that –

i)   Ireland supports a balanced *enlargement of the Security Council* which would improve the representation of both developed and developing countries.

ii)   Within the context of such an enlargement, Ireland also supports an *increase in the number of permanent members* of the Security Council, based on a balanced regional distribution of new permanent members.

iii)   Ireland does not favour extending the *use of the veto*, and supports efforts to confine its potential use by existing permanent members to the imposition of sanctions and other enforcement measures under Chapter VII of the Charter.

iv)   Ireland favours the inclusion of an inbuilt *review mechanism* in any new procedure.

v)   Ireland supports recent efforts to ensure *greater consultation* between the Security Council and the general membership to give legitimacy to the Security Council's claim to act on behalf of the Organisation as a whole. In particular, we support the provision of a formal basis for –

     —   improved consultations with troop-contributing countries;

     —   improved consultations with those directly involved in or affected by a dispute; and

     —   a more transparent system in relation to the imposition and application of sanctions.

5.52   The Government believe that membership of the Security Council should be open to all member states. Ireland served on the Security Council for a part term in 1962 and for a full term in 1981-82. The Government have decided that Ireland will seek election to the Council in the year 2000.

ECOSOC

5.53   The United Nations was established
with a mandate to promote the economic and social advancement of all
peoples as an indispensable dimension to the maintenance of peace and
security. The activities of the United Nations in the field of peace-building,
on the one hand, and in the fields of international development and
economic and social cooperation, on the other, should be considered as
mutually supportive and complementary.

5.54   In the coming years, the United
Nations has a unique opportunity to agree on a new framework for
international cooperation and development. The Government believe that
this is an opportunity that must be grasped. Such a new partnership will
advance the rights, aspirations and dignity of all by full development of the
multilateral system to the benefit of all. This will require a significant
strengthening of the United Nations system at all levels in the field of
international development so that the just requirements of the developing
countries are fully and adequately addressed.

5.55   The Charter of the United Nations
assigns to the Economic and Social Council (ECOSOC) the primary task
of coordinating the activities of agencies and programmes in the economic
and social sectors of the United Nations system. In recent years, ECOSOC
has gained new visibility and importance as a consequence of the holding
of a number of important international Conferences in the economic and
social spheres. These have included the United Nations Conference on
Environment and Development (Rio de Janeiro, 1992), the World
Conference on Human Rights (Vienna, 1993), the International
Conference on Population and Development (Cairo, 1994), the World
Summit for Social Development (Copenhagen, March 1995) and the
Fourth World Conference on Women (Beijing, September 1995).

5.56   Ireland, which is a member of
ECOSOC for the period 1994–96, considers that ECOSOC has an

essential role to play in the accelerating international dialogue on development and in ensuring greater coherence and coordination between the activities of the UN in the economic and social fields. Some specific reforms to enhance the effectiveness of ECOSOC have already taken place but much more remains to be achieved.

5.57 Ireland will work vigorously to ensure that the United Nations system, at all levels, plays an increasingly active and effective role in the field of international economic and social development involving the highest possible standards of coordination and accountability. We will, in particular, play a full and active role in the revitalisation of ECOSOC as an important element in advancing the goals set by the United Nations in *An Agenda for Development*, which is under consideration within the United Nations at present.

5.58 Together with the rest of the international community, we will seek to lay the foundations for a new international consensus on global development that can provide a firm basis for a new way forward. We will play our full part in promoting a new level of commitment by the international community in addressing the just needs of the developing countries and in building a new and more equitable relationship between developed and developing countries.

The Financial Crisis

5.59 The crisis in the Organisation's finances is one of the most serious constraints on the effective operation of the United Nations. As of the end of December 1995, the UN was owed some $3.3 billion by member states, $1.7 billion of which related to peacekeeping operations. Signifying its commitment to the UN, Ireland is consistently amongst the minority of member states which pay their assessed contributions in full and on time.

5.60 The Organisation's present financial situation is untenable. As the Secretary-General explained in *An Agenda for*

Peace, "the foundations of the Organisation daily grow weaker, debilitating its political will and practical capacity to undertake new and essential activities". Detailed discussions are taking place in New York on all issues relating to the financial crisis including capacity to pay, the present scale of assessment and the problem of arrears. (The question of arrears owed to Ireland in respect of peacekeeping operations is dealt with in Chapter 7, paragraphs 23 to 25). With our EU partners, Ireland will continue to play a very active role in these discussions, in order to find an equitable and workable solution to the problem and one which will secure the widest possible agreement.

The European Union and the UN

5.61   The EU is, through the contributions of its member states, the major contributor to the United Nations budget. We will work with our partners to promote and strengthen the role of the UN as the centre of a system for effective international action to ensure international peace and security in its broadest sense.

5.62   Article J.5 of the Treaty on European Union requires EU member states which are also members of the United Nations Security Council to concert and keep the other EU member states fully informed. The Article also provides that those EU member states which are also permanent members of the Security Council will, in the execution of their functions, ensure the defence of the positions and the interests of the Union, without prejudice to their responsibilities under the provisions of the United Nations Charter. The Government will work with our EU partners to give greater practical effect to these provisions.

Irish Policy across the UN System

5.63   Consistency and coherence in the work of the UN and its agencies require that these qualities inform national policies towards the UN and its agencies. In the past, co-ordination of Irish policy across the UN system has been conducted on an ad-hoc basis. The

Government have therefore decided to establish an Interdepartmental Liaison Group to ensure a more focused national position in the various UN bodies. The Liaison Group will meet regularly to discuss issues which are relevant to the UN system as a whole. A long-term strategy will be developed regarding elections to UN bodies, executive boards and expert committees which reflect Ireland's particular concerns. The Liaison Group will be able to make recommendations in this regard.

The UN and the Irish Public

5.64 The Irish people have always shown a strong commitment to and interest in the United Nations. The Irish United Nations Association has played its part in developing this interest. In recent years Irish NGOs have participated in and made significant contributions to the work of UN Conferences. In advance of several recent UN conferences relevant Departments have consulted with representatives of the NGO community and have supported their participation in these meetings. The Government will ensure that this approach continues and, where possible, is developed further.

5.65 To ensure greater transparency in our policy at the UN, the Minister for Foreign Affairs will publish annually a report on issues at the United Nations and on Ireland's voting record on these issues.

FOOTNOTES

1   Chapter VII of the Charter, titled *Action with respect to Threats to the Peace, Breaches of the Peace, and Acts of Aggression,* provides the legal basis for the Security Council to determine peace-enforcement measures.

Chapter 6

DISARMAMENT AND ARMS CONTROL

Introduction

6.1   Disarmament and arms control policy
play a central role in Irish foreign policy. They form a key element in our
contribution towards international security and the maintenance of peace.
The excessive accumulation of arms is one of the major contributory causes
to international tension and conflict.

6.2   Ireland's approach to issues of
disarmament and arms control is closely related to other aspects of our
foreign policy. For example, there are close links with our policy on human
rights abuse — the prohibition of inhumane weapons, the elimination of
weapons of mass destruction and controls on arms exports are all issues
with a strong human rights dimension. There are also close links with our
policy for development in the Third World, where the diversion of scarce
resources to arms procurement and the consequences of excessive
accumulations of arms are important issues.

11. Statue of St George, at the UN New York.

6.3   The acquisition and deployment of
military power has never been an instrument of Irish foreign policy, other
than in the context of essential security needs and involvement in UN
peacekeeping. The Defence Forces maintain weapons at the minimum level
needed to ensure the security of the State and carry out responsibilities in
areas such as peacekeeping. This level has, historically, been lower than the
level of armaments maintained by most other European states. We have no
indigenous arms industry and thus no economic dependence on arms
exports.

6.4   Ireland has sought to focus its
disarmament efforts at the political level in the major multilateral fora,
where we can be most effective in advancing our views and winning
support for concerted international action. These are primarily the United
Nations General Assembly and the UN Disarmament Commission;
conferences relating to specific international agreements; the Organisation
for Security and Cooperation in Europe (OSCE), whose Security Forum
has responsibilities in this area; and our participation in the Common
Foreign and Security Policy of the European Union.

6.5   In addition, Ireland participates in a
number of regimes and arrangements designed to combat proliferation.
These include the Australia Group, which is concerned with chemical and
biological weapons; the Nuclear Suppliers Group; the Missile Technology
Control Regime; and the negotiations for a new multilateral export control
arrangement. Our involvement in the work of bodies such as the
International Atomic Energy Agency (IAEA) is also closely linked to our
disarmament objectives.

6.6   The ending of the Cold War has had
major implications for disarmament and arms control. The abandonment
of the nuclear arms race, the ending of superpower confrontation and the
division of Europe have resulted in a far-reaching reassessment of the need
to maintain large arsenals. This has given a major impetus to multilateral
disarmament activities in relation both to weapons of mass destruction and
to conventional weapons.

6.7   For Ireland, the new situation has made possible significant progress towards the achievement of many of our long-standing disarmament objectives. It has also opened up   new challenges and opportunities which did not exist hitherto.

Nuclear Weapons

6.8   From the earliest days of our UN membership, Ireland has worked to halt the proliferation of nuclear weapons and to promote nuclear disarmament. Resolution 1665, which was adopted unanimously by the General Assembly on 4 December 1961 is still referred to as "the Irish Resolution".

6.9   The resolution contained the essence of the Non-Proliferation Treaty (NPT) which over the past 25 years has developed into a strong, global norm of nuclear non-proliferation. The NPT also contains the only legally-binding commitment to pursue nuclear disarmament which has been undertaken by the five recognised nuclear weapon states: China, France, the Russian Federation, the United Kingdom and the United States.

Complete abolition of nuclear weapons

6.10   Twenty-five years after the entry into force of the NPT and five years after the end of the Cold War, the Government see no justification for the stocks of nuclear weapons and fissile materials that exist today. Successive Irish Governments have advocated the complete abolition of nuclear weapons and have worked for and encouraged concrete steps to that end.

6.11   Since the ending of the Cold War, some progress has been made in reducing the massive stocks of nuclear weapons in the world. The cessation and reversal of the nuclear arms race between the US and the former Soviet Union has meant that each is currently destroying about 2000 nuclear weapons a year. Full and timely implementation of the START II Treaty, which has yet to be ratified, would leave 3,000 and 3,500 strategic nuclear weapons in Russia and the US, respectively, by the year 2003. While none of the smaller nuclear powers has to date pursued negotiations on nuclear disarmament as envisaged in the NPT, the UK and France appear to have made some limited unilateral reductions in their nuclear arsenals.

6.12   Ireland supported the adoption at the NPT Review and Extension Conference on 11 May 1995 of a set of principles and objectives for nuclear non-proliferation and disarmament. One element is especially relevant for nuclear disarmament.

6.13   The determined pursuit by the nuclear weapon states of systematic and progressive efforts to reduce nuclear weapons globally, with the ultimate goal of eliminating those weapons, is now a solemn undertaking which the nuclear weapon states cannot disregard. The Government will work to ensure that the nuclear weapon states are held to their pledge.

Nuclear non-proliferation

6.14   The fundamental objective of nuclear non-proliferation is to ensure that those who possess nuclear weapons and nuclear weapons technology do not pass on such weapons or such technology to non-nuclear weapon countries. Ireland is committed to strengthening the NPT as the indispensable cornerstone of the international nuclear non-proliferation regime. The other components of the regime, namely the safeguards system of the International Atomic Energy Agency (IAEA) and the systems developed to control nuclear exports, have their basis in the Treaty.

6.15   The Government welcomed the decision of the states party to the NPT on 11 May 1995 to extend the Treaty indefinitely. This decision has secured the future of the international non-proliferation regime and has also opened the way to further strengthening it to meet future proliferation challenges.

6.16   Ireland has always advocated universal adherence to the NPT and we are encouraged at the considerable progress that has been made in this direction. By the end of 1995, 182 states were party to the Treaty. Of these, 177 are non-nuclear weapon countries which have accepted an international legally-binding commitment not to acquire nuclear weapons or nuclear explosive devices, and to accept IAEA safeguards on all their nuclear activities.

6.17　　　　　　　　　Only 9 states still remain outside the Treaty and that number is set to shrink further. The NPT Conference brought together representatives of 175 states. These numbers attest to the enormous importance accorded to the NPT by the international community.

6.18　　　　　　　　　The handful of states which remain outside the Treaty, particularly India, Israel and Pakistan, which operate unsafeguarded nuclear facilities in regions of tension, will now come under further pressure to reconsider their position.

6.19　　　　　　　　　An effective NPT requires a system of reviews which can regularly inject political momentum into the achievement of the non-proliferation and disarmament objectives of the Treaty.

6.20　　　　　　　　　The Government have been active in urging the adoption of enhanced review procedures. Ireland supported, at the recent Conference, the pattern of five-yearly review conferences and the adoption of the provision for preparatory meetings in three out of four of the intervening years of the cycle. The new procedure specifies that review conferences should look forward as well as back, identifying the areas in which, and the means through which, further progress may be sought.

6.21　　　　　　　　　The Government intend to make full use of the increased opportunities afforded by the new review arrangements, including the new yardstick for the measurement of the performance of states party to the Treaty provided by the set of principles and objectives for nuclear non-proliferation and disarmament which was adopted by the Conference. It will seek to ensure that the Review Conference in the year 2000 addresses these issues in a comprehensive and effective manner.

Nuclear testing

6.22　　　　　　　　　The first and obvious step in moving to complete nuclear disarmament is to end the development of nuclear

173

weapons. The Government therefore want to see a permanent end to nuclear testing. Successive Irish Governments have held that a halt to testing and rapid conclusion of a Comprehensive Test Ban Treaty (CTBT) would provide the single clearest proof which the nuclear weapon states could offer of their commitment to total nuclear disarmament and of their determination to control the qualitative development of the arms race.

6.23 Unilateral moratoria on nuclear testing introduced by the US, Russia, the United Kingdom and France eventually cleared the way in 1993 for the start of negotiations in the UN Conference on Disarmament in Geneva for a test ban treaty. Complex technical negotiations continued throughout 1994 and 1995.

6.24 The NPT Conference agreed on the completion, no later than 1996, of a universal, and internationally and effectively verifiable, Comprehensive Test Ban Treaty.

6.25 Pending the entry into force of a CTBT, the Conference called on the nuclear weapon states to exercise the utmost restraint. The Government believe that it is of great importance for the timely conclusion of a CTBT that all nuclear weapon states refrain totally from nuclear weapons testing.

6.26 It was with considerable regret and disappointment therefore that the Government viewed the resort to nuclear tests by China and France just a short time after the conclusion of the NPT Review Conference.

6.27 The Government sought to persuade China and France, through available diplomatic channels, bilateral and multilateral, that a prompt and definitive cessation of all nuclear tests is the only way forward. The end of French nuclear testing is positive. The Government wish to see, as an immediate priority, the ending of all nuclear testing.

6.28 The Government remain committed to the conclusion of a truly comprehensive Test Ban Treaty in 1996. In this context, they have noted with interest the stated intention of France,

Britain and the United States to achieve a truly comprehensive ("zero yield") Test Ban Treaty. The Government have also noted as a significant development the intention of these three states to sign in 1996 the Protocols to the Treaty of Rarotonga, which established a South Pacific Nuclear Weapons Free Zone.

Ban on the production of fissile materials for nuclear weapons

6.29　　　　　　　The world today has an enormous excess of fissile materials for weapons purposes. There is no legal obstacle to the continued production of such materials by the nuclear weapon states. However, the United States and the United Kingdom have taken certain steps unilaterally towards halting their production of these materials. It is imperative, on non-proliferation grounds, but also on those of health, safety and the environment, that the window of opportunity afforded by these unilateral measures be used to the full.

6.30　　　　　　　The Government supported, at the NPT Conference, a decision on the immediate commencement, and early conclusion, of negotiations for a treaty banning the production of fissile material for nuclear weapons and other explosive devices.

6.31　　　　　　　Importantly, the Conference specified that these negotiations should be based on the mandate stated by the Special Coordinator of the Conference on Disarmament, which recognises that the problem of existing stocks of plutonium will be raised, even though the focus of the negotiations will be on capping production.

6.32　　　　　　　The objective of the Government is to secure an end to the production and stockpiling of materials, in particular plutonium, for use in the manufacture of nuclear weapons.

IAEA safeguards

6.33　　　　　　　The safeguards system of the IAEA provides assurances that states party to the NPT are complying with their non-proliferation commitments. The system was seriously challenged by the discovery of a clandestine nuclear weapons programme in Iraq and of incomplete declarations of nuclear material by the Democratic Peoples' Republic of Korea.

175

6.34   As a member of the Board of the IAEA, Ireland strongly supported the Agency in its elaboration of a comprehensive programme for strengthening the safeguards system. The Government would like to see decisions on this programme, the general direction of which has already been endorsed by the Board, taken as soon as possible.

6.35   The Government believe that the safeguards system should provide credible assurances both of the non-diversion of nuclear material from declared peaceful activities and of the absence of undeclared nuclear activities. An effective safeguards system will make an important contribution to confidence and trust between states.

6.36   The Government will work for agreement on an enhanced ability to detect undeclared nuclear activities which would add significantly to the effectiveness of the system, even if this necessitates a more intrusive inspection system than exists at present.

Nuclear safety

6.37   Successive Irish Governments have opted not to use nuclear energy for power generation. In view of our close proximity to a large proportion of the world's nuclear reactors as well as to a number of major fuel-cycle facilities, Ireland's policy in relation to the peaceful uses of nuclear energy in international fora places strong emphasis on nuclear safety issues, including radiological protection and the safe management of nuclear waste. Our experience of Sellafield, in particular, has reinforced that concern.

6.38   Countries such as Ireland, which have opted to forego the nuclear power option themselves, have a legitimate right to expect that, in making decisions about nuclear fuel, other countries will take into account also the possible effects of their decisions on human health and the environment beyond national boundaries.

6.39   The Government intend to ensure that the environmental, health and safety issues associated with the nuclear industry are effectively addressed in all the relevant fora. In this context, the IAEA has a key function as the universal forum for the promotion of internationally acceptable safety standards in the nuclear industry. The Government will promote concern for nuclear safety as a key factor shaping the Agency's activities in the promotion of the peaceful uses of nuclear energy. We will also seek determined action to address and resolve the health, safety and environmental issues associated with the nuclear industry as the essential condition for continued use of nuclear power.

Nuclear weapons: legality issues

6.40   The complex issue of the legality of nuclear weapons under international law is currently before the International Court of Justice in The Hague, following the referral of specific questions to it by the World Health Assembly in 1993 and the UN General Assembly in 1994. These questions relate to the legality of the threat or use of nuclear weapons. The advisory opinion of the Court is expected to clarify the legal issues which arise for states in relation to nuclear weapons.

6.41   The Government have taken steps to ensure that the Court is informed of the approach of successive Irish Governments to the issues of nuclear weapons. The Court's Advisory Opinion is expected in 1996.

Other Weapons of Mass Destruction

Biological and toxin weapons

6.42   Ireland has long supported the prohibition of the spread of disease as a means of warfare. We were a signatory of the 1972 Biological and Toxin Weapons Convention which bans the development, production, stockpiling, acquisition, or retention of biological agents or toxins except for peaceful purposes. It also bans weapons, equipment or means of delivery designed to use biological agents or toxins for hostile purposes or in armed conflict.

6.43   Efforts are currently under way to strengthen the effectiveness of the Convention by developing a system of measures to promote compliance with its provisions. The next Biological and Toxin Weapons Convention Review Conference will take place during Ireland's Presidency of the European Union.

6.44   The Government will promote the strongest possible outcome to the process aimed at strengthening compliance with the Convention, so as to enhance its effectiveness in preventing the proliferation of biological and toxin weapons. They will devote particular attention, in the context of Ireland's Presidency responsibilities, to the promotion of a successful outcome to the Review Conference.

Chemical weapons

6.45   The commitment of the international community to rid the world of the threat of chemical warfare dates back many years but it was only in the improved international climate following the end of the Cold War that a breakthrough became possible, leading to the signature of the Chemical Weapons Convention in 1993. Ireland, which was an original signatory of the Convention, is strongly committed to its obligations.

6.46   Some 160 countries have signed the Convention and it will enter into force when 65 of these have ratified it. By the end of 1995, 47 countries including 10 of our EU partners had ratified. The progress of others towards ratification is expected to permit entry into force before the end of 1996.

6.47   The Convention represents a qualitative leap in the content of international disarmament agreements. Like the Biological and Toxin Weapons Convention, the Chemical Weapons Convention imposes a total ban on the development, production, stockpiling or use of an entire category of weapons. It requires the destruction of all stocks of chemical weapons and production facilities within a set time-frame. It also includes the most intrusive inspection regime ever established in a disarmament agreement.

6.48   This involves rigorous monitoring of the destruction of chemical weapons stocks and production facilities; a comprehensive regime for routine international monitoring of chemicals production by Governments and by industry; and a system of short notice "challenge inspections" under which sites in any state party can be inspected if another state party suspects infringements of the Convention.

6.49   In view of our traditional policy of advocating comprehensive multilateral disarmament measures, Ireland has been a strong supporter of the principles underlying the Chemical Weapons Convention since negotiations on it first began. The Government welcome the strong verification provisions of the Convention and believe that they provide a model for strengthening other disarmament agreements.

6.50   The Government intend, therefore, that Ireland should be a party to the Convention as soon as it enters into force. Although Ireland has never possessed chemical weapons or facilities for their production, we will have mandatory obligations under the Convention in the area of monitoring production and use of toxic chemicals by the Irish chemical industry. The Government are taking the steps necessary to enable Ireland to ratify at the earliest possible date.

Other non-proliferation control regimes

6.51   The ending of the Cold War has also stimulated closer international cooperation to prevent the proliferation of the materials and technologies necessary for the manufacture of weapons of mass destruction to countries which may be seeking to acquire such weapons for offensive purposes. Concern that the ending of central control in the former Soviet Union could lead to uncontrolled exports of nuclear, chemical and biological materials and even to the sale of expertise in these fields to countries with clandestine weapons programmes has been an additional incentive.

6.52   One of the most concrete ways of contributing to efforts to reduce proliferation risks is to adhere to the relevant export control guidelines. Ireland is a member of the Nuclear Suppliers Group, the Missile Technology Control Regime and the Australia Group (this last concerns chemical and biological weapons). The purpose of these export control regimes is to make it more difficult for potential proliferators to acquire the materials and technology necessary to develop nuclear weapons, ballistic missile programmes, and chemical and biological weapons, respectively. As controls become more effective, potential proliferators become more sophisticated in their methods.

179

6.53   As part of the Single Market, Ireland
bears an important responsibility for ensuring that it is not used to
circumvent export controls of other EU states. The Department of Tourism
and Trade, as the Irish export licensing authority, has taken the steps
necessary to give effect in full in Ireland to all the export control guidelines
to which we adhere. The Department of Foreign Affairs, which is
responsible for servicing the non-proliferation regimes, maintains close
liaison with the Department of Tourism and Trade and is consulted on
specific cases.

6.54   The European Union has also taken
action pursuant to international non-proliferation commitments
undertaken by member states. With effect from 1 July 1995, exports of
dual-use goods from the European Union to third countries are subject to
a Community régime.

6.55   This régime is designed to ensure that
such goods, which have military as well as civilian applications, will not be
exported to destinations where they might be used to produce weapons of
mass destruction.

6.56   The Government will ensure that
vigilance is exercised in preventing the export from Ireland of arms or dual-
use goods which would give rise to proliferation concern.

Conventional Weapons

6.57   Progress in the area of conventional
weapons since the ending of the Cold War has, so far, been disappointing.
Although in Europe the Treaty on Conventional Forces in Europe (CFE)
marked a turning point with regard to major weapons reductions, at the
global level the easing of tensions which followed the ending of the Cold
War has not resulted in dramatic reductions.

6.58   Indeed, significant overcapacity in
world defence production, declining national defence markets and the
limited success to date of efforts to convert military industries to civilian
uses have increased the economic incentive to sell weapons abroad. The
economies of many central and eastern European countries which were

heavily dependent on arms production and export have suffered, and major economic restructuring is required.

Over-Armament in the Third World

6.59　　　　　　　　　　Acute problems have arisen from the destabilising effects of stockpiles of weaponry, especially in the Third World. The spread of sophisticated conventional weapon technologies to areas of potential conflict has emerged as a major security challenge of the 1990s. Whether acquired abroad or produced indigenously, the introduction of sophisticated conventional weapons into volatile regions undermines stability, poses a threat to neighbouring states and frustrates arms control initiatives.

6.60　　　　　　　　　　There is also an extensive trade in small arms, including hand-held automatic weapons, hand grenades and, most devastatingly of all, landmines.

Restraint in arms transfers

6.61　　　　　　　　　　At the global level, there are no general guidelines or multilateral agreements governing the transfer of weapons. The Government believe that it is essential that states accept the need to exercise restraint and responsibility in their exports and imports of conventional arms and that they agree to observe certain principles in the matter.

6.62　　　　　　　　　　No single arms-exporting country is likely to be willing, unilaterally, to exercise restraint at the risk of losing export markets to its competitors. A cooperative arrangement involving all the major arms producers is, therefore, needed. In this context, the outcome of the current discussions on the successor to COCOM (see paragraphs 6.88 to 6. 90, below) will be important in shaping international restraint in the future on exports of arms and conventional weapons-related dual use goods.

Action to date and how it can be developed further

6.63　　　　　　　　　　There is growing recognition of the need for a more systematic international approach to restricting sales of conventional weapons so as to prevent regional arms races and limit the consequences of regional instability. However, the Government regret that there continues to be inadequate international acceptance of the need for all aspects of arms transfers to be the subject of concerted action by the international community.

6.64   The Government believe that the threat posed by excessive accumulations of conventional weapons in many regions of the world deserves much greater attention from the international community. In this context, they are committed to promoting restraint in the manufacture, possession, transfer and sale of all conventional weapons.

UN Register

6.65   Ireland, together with its partners in the EU, proposed the establishment in 1991 of the United Nations Register of Conventional Armaments, to which member states provide information regarding certain categories of major weapons' exports and imports. The Register can contribute in a practical way to building confidence among states by promoting transparency in military matters.

6.66   The Government believe that the value of the Register can be enhanced — for example, by its consolidation through wider participation and qualitative improvement of the data submitted to it. This would indirectly prepare countries to show restraint in the accumulation of arms. The sensitive question of adding other weapon categories to the seven now covered by the Register needs also to be addressed.

6.67   The Government, in line with its support for increased UN attention to the problems posed by excessive accumulations of conventional weapons, will work with EU partners and other like-minded countries for the further development of the Register as a unique instrument in the field of conventional arms transfers.

Code of Conduct for Conventional Arms Transfers

6.68   At Ireland's initiative, a proposal to develop a code of conduct for conventional arms transfers was tabled at the UN General Assembly in 1994 on behalf of the EU and a number of eastern European countries. The code would encourage states to exercise voluntary responsibility and restraint in their exports and imports of conventional arms, and set out common principles to be observed in this area.

6.69   These principles include respect for international commitments, respect for human rights, and restraint in exports to areas of tension or armed conflict.

6.70   Discussions to date have shown that, while there is growing recognition of the need for international action in this area, a number of states, notably certain developing countries, remain to be convinced. Ireland will maintain its efforts to broaden the political acceptance at the United Nations of certain principles in the area of international arms transfers.

6.71   We are working, on the one hand, to ease the fears of some developing countries that acceptance of such principles might interfere with their legitimate right under Article 51 of the UN Charter to provide for their own self-defence and, on the other, to expand the consensus in favour of reducing over-armament through restraint in conventional arms transfers.

6.72   The OSCE has already approved a set of principles governing conventional arms transfers and the EU has identified common criteria in this area. The Government will work, in the OSCE and in the EU, to develop further this approach and to promote its application by the member states.

EU Criteria for National Policies on Arms Exports

6.73   Ireland attaches great importance to the development and application by the EU and its member states of criteria to govern arms exports and seeks to promote their practical relevance in the arms export policies of our partners. Certain steps have already been taken in this regard.

6.74   The European Council has agreed that far-reaching international action is needed to promote restraint and transparency in the transfers of conventional weapons and of technologies for military use, in particular towards areas of tension. In this context, it has identified a number of common criteria on which the national policies of member states on arms exports are based.

6.75   In addition, under the CFSP, member states increasingly inform and consult each other on matters of arms export policy. This process is intended to contribute to transparency and to promote a common understanding of the criteria to which all partners adhere.

6.76   While these steps are welcome, the Government believe that further progress is necessary to promote restraint and to develop more effective controls on the export of arms from EU countries. They will continue to work for these objectives within the European Union.

6.77   The report of the Reflection Group set up to prepare for the EU Intergovernmental Conference noted the views of a majority of EU partners that the question of European armaments cooperation is one that the IGC should consider (see Chapter Four — International Security — paragraphs 4.96 to 4.103). This issue has arisen many times over the years. The Government's approach to the issue of armaments derives in the first instance from our strong and enduring commitment to disarmament and arms control. Our primary concern therefore will be to ensure that any developments in this area are consistent with our priorities in disarmament and arms control and our overall approach to international peace and security. Ireland is not a producer of armaments and will not become one. The Government will continue to work for enhanced EU cooperation on arms export policy to achieve the maximum possible transparency and restraint in arms transfers.

Inhumane Weapons

6.78   Ireland was an original signatory of the 1981 Inhumane Weapons Convention which followed the 1968 International Conference on Human Rights, held in Tehran. The Convention enshrined the basic principles that certain conventional weapons should neither inflict excessive injury, nor cause unnecessary suffering, that they should be directed only at military forces and that they should not be used indiscriminately to harm the civilian population.

6.79 Three Protocols annexed to the Convention set out prohibitions or restrictions on the use of fragmentation weapons, mines in populated areas and incendiary weapons. Ireland does not manufacture or trade in any of the weapons covered by the Inhumane Weapons Convention nor are these used by the Defence Forces except for the essential purposes of military training. We do not propose to allow such manufacture in the future.

6.80 A Conference to review the scope and operation of the Inhumane Weapons Convention began in Vienna on 25 September 1995 with a view to strengthening and widening the provisions of the Convention, especially Protocol II on landmines. Ireland, having ratified the Convention on 13 March 1995, is participating as a state party in the Review Conference. The Conference, which was unable to reach agreement in the time initially allocated, reconvened in Geneva in January and is scheduled to conclude on 3 May this year.

Landmines

6.81 The devastating effects of landmines, especially in developing countries, raise issues not only of disarmament and arms control but also of international humanitarian law and of development policy.

6.82 Official estimates put the number of active landmines around the world in the range 85–100 million. Anti-personnel landmines continue to cause deaths and injuries to civilians long after conflicts have ceased. Until it is de-mined, agricultural land remains unusable, thus retarding the development, rehabilitation and reconstruction of many poor countries. Non-governmental organisations, especially humanitarian and relief agencies, have campaigned tirelessly and with considerable success to raise international awareness of the devastation caused by landmines and of the imperative of urgent international action.

6.83 The Government are totally opposed to the indiscriminate nature, production, stockpiling, use and trade of anti-personnel landmines and are seeking support for a total ban on these weapons. The Government will encourage the adoption of moratoria on

mine exports and the broadening, to the maximum extent possible, of the prohibitions and restrictions on landmines contained in Protocol II of the Inhumane Weapons Convention.

6.84 The Government are also committed to the provision of increased assistance to de-mining activities. Our assistance grew substantially in 1995 when the Government made a first-time contribution to the UN Voluntary Trust Fund for Assistance in Mine Clearance, as well as providing continued support for de-mining programmes in Mozambique and Cambodia.

6.85 Ireland has supported concerted action on landmines at EU level. The General Affairs Council on 10 April 1995 agreed a Joint Action on anti-personnel landmines, comprising a common moratorium on exports of anti-personnel mines, active preparation of the Inhumane Weapons Convention Review Conference and an EU contribution to international mine clearance. The Government believe that a strong EU profile in this crucial disarmament area will have a significant political impact and contribute to real progress on the issues.

6.86 The Government are concerned at the limited nature of the measures which are being negotiated in the Review Conference to strengthen Protocol II to the Inhumane Weapons Convention. These fall far short of a total ban on anti-personnel landmines. The fact that only a small number of states, some 50 in total, as parties to the Convention have accepted any restraints on the use of landmines is also an important consideration. One factor in the slow progress in this area is the fact that many states, particularly in the developing world and those with land frontiers, see the use of landmines, including anti-personnel landmines, which are cheap, plentiful and easy to manufacture, as essential elements in their national defence.

6.87 The Government welcomed the decision of the Vienna Review Conference to agree a new Protocol which bans the use of blinding laser weapons. This is a welcome example of the international community acting pre-emptively, in the light of continuous developments in warfare technology, to prevent the spread of a new category of inhumane weapons.

Multilateral Export Controls

6.88   Ireland is participating in negotiations for a New Multilateral Export Control Arrangement whose objective would be to prevent the acquisition of armaments and sensitive dual-use items for military end-uses, if the behaviour of a state is or becomes a cause of serious concern.

6.89   Though not a member of the earlier Coordinating Committee for Multilateral Export Controls, known as COCOM, Ireland adhered to COCOM guidelines, in part in order to facilitate inward investment in high technology areas. In the new international environment following the end of the Cold War, the COCOM arrangement lapsed in March 1994.

6.90   The Government support the establishment of a new arrangement that is open on a global, non-discriminatory basis to prospective members who adhere to effective export controls, to non-proliferation policies and to appropriate national policies. It is hoped that such an arrangement, covering both dual-use items and arms, will be in place early in 1996.

Priorities for Future Action

Participation in international fora

6.91   In order to enhance the effectiveness of Ireland's contribution to the work of international disarmament and arms control fora, the Government will –

* ensure that Ireland uses to the full the opportunities provided by the Common Foreign and Security Policy of the EU to advance the Government's disarmament objectives;

* in this connection, give appropriate priority to disarmament issues during the Irish Presidency of the European Union;

* seek to achieve membership for Ireland of the Conference on Disarmament in Geneva in the context of enlargement of membership of that body;

- be represented at a high level at the forthcoming United Nations Review Conference on the Biological and Toxin Weapons Convention;

- strengthen Ireland's representation at the Security Forum of the OSCE in Vienna.

Weapons of mass destruction

6.92   The Government are determined to pursue the elimination of all weapons of mass destruction. In this context the Government will –

- continue to promote the abolition of nuclear weapons, seeking, in particular, to ensure that the nuclear weapon states pursue systematic and progressive efforts to reduce such weapons, with the ultimate goal of eliminating them;

- work to strengthen further the international nuclear non-proliferation regime, using to the full the enhanced arrangements for review and the principles and objectives for nuclear non-proliferation and disarmament adopted in May 1995;

- press for a permanent end to nuclear testing and, in this context, for the conclusion in 1996 of a Comprehensive Test Ban Treaty;

- urge an immediate start to, and early conclusion of, negotiations on a treaty banning production of plutonium for weapons purposes, with appropriate attention being given to the problem of existing stocks;

- give priority to ratification by Ireland of the Chemical Weapons Convention at the earliest possible date;

- encourage effective adherence to export control guidelines designed to prevent the proliferation of materials and technology for making weapons of mass destruction.

Conventional weapons

6.93   The Government will endeavour to focus international attention on the problems caused by the excessive accumulation of conventional arms in many parts of the world. They are committed to promoting restraint in transfers of conventional weapons and further prohibitions and restrictions on the use of inhumane weapons. Accordingly, the Government will –

- pursue at the United Nations Ireland's proposal for a code of conduct for conventional arms transfers;

- promote the uniform and strictest application of the EU's common criteria for conventional arms exports;

- seek support for a total ban on anti-personnel landmines;

- seek, in the context of the review of the Inhumane Weapons Convention, the broadening, to the maximum extent achievable, of the prohibitions and restrictions on landmines contained in Protocol II to the Convention;

- support the establishment of a new multilateral export control arrangement to cover arms and sensitive dual-use items.

UNITED NATIONS TRAINING SCHO

IRELAND

Chapter 7

PEACEKEEPING

The United Nations and Peacekeeping

7.1   The concept of the deployment of
military and police personnel for international peacekeeping purposes was
first developed by the United Nations. Although not specifically mentioned
in the Charter, it represented a logical development of the Organisation's
capacity to deal with the question of conflict prevention and conflict
resolution. The Secretary-General's *Agenda for Peace* defines peacekeeping
as "a technique that expands the possibilities for both the prevention of
conflict and the making of peace."

7.2   In 1948, UN military observers were
deployed for the first time. Their task was to monitor the truce which
marked the end of Arab-Israeli hostilities. The *United Nations Emergency
Force* which was established in 1956 in the context of a resolution of the
Suez crisis, was the first large-scale peacekeeping operation involving the
use of armed troops.

12. Defence Forces UN Training School.

7.3   The members of a UN peacekeeping
force, although remaining in their national service, operate as international
personnel under the authority of the United Nations and subject to the
instructions of the Force Commander. Members of the force are expected
to discharge their functions on the basis of the mandate established by the
Security Council.

7.4   During the first forty years of UN
peacekeeping the Security Council established only 13 peacekeeping
operations, but a further 29 operations have been set up since 1988. The
end of the Cold War was followed by increased demands for UN
involvement in peacekeeping activities. Seventy countries now contribute
troops to UN peacekeeping operations and the annual cost of these
operations has grown to approximately $3.3 billion.

The evolution of Peacekeeping

7.5   Traditionally, the following
conditions have been required for the deployment of UN peacekeeping
forces –

•   the consent of the parties to the conflict;

•   the support of the Security Council;

•   the willingness of the international community to commit personnel;

•   impartiality in the discharge of the UN mandate;

•   control of the forces vested in the Secretary-General;

•   the non-use of force other than in self-defence.

7.6   The classic peacekeeping operation of
the Cold War era was primarily concerned with policing a cease-fire and
containing tension. In response to the changing international situation the

nature and scale of peacekeeping operations have altered significantly. In recent years this has led to UN operations which have involved organising and monitoring elections, participating in civil administration, monitoring human rights situations and assisting in the repatriation of refugees.

7.7 A further development of peacekeeping has been the evolution of the concept of preventive deployment which permits the positioning of UN military on one or both sides of a border with the object of deterring the escalation of tension into armed conflict. The UN has deployed a mission for this purpose in the Former Yugoslav Republic of Macedonia.

7.8 UN peacekeeping operations have become politically, administratively and logistically more complex. They are now more likely to be deployed in intra-state conflicts; all but 2 of the 19 operations established since January 1992 relate to such situations. In some cases there is no peace to monitor and the acceptance by the parties of the United Nations' role and mandate is less than wholehearted. On occasion the UN is required to act in situations where there has been a virtual breakdown of the political, administrative and judicial systems. In these circumstances, Member States are showing increasing unwillingness to provide troops for UN operations.

7.9 In some cases the effectiveness of peacekeeping operations has been hampered by the establishment of unrealistic mandates. In others, mandates have been changed in the course of a mission to allow enforcement action. Such developments may jeopardise the original mission objectives. In this context, the Secretary-General has pointed out that "the logic of peacekeeping flows from political and military premises that are quite distinct from those of enforcement and the dynamics of the latter are incompatible with the political process that peacekeeping is intended to facilitate. To blur the distinction between the two can undermine the viability of the peacekeeping operation and endanger its personnel".

Ireland and UN Peacekeeping

7.10   Since 1958, over 42,000 members of
the Defence Forces and the Garda Síochána have served with distinction as
UN peacekeepers. 75 have died on UN service. Ireland currently provides
some 750 personnel to 11 UN missions. Our involvement in peacekeeping
represents a major contribution to international peace and security. The
Irish people are justly proud of the commitment and professionalism of our
peacekeepers and the regard in which they are held internationally.

7.11   The service of Irish personnel in UN
peacekeeping missions is governed by the Defence Act and the Garda
Síochána Act. In 1993, the Defence Act was amended to remove the
previous limitation on personnel serving on United Nations operations
solely "for the performance of duties of a police character". This enabled
Irish troops to participate in the UNOSOM II operation in Somalia,
although the Irish contingent was not itself involved in enforcement
activities. It might be noted that the UN operation in the former Congo
(ONUC), in which Ireland participated from 1961-64, while not a
Chapter VII operation, did permit the use of force to prevent secession and
remove mercenary forces.

7.12   Given the unique role and authority
of the United Nations and the fact that its peacekeeping activities have
proved an important element in containing conflict, the Government are
committed to sustaining the overall level of Ireland's contribution to
peacekeeping.

7.13   However, in view of the number, size
and complexity of current peacekeeping operations it will be necessary to
develop a selective response to future requests from the United Nations.

The factors which will inform the Government's consideration of such requests will include –

- an assessment of whether a peacekeeping operation is the most appropriate response to the situation;

- consideration of how the proposed mission relates to the priorities of Irish foreign policy;

- the degree of risk involved for UN personnel;

- the extent to which the particular skills or characteristics required relate to Irish capabilities;

- the existence of realistic objectives and a clear mandate which has the potential to contribute to a political solution;

- whether the operation is adequately resourced;

- the level of existing commitments to peacekeeping operations.

7.14 Close contact exists between the Departments of Foreign Affairs, Defence and Justice on issues relating to peacekeeping operations. In order to increase further the effectiveness and coherence of policy in this area, the Government have decided to establish a Standing Inter-Departmental Committee on Peacekeeping which will consider issues relating to Irish involvement in peacekeeping operations. In addition, the appointment of a military adviser to serve in the Permanent Mission to the United Nations in New York is envisaged.

Command and Control

7.15 In his *Agenda for Peace,* the Secretary-General stressed the importance of unity of command and control. With the recent growth in the complexity of operations, issues related to command and control have taken on an even greater urgency. The Government agree with the Secretary-General's view that it is both useful and necessary to distinguish between the political control of peacekeeping operations provided by the Security Council, the executive control provided by the Secretary-General, and the operational control which resides with either the Secretary-General's Special Representative or the Force Commander.

7.16 In connection with executive control, Ireland fully supports the Secretary-General's assessment that the UN Secretariat's capacity for executive direction and management of peacekeeping operations needs to be strengthened further. The Government will support efforts to ensure that the Secretariat is provided with the additional resources which may be required.

7.17 On the issue of operational control, Ireland has long subscribed to the view that unity of command in the field is essential to ensure the effective implementation of UN peacekeeping mandates.

Participation by Irish units in UN peacekeeping operations has always been based on the premise that full operational command in the field must reside with the Force Commander or Head of Mission, as appropriate. Any departure from this principle is one which is likely to jeopardize both the effectiveness of a mission and the safety and security of its personnel.

Safety of UN Personnel

7.18 The safety of Irish personnel is of paramount concern to the Government. For this reason Ireland co-sponsored the resolution to establish a *Convention on the Safety of United Nations and Associated Personnel.* The Convention provides that each state party should make it a crime under its national law to attack UN personnel. The Government intend to sign and ratify the Convention at an early date.

Peacekeeping and Human Rights

7.19 Human rights abuses have characterised many of the situations in which the UN is called upon to operate. Ireland will support efforts to ensure that mandates of peacekeeping missions take human rights considerations into account including, whenever appropriate, specific provisions which would require personnel to report on any human rights violations which they witness.

Training

7.20 The provision of peacekeeping training is an essential component to the success of a mission. Ireland has always attached high priority to equipping its peacekeepers with the skills and knowledge which they require for service overseas. The UN Training School recently established by the Defence Forces at the Curragh contributes to this objective.

7.21 As a result of the expansion of UN operations, many countries have become involved in peacekeeping operations for the first time. The Government will seek to make use of Ireland's expertise in peacekeeping, such as that available at the Defence Forces' UN Training School, to assist other countries endeavouring to develop their own training facilities.

Consultations between Troop Contributors and the Security Council

7.22 Ireland will continue to work with like-minded countries to enhance the present arrangements for consultations between the Security Council and troop-contributing countries, and to place them on a more formal basis. In particular, we will support the establishment of a subsidiary body of the Security Council for this task.

Finance

7.23 The scale of operations and the number of personnel now deployed on UN peacekeeping operations probably represent the limit of the Organisation's capacity. The escalation in the number and size of missions has contributed to the financial crisis facing the Organisation. The fact is that too few countries are prepared, as Ireland is, to pay their assessed contributions to UN operations in full and on time. At the end of December 1995, the UN peacekeeping budget was owed $1.7 billion due to arrears of payment on the part of several member states. The unilateral reduction in its contribution by the United States has exacerbated the crisis facing the financing of UN peacekeeping operations.

7.24 Together with other troop-contributing countries, Ireland is owed substantial arrears arising from its participation in peacekeeping operations. The Government will continue to use every opportunity to press for the settlement of this problem.

7.25 In concert with our EU partners Ireland will continue to work towards an improved system for financing UN peacekeeping operations.

Rapid Reaction

7.26 Recent experience highlights the need to reduce the time which it takes to deploy peacekeeping missions. In order to enhance the UN's capacity to plan for and respond more quickly to emergency situations the Secretary-General has, through his *United Nations Standby Arrangements System (UNSAS)*, asked member states to indicate the forces which they would be prepared to designate for use in peacekeeping operations. While the UNSAS is not the complete answer (none of its members agreed to contribute troops to Rwanda in May 1994), it should improve the capacity of the UN to respond to emergency situations.

7.27 The Government will consider whether, following the outcome of the Defence Forces Review, Irish units should be included within the UNSAS. Participation in the UNSAS will be subject to the existing requirements which require Dáil approval for the despatch of a contingent to participate in a specific operation.

7.28 While there are many complexities and difficulties involved in giving the Security Council an independent military capacity, the Government believe that there is scope for considering what more can be done, in addition to the UNSAS, to provide standby units of military and police for use by the United Nations in sudden conflicts and humanitarian emergencies.

A number of proposals have been advanced for such rapid standby units and standby UN military headquarters staff and the Government believe that they merit full consideration by member states.

Enforcement Action

7.29 Enforcement provisions are an essential element of the system of collective security envisaged by the UN Charter. The Secretary-General has pointed out that "neither the Security Council nor the Secretary-General at present has the capacity to deploy, direct, command and control troops for this purpose, except perhaps on a very limited scale". He points out that in the past groups of member states were mandated to carry out such action in Korea, Iraq and Haiti.

7.30 Two issues arise for the Government:

(i) Ireland's attitude to participation in future peace-enforcement operations, and

(ii) our attitude to such mandates being given to non-UN forces.

7.31   Taking account of the experience of
Somalia, the Government's approach to participation in future
enforcement operations will be guided by the following criteria –

•   that the operation derives its legitimacy from decisions of the
        Security Council;

•   that the objectives are clear and unambiguous and of sufficient
        urgency and importance to justify the use of force;

•   that all other reasonable means of achieving the objectives have been
        tried and failed;

•   that the duration of the operation be the minimum necessary to
        achieve the stated objectives;

•   that diplomatic efforts to resolve the underlying disputes should be
        resumed at the earliest possible moment;

•   that the command and control arrangements for the operation are in
        conformity with the relevant decisions of the Security Council, and
        that the Security Council is kept fully informed of the
        implementation of its decisions.

7.32   Where multinational forces are
mandated to carry out an operation with the authority of the United
Nations it is essential that the mission should operate strictly within the
terms laid down by the UN. To ensure this, there could be an advantage in
the establishment of a UN observer mission to monitor and report to the
Security Council on the manner in which the mandate is being
implemented.

Regional Organisations and Peacekeeping

7.33   In light of the growing demands on
the UN, the Organisation has been considering how it can better utilise the

provisions of Chapter VIII of the UN Charter which describes the role which regional organisations can play in the maintenance of international peace and security.

In September 1993, the General Assembly adopted a resolution which amongst other provisions encouraged regional organisations, in their fields of competence, to consider ways and means for promoting closer cooperation and coordination with the United Nations with the objective of contributing to the purposes and principles of the Charter.

In August 1994, the Secretary-General convened the first-ever meeting of heads of regional organisations in order to assess and enhance the present level of cooperation.

7.34   In view of the burden on the UN in the new international situation the Government accept that the development of regional organisations, in accordance with Chapter VIII of the Charter, is both necessary and welcome. A key question for Ireland is how best we can contribute to the development of peacekeeping capacity in our region.

7.35   Existing legislation permits service outside the state by members of the Permanent Defence Forces and the Garda Síochána as "part of an international force or body established by the Security Council or the General Assembly" of the United Nations. In cases involving the participation of an armed contingent consisting of more than twelve members of the Defence Forces, Dáil approval is required.

In response to the trend towards greater cooperation between the UN and regional organisations, the Government are considering such changes as may be necessary to the Defence and Garda Síochána Acts to enable Ireland to be in a position to respond to requests to participate in such missions.

OSCE

7.36   In response to the serious regional and ethnic tensions surfacing in Yugoslavia and elsewhere, including in the former Soviet Union, it was recognised that the OSCE[1] urgently required additional instruments to address tensions before violence erupted and to handle crises when they developed. The 1992 Helsinki meeting adopted a number of measures to develop the OSCE's capacities for early warning, conflict prevention and crisis management, including the possibility of peacekeeping activities, either directly under the OSCE's own aegis or in close cooperation with other regional and transatlantic security organisations.

7.37 The Helsinki Summit conclusions make clear that such peacekeeping: "will be undertaken with due regard to the responsibility of the UN . . . and will at all times be in conformity with the Purposes and Principles of the Charter of the UN. CSCE peacekeeping will take place in particular within the framework of Chapter VIII of the Charter of the United Nations." This development is intended to be complementary to UN peacekeeping. The UN and the OSCE have subsequently deepened cooperation and contacts in this area.

7.38 The Summit also foresaw that the OSCE might benefit from the resources and expertise of existing organisations, such as the EC, NATO and WEU, in carrying out peacekeeping activities.

7.39 Against the background of an increasingly overburdened UN peacekeeping capability, and the OSCE's status as a regional arrangement under Chapter VIII of the UN Charter, Ireland strongly supported this new departure. The Government view OSCE peacekeeping as a necessarily broad concept, comprising both observer and monitor missions as well as classic UN-style peacekeeping operations. They welcome the exclusion of enforcement action which will remain the responsibility of the UN Security Council. OSCE peacekeeping is an addition to the organisation's existing range of dispute settlement and conflict prevention mechanisms, allowing a flexible and graduated response to diverse crisis situations in the OSCE area. The Government believe that OSCE peacekeeping must match the high standards set by the UN and, in order to avoid duplication, must avail itself of the UN's technical experience and assistance.

7.40 Since 1992 the OSCE has established nine long-term missions to assist in the easing of tensions and the settlement of conflicts. Such missions are currently operating in the Former Yugoslav Republic of Macedonia, Georgia, Estonia, Moldova, Latvia, Tajikistan, Bosnia-Herzegovina, and Ukraine. The OSCE is also involved in assisting in the implementation of certain bilateral agreements between Russia and two of the Baltic States. Missions also operate, under the aegis of the OSCE, in each of the states neighbouring Serbia and Montenegro to assist in the implementation of UN sanctions against Belgrade.

7.41 The development of these OSCE missions can be seen as similar to the development of UN peacekeeping operations in that they can be mandated and staffed to respond to the broad range of issues and problems that need to be addressed in some potential or actual conflict situations, and not just to the military aspects alone.

7.42 On the basis of its extensive UN experience, Ireland regarded itself as well-placed to contribute to this new initiative and to the possible development of a regional peacekeeping capability in Europe. Irish military officers have been seconded to the OSCE Mission to Georgia since April 1994 and Irish customs officers are serving with the Sanctions Assistance Mission in Skopje since January 1994.

7.43 A full-scale OSCE peacekeeping operation, on the lines of those mounted by the UN, has yet to be established. The OSCE holds special responsibility for efforts to achieve a peaceful settlement to the crisis in Nagorno-Karabakh (involving Armenia and Azerbaijan).

The Budapest Summit in December 1994 decided that a multinational peacekeeping force in the region is an essential element of a political settlement. The Summit approved the establishment of a High Level Planning Group to make recommendations on the size of such a force, command and control, logistics, rules of engagement etc.

Ireland views this Group as an important opportunity to lay the groundwork for future OSCE regional peacekeeping. An experienced Irish military officer has been seconded by the Government to assist its planning operations.

7.44 The development of the OSCE's conflict prevention and crisis management capacity is ongoing. Ireland will support the further development of OSCE peacekeeping and contribute as far as possible to OSCE missions. We will continue to press for closer coordination between the OSCE and the UN in the area of peacekeeping and for the development, within the OSCE Secretariat in Vienna, of a permanent peacekeeping unit.

Regional Organisations outside Europe

7.45 The potential for the involvement of regional organisations in peacekeeping operations under Chapter VIII of the Charter is not confined to Europe. One region which has seen significant developments in recent years is Africa, where conflicts in areas such Rwanda, Burundi, Somalia, Liberia and Sierra Leone have underscored the need for effective regional conflict prevention and resolution mechanisms. This was reflected by the UN Security Council in its Presidential Statement of 22 February 1995[2] which encouraged greater cooperation between the UN and regional groups under Chapter VIII of the UN Charter, with particular emphasis on Africa.

7.46 Since November 1993, when the Organisation of African Unity (OAU) approved the establishment of a mechanism for conflict prevention, management and resolution, the OAU has been in consultation with the UN, the EU and other parties. The aim of these consultations has been to establish how the international community can cooperate with the OAU and its 52 member states in the development of its conflict management initiative. There has been particular emphasis on practical cooperation in areas such as improving early warning systems designed to identify potential conflicts, encouraging preventive diplomacy, and expanding the capacity and speed of deployment of peacekeeping resources.

FOOTNOTES

1   Known as the CSCE until December 1994.

2   (S/PRST/1995/9).

205

UNIVERSAL DECLARATION
OF HUMAN RIGHTS

Article 1. All human beings are born free and equal in dignity and rights. They are endowed with reason and conscience and should act towards one another in a spirit of brotherhood.

Article 2. Everyone is entitled to all the rights and freedoms set forth in this Declaration, without distinction of any kind, such as race, colour, sex, language, religion, political or other opinion, national or social origin, property, birth or other status.

Furthermore, no distinction shall be made on the basis of the political, jurisdictional or international status of the country or territory to which a person belongs, whether it be independent, trust, non-self-governing or under any other limitation of sovereignty.

Article 3. Everyone has the right to life, liberty and the security of person.

Article 4. No one shall be held in slavery or servitude; slavery and the slave trade shall be prohibited in all their forms.

Article 5. No one shall be subjected to torture or to cruel, inhuman or degrading treatment or punishment.

Article 6. Everyone has the right to recognition everywhere as a person before the law.

Article 7. All are equal before the law and are entitled without any discrimination to equal protection of the law. All are entitled to equal protection against any discrimination in violation of this Declaration and against any incitement to such discrimination.

Article 8. Everyone has the right to an effective remedy by the competent national tribunals for acts violating the fundamental rights granted him by the constitution or by law.

Article 9. No one shall be subjected to arbitrary arrest, detention or exile.

Article 10. Everyone is entitled in full equality to a fair and public hearing by an independent and impartial tribunal, in the determination of his rights and obligations and of any criminal charge against him.

Article 11. (1) Everyone charged with a penal offence has the right to be presumed innocent until proved guilty according to law in a public trial at which he has had all the guarantees necessary for his defence.

(2) No one shall be held guilty of any penal offence on account of any act or omission which did not constitute a penal offence, under national or international law, at the time when it was committed. Nor shall a heavier penalty be imposed than the one that was applicable at the time the penal offence was committed.

Article 12. No one shall be subjected to arbitrary interference with his privacy, family, home or correspondence, nor to attacks upon his honour and reputation. Everyone has the right to the protection of the law against such interference or attacks.

Article 13. (1) Everyone has the right to freedom of movement and residence within the borders of each state.

(2) Everyone has the right to leave any country, including his own, and to return to his country.

Article 14. (1) Everyone has the right to seek and to enjoy in other countries asylum from persecution.

(2) This right may not be invoked in the case of prosecutions genuinely arising from non-political crimes or from acts contrary to the purposes and principles of the United Nations.

Article 15. (1) Everyone has the right to a nationality.

(2) No one shall be arbitrarily deprived of his nationality nor denied the right to change his nationality.

Article 16. (1) Men and women of full age, without any limitation due to race, nationality or religion, have the right to marry and to found a family. They are entitled to equal rights as to marriage, during marriage and at its dissolution.

(2) Marriage shall be entered into only with the free and full consent of the intending spouses.

(3) The family is the natural and fundamental group unit of society and is entitled to protection by society and the State.

Article 17. (1) Everyone has the right to own property alone as well as in association with others.

(2) No one shall be arbitrarily deprived of his property.

Article 18. Everyone has the right to freedom of thought, conscience and religion; this right includes freedom to change his religion or belief, and freedom, either alone or in community with others and in public or private, to manifest his religion or belief in teaching, practice, worship and observance.

Article 19. Everyone has the right to freedom of opinion and expression; this right includes freedom to hold opinions without interference and to seek, receive and impart information and ideas through any media and regardless of frontiers.

Article 20. (1) Everyone has the right to freedom of peaceful assembly and association.

(2) No one may be compelled to belong to an association.

Article 21. (1) Everyone has the right to take part in the government of his country, directly or through freely chosen representatives.

(2) Everyone has the right of equal access to public service in his country.

(3) The will of the people shall be the basis of the authority of government; this will shall be expressed in periodic and genuine elections which shall be by universal and equal suffrage and shall be held by secret vote or by equivalent free voting procedures.

Article 22. Everyone, as a member of society, has the right to social security and is entitled to realization, through national effort and international co-operation and in accordance with the organization and resources of each State, of the economic, social and cultural rights indispensable for his dignity and the free development of his personality.

Article 23. (1) Everyone has the right to work, to free choice of employment, to just and favourable conditions of work and to protection against unemployment.

(2) Everyone, without any discrimination, has the right to equal pay for equal work.

(3) Everyone who works has the right to just and favourable remuneration ensuring for himself and his family an existence worthy of human dignity, and supplemented, if necessary, by other means of social protection.

(4) Everyone has the right to form and to join trade unions for the protection of his interests.

Article 24. Everyone has the right to rest and leisure, including reasonable limitation of working hours and periodic holidays with pay.

Article 25. (1) Everyone has the right to a standard of living adequate for the health and well-being of himself and of his family, including food, clothing, housing and medical care and necessary social services, and the right to security in the event of unemployment, sickness, disability, widowhood, old age or other lack of livelihood in circumstances beyond his control.

(2) Motherhood and childhood are entitled to special care and assistance. All children, whether born in or out of wedlock, shall enjoy the same social protection.

Article 26. (1) Everyone has the right to education. Education shall be free, at least in the elementary and fundamental stages. Elementary education shall be compulsory. Technical and professional education shall be made generally available and higher education shall be equally accessible to all on the basis of merit.

(2) Education shall be directed to the full development of the human personality and to the strengthening of respect for human rights and fundamental freedoms. It shall promote understanding, tolerance and friendship among all nations, racial or religious groups, and shall further the activities of the United Nations for the maintenance of peace.

(3) Parents have a prior right to choose the kind of education that shall be given to their children.

Article 27. (1) Everyone has the right freely to participate in the cultural life of the community, to enjoy the arts and to share in scientific advancement and its benefits.

(2) Everyone has the right to the protection of the moral and material interests resulting from any scientific, literary or artistic production of which he is the author.

Article 28. Everyone is entitled to a social and international order in which the rights and freedoms set forth in this Declaration can be fully realized.

Article 29. (1) Everyone has duties to the community in which alone the free and full development of his personality is possible.

(2) In the exercise of his rights and freedoms, everyone shall be subject only to such limitations as are determined by law solely for the purpose of securing due recognition and respect for the rights and freedoms of others and of meeting the just requirements of morality, public order and the general welfare in a democratic society.

(3) These rights and freedoms may in no case be exercised contrary to the purposes and principles of the United Nations.

Article 30. Nothing in this Declaration may be interpreted as implying for any State, group or person any right to engage in any activity or to perform any act aimed at the destruction of any of the rights and freedoms set forth herein.

Adopted by the General Assembly on 10 December 1948

Issued by the Department of Foreign Affairs, Ireland on the occasion of the fortieth anniversary of the Universal Declaration of Human Rights.

10 December 1988

UNITED NATIONS

Chapter 8

HUMAN RIGHTS

8.1   Human rights have traditionally been
a central concern of Irish foreign policy. A variety of factors has
underpinned this emphasis, including our own historical experience, Irish
involvement with developing countries, and the human rights dimension
to the problem of Northern Ireland. The emphasis on human rights issues
is rightly seen as an essential part of the approach to foreign policy adopted
by Ireland, particularly in the United Nations.

8.2   As a reflection of its concern, the
Government have decided to take a number of measures, including the
allocation of additional resources, to ensure a continuing strong profile for
human rights issues in Irish foreign policy.

8.3   Within Ireland, these measures
include the establishment of a Human Rights Unit within the Department
of Foreign Affairs and the creation of structures to link this Unit to other
actors in the human rights field.

13. *UN Declaration of Human Rights,*
adopted by the General Assembly on
10 December, 1948.

8.4 Externally, the Government intend to place a strong emphasis on human rights issues during the Irish Presidency of the EU, and to initiate a campaign to seek membership of the UN Commission on Human Rights. In addition, the focus on human rights and democratisation in the Irish Aid programme will be strengthened.

The Development of International Human Rights Instruments

8.5 The Charter of the United Nations lists as one of the purposes of the Organisation a commitment "to achieve international co-operation in promoting and encouraging respect for human rights and fundamental freedoms for all without distinction as to race, sex, language, or religion". This was the first time in a major international agreement that such an objective, however general and cautiously phrased, was described as properly the concern of the international community.

8.6 When it adopted the *Universal Declaration on Human Rights on* 10 December 1948, the United Nations General Assembly built on the concepts contained in the Charter to express a comprehensive view of the international community on human rights. Through its accession to the United Nations on 14 December 1955, Ireland accepted the Purposes and Principles of the Charter and the moral force of the Universal Declaration, and joined in the work which was then underway to elaborate two covenants on human rights which would be legally binding on contracting states.

8.7 A very considerable part of the Declaration is devoted to civil and political rights which benefit man as an individual; the right to self determination of peoples, for example, was not mentioned as a basic human right. The period between the adoption of the Universal Declaration and the more detailed standard setting of the *International Covenant on Civil and Political Rights* and the *International Covenant on Economic, Social and Cultural Rights* in 1966 was marked by the admittance of increasing numbers of developing countries to the

United Nations as well as the emerging ideological role of the eastern bloc. The two International Covenants of 1966, the *Convention on the Elimination of All Forms of Racial Discrimination* (1965), the *Convention on the Suppression and Punishment of the Crime of Apartheid* (1973), the *Convention on the Elimination of All Forms of Discrimination Against Women* (1979) and the *Convention on the Rights of the Child* (1989) reflect an increasing concern with economic, social and cultural rights.

8.8 Despite approaches to human rights which differ from one culture to another, the *Vienna Declaration and Programme of Action* marked a breakthrough in the promotion of the universality of human rights. Its adoption *by consensus* by the World Conference on Human Rights in July 1993 may be said to have signalled the acceptance, at least in a formal sense, of the validity of universal human rights standards by virtually the entire international community. Article 5 of the Declaration states –

> 'All human rights are universal, indivisible and interdependent and inter-related. The international community must treat human rights globally in a fair and equal manner, on the same footing, and with the same emphasis. While the significance of national and regional particularities and various historical, cultural and religious backgrounds must be borne in mind, it is the duty of the states, regardless of their political, economic and cultural systems, to promote and protect all human rights and fundamental freedoms'.

8.9 *The Helsinki Final Act* of 1975, adopted by the 34 participating countries in the Helsinki Conference, including Ireland, has been another formative influence in the evolution of European thinking on human rights and had a direct influence on the major changes of recent years in central and eastern Europe. Its provisions have been developed today into the Human Dimension activities of the Organisation for Security and Co-operation in Europe (OSCE).

Ireland and the System of Human Rights Monitoring

8.10   Ireland has a strong moral and legal commitment to international human rights instruments. In 1976, we became a party to the UN Convention on the *Prevention and Punishment of the Crime of Genocide*. In recent years, substantial progress has been made in the ratification of the six main UN human rights instruments. The two International Covenants of 1966 forming part of the *International Bill of Human Rights* were ratified on 7 December 1989. Ireland also became a party to the *First Optional Protocol to the Covenant on Civil and Political Rights* (1966), which provides for the right of individual communication.

8.11   On 18 June 1993, Ireland, having abolished the death penalty, ratified the *Second Optional Protocol* to the Covenant on Civil and Political Rights (1989) aiming at the international abolition of the death penalty. Ireland is one of only twenty-nine UN member states (as of 30 December 1995) to do so.

8.12   States party to the UN human rights treaties are generally required to submit periodic reports to various monitoring bodies established thereunder on the measures they have adopted to give effect to the provisions of the treaties. The presentation, at a public hearing in Geneva from 12-14 July 1993, of Ireland's first national report under the International Covenant on Civil and Political Rights to the *Human Rights Committee*, established under the Covenant, marked a significant development in the State's international human rights reporting.

8.13   The Human Rights Committee raised some concerns about Ireland's implementation of the Covenant, as is normal when it considers state party reports. However, it expressed its satisfaction with the high quality of the report and the constructive dialogue which it had with the high-level Irish delegation led by the then Attorney-General. Since the hearing, some of the concerns expressed by the Committee have been addressed e.g. the rescinding of the Ministerial Order made under section 31 of the Broadcasting Authority Act, 1960, as amended, and the ending of the state of emergency.

8.14   Ireland's first national report under the UN Convention on the Rights of the Child will shortly be presented to the monitoring committee established under that Convention.

8.15   Our first national report under the International Covenant on Economic, Social and Cultural Rights is in preparation.

Ireland and Human Rights in International Organisations

The United Nations

8.16   The main UN bodies concerned with human rights are the Third Committee of the UN General Assembly (UNGA), the Economic and Social Council (ECOSOC) and the Commission on Human Rights (CHR). Ireland has been active in these bodies over the years. Each year the Irish delegation introduces a draft resolution on *Religious Intolerance* in the Third Committee and in the CHR. Ireland is currently a member of ECOSOC (for the period 1994–96) and has worked, together with its EU partners, to reinforce the system of CHR Special Rapporteurs, whose mandates must be approved by ECOSOC.

8.17   From 1983–88, Ireland served two consecutive three-year terms as a member of the CHR. It has been active as an observer delegation since then. During the last Irish Presidency of the EC, in 1990, Ireland sponsored a significant advance in the level of cooperation in the CHR between the then twelve member states. The EU profile in the CHR has continued to develop and the fifteen member states of the European Union, whether members or observers in the CHR, now act together as a group during its annual six-week session.

8.18   The Government have decided that Ireland will seek membership of the CHR for the 1997–99 term. The elections for this term will be held during 1996 in ECOSOC.

211

8.19   In the CHR, as in UNGA and
ECOSOC, Ireland will pursue the following priorities –

- the development of the mandate of the UN High Commissioner of Human Rights and the strengthening of the role of that office including its management of the UN Centre for Human Rights in Geneva;

- the establishment of a standing team of human rights monitors at the disposal of the High Commissioner and the strengthening of the system of Special Rapporteurs and related Working Groups;

- the allocation of additional resources to human rights in the UN system under the overall direction of the Secretary-General and the High Commissioner;

- the establishment of a Permanent International Criminal Court to try those accused of war crimes and massive human rights violations wherever they occur;

- a system-wide approach in the UN to women's rights as an integral part of universal human rights;

- the rights of the child;

- the rights of persons with disabilities;

- the further integration of human rights concerns into peacekeeping mandates;

- the promotion of a dialogue with the developing countries on human rights, democracy and development, including the right to development;

- the adoption of an acceptable *Declaration on Human Rights Defenders.*

The Council of Europe

8.20   In the area of human rights mention
should also be made of the Council of Europe, of which Ireland was one of

the founding members in 1949. The success of the Council in human rights standard setting has been its greatest achievement. On 25 February 1953, Ireland was one of the first member states to ratify the *Convention for the Protection of Human Rights and Fundamental Freedoms,* better known as the *European Convention on Human Rights.* The European Convention on Human Rights was the first important multilateral convention which gave rights to individuals. This was a major innovation in international law at the time the Convention was adopted in 1950.

8.21 In recent years, with the emergence of the newly independent states of the former Soviet Union and of the countries of central and eastern Europe, the number of states party to the Convention has greatly increased. Countries in central and eastern Europe which are not yet parties to the Convention are incorporating its provisions into their laws with a view to becoming parties as early as possible. Ireland views their success in adhering to the standards set by the Council of Europe in the field of human rights as an important indication of their commitment to democratic values.

8.22 The Convention and the jurisprudence of its supervisory organs, namely the European Court and Commission of Human Rights, continue to have a major impact on the human rights provisions contained in the domestic laws of member countries. The Convention remains today the most advanced regional provision for the protection and promotion of human rights. It has had a major influence in the development of our own national understanding of human rights.

8.23 The European Union has undertaken to respect the rights guaranteed by the Convention. In addition, the Convention has served as a model for the domestic laws of many countries in Africa, Asia and the Caribbean.

8.24 Ireland attaches particular importance to the role of the Commission and Court in their evolving interpretation of the rights set out in the Convention. The rights contained in the Convention are primarily civil and political, although the Court of Human Rights has recognised the social and economic nature of many of these rights. More than half of the cases referred to the Court are concerned with Article 5 of the Convention which guarantees the right to liberty and security of the person, and with Article 6 which guarantees the right to a fair and public hearing. By virtue of these provisions the rights of persons in detention have been greatly strengthened in contracting states. Other provisions which have had a substantial impact on the protection of human rights in contracting states are those relating to: respect for private and family life, home and correspondence; freedom of expression; freedom of thought, conscience and religion; and the right to peaceful enjoyment of possessions.

8.25 Ireland was among the first member states of the Council of Europe to accept for an indefinite period the competence of the European Commission of Human Rights to receive petitions from individuals and to accept the compulsory jurisdiction of the European Court of Human Rights. On 11 May 1994, Ireland signed the latest Protocol to the European Convention on Human Rights (No. 11) which, on entry into force, will provide for the creation of a new permanent court of human rights in Strasbourg to replace the existing Commission and Court of Human Rights. The Government are committed to ratifying both Protocol No.11 and Protocol No. 7, which is concerned, inter alia, with the rights of aliens, equality of spouses and compensation for wrongful conviction, at the earliest possible date.

8.26 The Council of Europe has also played an important role in standard setting in areas other than human rights. Many conventions in areas such as the civil, criminal, educational, cultural, public health and social security fields have been adopted by the Council of Europe and have attracted wide participation. The important work of the Council in the cultural field is dealt with in Chapter 14.

The Organisation for Security and Cooperation in Europe

8.27   At the European regional level, in
parallel with the important work on human rights in the Council of
Europe, the OSCE (formerly known as the CSCE) has developed as an
essential forum for the promotion of human rights. With the adoption of
the Helsinki Final Act in 1975, the countries of Europe, then divided
between East and West, committed themselves to the development of a
community of shared values in the interests of their shared security and
placed the protection of human rights at the centre of the CSCE's broad
concept of security.

8.28   Since 1975, the CSCE/OSCE has
developed a comprehensive and responsive approach to human rights
issues. OSCE states have accepted that the protection of human rights is of
concern to all participating states, and that state sovereignty cannot be used
as a shield for human rights abuses. The development of the concept of the
"Human Dimension" in the OSCE encompasses a broad definition of
human rights and fundamental freedoms, democracy and the rule of law. It
also provides for a range of mechanisms and procedures to encourage full
compliance with human dimension commitments.

8.29   Ireland has attached particular
importance to the development of the Human Dimension, which we
regard as among the most important achievements of the OSCE process.
Most recently, at the Budapest Review Conference and Summit, in
December 1994, Ireland, together with our EU partners, sought the closer
integration of the OSCE human dimension activities into the mainstream
of OSCE activities, and underlined the importance of the human
dimension in the pursuit of early warning and preventive diplomacy.

8.30   The next OSCE Review Conference
and Summit is scheduled to take place in Lisbon during Ireland's EU
Presidency in the second half of this year.

This will provide a further opportunity to ensure an enhanced role for
the OSCE human dimension. The following are the Government's main

objectives in the OSCE in relation to the human dimension –

- to ensure that the Human Dimension remains at the centre of the OSCE's broad concept of security and that it is fully integrated into other OSCE activities, including the mandates for OSCE missions; and

- to encourage more active use of the OSCE Human Dimension mechanisms and procedures to address human rights abuses in the OSCE area.

The European Union

8.31 The Maastricht Treaty, which entered into force in November 1993 pledged the Union to respect as general principles of Community law, fundamental rights as guaranteed by the European Convention on Human Rights and as they result from the constitutional traditions common to the member states.

8.32 The question of the accession of the European Community to the European Convention has since arisen on foot of a proposal from the Commission. In April 1994 the Council asked the EU Court of Justice for an opinion, which is awaited, on whether the European Community's accession to the European Convention on Human Rights is compatible with the existing Treaty establishing the Community.

8.33 This question, which gives rise to certain legal difficulties, is quite separate from the issue likely to arise at the 1996 Intergovernmental Conference of whether the existing EC treaty should be amended to permit accession of the EC to the European Convention on Human Rights. The Government will take a position on this question when the legal implications have been fully examined at European and national level.

8.34 The Maastricht Treaty also established a legal commitment to the promotion of human rights in the Union's external policies.

Article J.1.2 included among the objectives of the Union's Common Foreign and Security Policy (CFSP) a commitment "to develop and consolidate democracy and the rule of law, and respect for human rights and fundamental freedoms", while a new Article 130u, inserted into the EC Treaty, stated that Development Cooperation Policy will "contribute to the general objective of developing and consolidating democracy and the rule of law, and to that of respecting human rights and fundamental freedoms".

8.35 Human Rights are given a high priority across the full range of activity under the CFSP. A Human Rights working group monitors and advises on human rights issues. Ireland has sought to play a leading role in highlighting the human rights dimension of issues arising under the CFSP. The recent enlargement of the Union has tended to reinforce the existing support for our perspective on many human rights issues.

8.36 The Union places considerable importance on human rights questions in its dealings with third countries. It has become standard practice for agreements with third countries to include an article stating that respect for human rights is an essential element of the agreement. Also normal is a provision for the partial or total suspension of the agreement in the event of non-compliance with these essential elements.

8.37 Concern at an increase in the number of racially motivated incidents of a serious nature has led the European Union to seek to develop a strategy to combat racism and xenophobia. The European Council meeting at Corfu in June 1994 decided to establish a *Consultative Commission on Racism and Xenophobia* to make recommendations on the development of an overall strategy. This Commission, which included an Irish representative, reported to the European Council at Cannes at the end of June 1995. The European Council also took into account the recommendations of the Justice and Home Affairs, Education and Youth Affairs Councils. At Cannes, the Heads of State or Government asked the Commission to extend its work to study, in close cooperation with the Council of Europe, the feasibility of a European Monitoring Centre on Racism and Xenophobia.

8.38 As President in Office of the EU Council during the latter half of 1996, Ireland will have responsibility for coordinating the position of the Fifteen during the annual United Nations General Assembly (UNGA) session and, therefore, the opportunity in the human rights context to develop further the EU's presence in the Third Committee of UNGA. Our Presidency of the Council also means that until June 1997 Ireland will serve on the EU Troika which plays an important role in the human rights dialogue with third countries.

8.39 The Government believe that a continuing commitment to fundamental human rights values must be part of Ireland's approach to charting the future course of the European Union in cooperation with our partners.

Current Human Rights Issues

8.40 Almost 50 years after the adoption of the Universal Declaration, human rights abuse remains a major worldwide problem. Indeed, the emergence of various regional and ethnic tensions with the ending of the Cold War era have led to an increase in the problem in some areas of the world. In former Yugoslavia and in Rwanda the international community has been forced to confront again the horror of crimes of genocide and other human rights violations. It has struggled to find ways of adequately responding through the establishment of monitoring mechanisms and ad-hoc Tribunals to try the perpetrators of such crimes.

8.41 New issues are also being raised in the human rights field which will require careful consideration and which may conflict with more traditional or legalistic approaches. Many developing countries are seriously concerned about the international dumping of toxic waste and see this as a human rights issue.

The globalization of the world economy is stimulating debate on the relationship between labour standards and economic growth. The policies of multinational companies in marketing certain products in developing countries are seen by many as having human rights implications.

The development of a coherent approach to these issues, consistent with universal human rights standards, is likely to represent a major challenge for the international community in the years ahead. Ireland will emphasise the importance of maintaining a constructive dialogue with the developing world on all of these issues.

Impunity and the International Monitoring of Human Rights

8.42 Despite the existence of international monitoring mechanisms, it is clear that many of those responsible for gross violations of human rights act in the conviction that they are immune to prosecution for their crimes. The problem of impunity has attracted increased attention in recent years and the establishment of the ad-hoc Tribunals mentioned earlier represents an attempt to deal with it in the specific cases of former Yugoslavia and Rwanda.

8.43 The Government believe that there is need urgently to address the wider issue of establishing an *International Criminal Court* to ensure that human rights violators are made to answer for their crimes against the dignity of the human person. The Government also recognise the importance of measures which would give early warning of potential situations of human rights abuse. They consider that the UN High Commissioner for Human Rights, supported by human rights monitors, has a crucial role to play in this regard.

The Vienna Declaration and Programme of Action

8.44 As the United Nations expanded in membership, it was sometimes suggested that since many of the newer member states had not participated in the drafting of the Universal Declaration, they were not necessarily bound by its principles or those of the instruments which derived from it. It was argued that there were particular cultural or regional values which had not been reflected in the

Declaration. Ireland, although not a member of the UN at the time the Universal Declaration was adopted, has always accepted that the human rights values enshrined in the Universal Declaration and the instruments which flow from it are indeed universal and indivisible.

8.45 The World Conferences on Population (Cairo, 1994); Social Development (Copenhagen, March 1995); and Women (Beijing, September 1995) have also addressed human rights issues. Despite clear evidence that some states continue to resist the implications and implementation of the Vienna Declaration, it is the standard by which future developments in the human rights field will be judged. Ireland will continue to work with its EU partners to ensure that the progress represented by the Vienna Declaration is maintained at future UN conferences.

8.46 It is now generally accepted that much has been accomplished in standard-setting, or the drafting of human rights instruments, and that there are sufficient international instruments in existence. While new standards may yet be elaborated in some specific thematic areas, and while work continues on detailed optional protocols to various existing instruments, there is wide agreement that the international community should now concentrate on the implementation of the provisions of these instruments.

8.47 The Vienna Declaration and Programme of Action is, again, the key point of reference. It calls, inter alia, for a concerted effort to be made to promote ratification of international human rights instruments with the aim of their universal acceptance. It contains many other provisions dealing with the various thematic concerns in the human rights field such as the eradication of torture.

Resources for Human Rights

8.48 The Vienna Programme of Action represents a comprehensive blueprint for international human rights action. Its adoption by consensus provides a major opportunity to improve global human rights observance.

8.49 However, Ireland, together with its partners in the EU, is concerned that its implementation will suffer unless there is a substantial increase in the proportion of the UN Regular Budget devoted to human rights activity. Although there has been some increase since the Vienna Conference, this percentage, now standing at about 1.8%, is still inadequate.

8.50 As a demonstration of Ireland's national commitment, the Government have again in 1995 and 1996 substantially increased our contributions to the various UN *Voluntary Funds* in the field of human rights. The Government will work with our EU partners to persuade others to do the same and, crucially, to agree in UNGA to a substantial increase in the proportion of the UN Regular Budget devoted to human rights, so that the Vienna Programme can be fully implemented.

Human Rights and Development

8.51 In promoting such an increase, it will be necessary to overcome the fears expressed by many of the developing countries in UNGA that spending on human rights means less spending on development. For Ireland, a commitment to human rights has always been a vital part of our expression of solidarity with the developing world. The Government are convinced of the intrinsic linkage between human rights, democracy and development as expressed in the November 1991 Declaration of the EC Council of Development Ministers, in Article 130u of the EC Treaty, and in various statements of Irish Aid policy.

8.52 The promotion of respect for human rights and of democracy has been a part of the Irish Aid programme since its inception. In the past two years, a specific democratisation and human rights programme has been developed as the Government have increased spending on overseas development assistance (ODA). Irish electoral

221

observers have participated in missions to a number of countries as part of this programme. Clauses on human rights and democracy now form a standard part of our cooperation agreements with developing countries.

8.53 The Government's commitment to annual increases in ODA spending will allow the further development of this integral element of our overall development effort. It reflects the reality that the promotion of human rights and democracy at all levels of society is itself a vital tool for economic and social development.

8.54 The violation of women's rights constitutes a major obstacle to development. The challenge is to empower women so that they become the agents as well as the beneficiaries of development. The Government will therefore give particular attention in the overall Irish Aid programme to gender-specific approaches and to countering violence against women.

8.55 The World Conference on Human Rights agreed on a definition of *the Right to Development*. However, a common understanding of what the implementation of this right requires in practice remains elusive and a source of difference between the developed and developing world. Friction surrounding the Right to Development in turn hinders efforts to increase UN spending on human rights generally. Ireland is well-placed, given its history and expanding development cooperation activities, to promote greater dialogue between the regions on the related questions of human rights and development. One of the challenges we face is to persuade more UN member states that spending on human rights is spending on development. Ireland will also seek to promote a more complete acceptance of the importance of all aspects of the Right to Development as defined in the Vienna Declaration.

8.56 Another source of contention with developing countries is the question of *conditionality* where aid or other forms of cooperation are linked to human rights observance. Within the EU and in other fora, discussion continues on the balance to be sought in such linkages. Ireland will continue to resist automatic mechanisms of conditionality which can in some circumstances harm the very poor in the developing world, rather than those wealthier Governments which fail to observe universal human rights standards. At the same time, the Government acknowledge that this is a difficult and complex issue and that sometimes firm action in defence of those standards will be required.

8.57 The Government recognise the potential contribution which Ireland's aid programme can make to the promotion and protection of human rights and the strengthening of the institutions of emerging democracies around the world.

8.58 With a view to realising this potential, the Government will provide support through Irish Aid for the following –

- human rights NGOs in the developing countries;

- assistance in the training of the judiciary, the police and the mass media;

- human rights education for police and military personnel, drawing on the expertise of the Garda Síochána and the Defence Forces.

Human Rights Education

8.59 The Vienna Declaration stresses the importance of human rights education. Human rights education in the domestic context is not strictly a foreign policy concern for review in this White Paper. However, the Government believe that it is a proper subject for further consideration in an interdepartmental framework, given the responsibility of the State to promote an awareness of the provisions of the various international human right instruments.

8.60 The work of Irish people in developing countries and areas of conflict has traditionally been imbued with a concern for human rights — what might be described as an informal human rights culture. Irish development workers have become advocates at home for the poor and oppressed whom they have met abroad. Irish military and Garda personnel on UN service have developed close relations with local communities based on an understanding for their values as well as a full awareness of international human rights standards. Respect for these standards is an integral part of the training of the Defence Forces and the Garda Síochána.

8.61　　　　　　　　　　　　　It is vital that all those who serve the UN or other international or regional bodies, whether in a peacekeeping or other capacity, should fully respect the highest human rights standards.

Human Rights in the Shaping of Ireland's Foreign Policy

8.62　　　　　　　　　　　　　The Government are determined that the traditional emphasis on human rights in Irish foreign policy will be maintained in the face of new challenges in the political, economic and security areas. This must apply in both bilateral and multilateral contexts. Drawing on the experience of other countries, particularly that of our EU partners, the challenge is to put in place structures which will ensure that the Irish approach to human rights issues is effectively presented at the European and international levels.

The Department of Foreign Affairs and Human Rights

8.63　　　　　　　　　　　　　In recent years, there has been a dramatic increase in the human rights- related work of the Department of Foreign Affairs. The dynamic contribution of the NGO community has heightened the profile of human rights issues. The range and immediacy of media coverage has also had a major impact on the extent to which the general public expect Government to respond to international crises involving violations of human rights. The Department is also regularly called upon to service the Oireachtas Joint Committee on Foreign Affairs in its frequent enquiries into situations of human rights abuse abroad.

8.64　　　　　　　　　　　　　As a result of the progressive ratification of UN human rights instruments, the State has undertaken a permanent and ongoing obligation to submit periodic reports on its implementation of the provisions required under the instruments. The preparation of these reports involves extensive consultation and co-ordination by the Department of Foreign Affairs with other Government Departments which have substantive responsibility for the implementation of the provisions of these instruments at the domestic level (the Department of Equality and Law Reform prepares the reports due under the Convention on the Elimination of All Forms of Discrimination Against Women).

The implications of judicial and administrative decisions and proposed legislation with implications for the State's international obligations in the human rights area must also be monitored.

8.65 These demands, together with the pressures of an increasingly complex international environment, require an improvement in coordination. This applies to coordination between the human rights work of the geographic and functional areas of the Department of Foreign Affairs, as well as to coordination with other Government Departments responsible for the domestic implementation of international human rights standards and with the Attorney-General's Office.

Establishment of a Human Rights Unit

8.66 In response to this situation, a Human Rights Unit is in the process of being established in the Political Division of the Department of Foreign Affairs. The Government have allocated additional resources for this Unit.

8.67 It is intended that the Unit's main function will be to take an overview of Ireland's approach to international human rights issues so that they are given full attention in all aspects of our foreign policy. Its role will essentially be to reinforce an active human rights culture in the Department of Foreign Affairs. Human rights work currently undertaken in all other areas of the Department's structure will continue as before in line with the long-standing principle that all line Divisions and Sections of the Department should address human rights issues pertaining to their normal work.

8.68　　　　　　　　　　The Human Rights Unit will also have a key role to play in ensuring that Irish perspectives on human rights issues around the world are brought forward in the context of the EU's Common Foreign and Security Policy. The Government expect that the establishment of the Unit will significantly enhance the human rights dimension of Ireland's Presidency of the EU.

8.69　　　　　　　　　　The Unit will have a lead role in coordinating the fulfilment of Ireland's international reporting and other human rights obligations with other Government Departments and Offices. In addition it will manage Ireland's participation in the UN human rights bodies with the involvement of other relevant sections of the Department of Foreign Affairs. It will seek to encourage a coherent overall approach to new issues in the field of human rights.

8.70　　　　　　　　　　The Unit will recommend to the Government, as appropriate, the nomination of Irish expert candidates for election to international human rights bodies.

8.71　　　　　　　　　　The Human Rights Unit will also pursue the ratification of human rights and international humanitarian law instruments. Work on the UN *Conventions on Torture and Racial Discrimination* is already underway in relevant Departments with a view to early ratification. Thereafter, the Human Rights Unit, in cooperation with other Government Departments, will be focusing its attention on the ratification of instruments such as the *1977 Additional Protocols to the 1949 Geneva Conventions* dealing with the protection of the victims of armed conflicts. Ireland became a party to the 1949 Geneva Conventions in the year in which they were adopted.

Interdepartmental Cooperation

8.72　　　　　　　　　　It has also been decided that the Head of the Human Rights Unit should chair a new standing Interdepartmental Committee to consider all aspects of Ireland's international human rights obligations. This Committee will be particularly concerned with ensuring the timely preparation of comprehensive national reports under the various international instruments already ratified and with expediting the legislation necessary for the ratification of additional instruments.

The Non-Governmental Community

8.73 A feature of the Irish presence at the World Conference in Vienna was the presence, with the support of the Department of Foreign Affairs, of a delegation representing the Irish non-governmental community at the NGO Forum. Their attendance reflected the remarkable growth of the NGO movement in Ireland in recent years. There are now a large number of NGOs concerned with human rights which are active on thematic, country situation or developmental issues. Their activity, and the public interest which it generates, already strongly influences the formulation of policy in the human rights field and the treatment of related issues in the Oireachtas. Various sections in the Department of Foreign Affairs maintain an ongoing and mutually beneficial contact with the NGOs, according to their area of interest.

8.74 The Irish NGOs have their counterparts around the world, in the international NGOs and the numerous human rights defenders who struggle at grassroots level for fundamental human dignity. Ireland, through, for example, its membership of the NGO Committee in ECOSOC and its support for the drafting of a *Declaration on the rights of Human Rights Defenders* in the CHR, strongly supports the work of the NGO community internationally.

A Joint Standing Committee

8.75 Contact between the Department of Foreign Affairs and the NGO community on the human rights aspects of foreign policy is now so intensive that it has been decided to establish a formal framework for a regular exchange of views between the Department and representatives of the NGO community. A Joint Standing Committee representing the Department, NGOs and experts in the human rights field will therefore be established. This Standing Committee is not intended to replace, or restrict, the current informal flow of information and views.

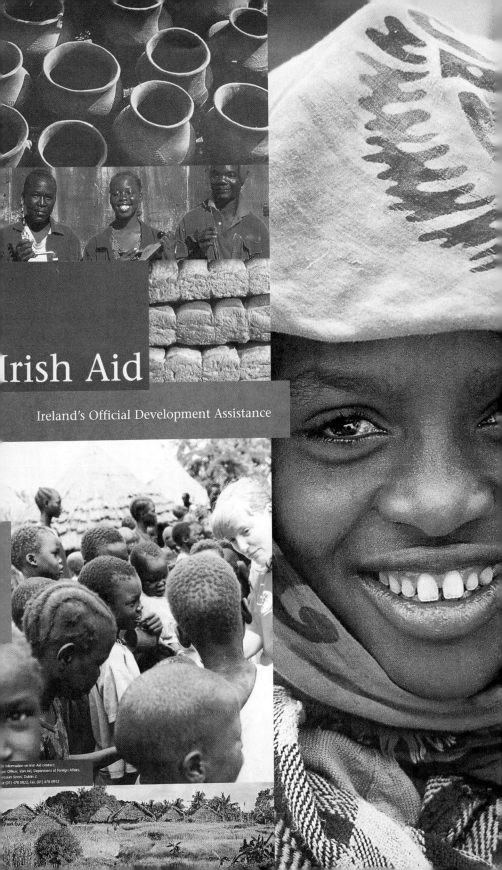

Irish Aid

Ireland's Official Development Assistance

For information on Irish Aid contact:
an Officer, Irish Aid, Department of Foreign Affairs,
rcourt Street, Dublin 2
e (01) 478 0822, Fax (01) 478 0952

Chapter 9

DEVELOPMENT COOPERATION

Development Policy

9.1   Ireland's relations with the developing countries form an integral part of our foreign policy. There is a demonstrable interconnection between the economic and social well-being of all the nations of the world and the maintenance of international peace and security. Irish Aid and Development Cooperation are practical expressions of Ireland's foreign policy commitment to peace and justice in the world.

9.2   Since the inception of the Irish Aid programme in 1974, virtually every Irish family has had involvement with Ireland's overall aid effort, either by way of a family member working in the developing world or by contributing financially to the work of one of the many Irish humanitarian NGOs.

9.3   The chief foreign policy mechanism through which the Government meet their responsibilities towards

14. Irish Aid poster

developing countries is Official Development Assistance (ODA). Implementation of the Government's ODA programme is primarily the responsibility of the Department of Foreign Affairs through its Development Cooperation Division and through Development Cooperation Offices and Embassies in partner countries.

9.4   In carrying out the programme, the Department acts in partnership with –

- *Governments* in the developing countries;

- *Intergovernmental Bodies* — the United Nations family, the EU, the World Bank;

- *International Aid Agencies and Non-Governmental Organisations* e.g. the International Committee of the Red Cross, Concern, Goal, Trócaire and Christian Aid.

9.5   The United Nations has set a target of 0.7% of GNP to be devoted towards development assistance. Between 1992 and 1995, Irish Aid expenditure has more than doubled. In 1996, it will amount to almost £106 million or almost 0.3% of GNP, the highest ever Irish transfer of funds to the developing countries both in cash terms and as a percentage of GNP. The Government aim to make further significant increases in ODA in the years ahead so as to put Ireland's ODA performance on a par with that of our partners in the European Union, and with the ultimate aim of meeting the UN target.

Objectives

9.6   The Government's objectives in the field of Development Cooperation are –

- to reduce poverty and promote sustainable development in some of the poorest countries in the world;

- to assist in establishing and maintaining peace in developing countries by fostering democracy, respect for human rights, gender and social equality and protection of the environment;

- to respond promptly to emergencies and humanitarian disasters, both natural and man-made, as they occur, and to support preventive measures so that such emergencies may, so far as possible, be avoided;

- to contribute to building civil society and social solidarity.

9.7   Ireland's standing in the developing world is high. Our historical experience and political outlook have struck a chord with many developing countries. The long history of involvement by Irish missionary orders has strengthened the impression of the willingness of the Irish people to give generously in the cause of others.

9.8   That tradition has been added to in recent years by the many Irish men and women working in developing countries, whether for non-governmental organisations (NGOs) or international agencies or for the Irish Aid programme including through APSO. The outstanding service and dedication shown by these personnel have enhanced the reputation of Ireland.

Development Assistance Programme

9.9   Ireland's Official Development Assistance programme was the subject of a study published by the Government in 1993, *Irish Aid: Consolidation and Growth — A Strategy Plan*. The principal instruments are those generally common to governmental aid programmes: multilateral funding, a bilateral programme, assistance towards volunteer service and emergency humanitarian assistance. A breakdown of the major components of the Irish Aid programme in 1996 is contained in the appendices.

9.10   While it is intended that all of these instruments should continue to be used, the Government recognise that they have an obligation to reassess continually how our aid can be most effective, to respond to the changing requirements of developing countries and to reorientate our programme as necessary.

9.11 The main target of Irish Aid has been sub-Saharan Africa. The priority countries are Lesotho, Sudan, Zambia, Tanzania, Ethiopia and Uganda. The latter two countries, which have experienced brutal civil wars and are struggling to establish democratic institutions in the face of immense constraints, were added to the list in 1994. A further priority country, Mozambique, also a newly emerged democracy, will be added in the course of 1996. The programme in Sudan, which has been categorised as a priority country, has remained static in volume and has been implemented only at local level in recent years because of the human rights situation in that country.

9.12 Countries which do not enjoy full priority status have also been recipients of significant funding. South Africa, Zimbabwe, the Palestinian Territories, Cambodia, Vietnam and Bangladesh are examples. In addition, the Government use two mechanisms — the Emergency Humanitarian Fund and the NGO Co-Financing Scheme — as the main channels for funding the work of NGOs. In this way, Government funding is put to good use in most parts of the world even if it is in some cases on a modest scale.

9.13 In recent years some donor countries have redirected funding to eastern Europe. While Ireland has joined with our EU partners in meeting needs in that region, the Government's intention, supported in the submissions received in the context of the White Paper, is that Ireland should continue to concentrate its efforts on sub-Saharan Africa.

9.14 Coherence of policy is important in our approach to the developing countries — both within the various aspects of development policy itself and between development policy and the other aspects of government policy. It is increasingly recognised that development assistance alone is not enough; development policy must take account of a range of factors including human rights, trade and investment, the arms trade, debt, the role of women, population and the environment. There is also a greater understanding of the need for the process to be a real partnership, with the beneficiary countries and communities being fully involved, instead of having models of development imposed upon them.

Conflict and Development

9.15 The pattern of global conflict is changing, with a clear tendency for conflicts to occur within, rather than between, states. The majority of such conflicts in recent years has taken place in the developing world. These conflicts have provoked a succession of complex humanitarian crises which are characterised by heavy loss of life, intense suffering due to hunger and disease, widespread violations of human rights, and regular and systematic targeting of civilian populations.

9.16 The conflicts have also been immensely destructive of governmental and civil structures in the countries in which they occur. In many cases, they have wiped away years of development investment and have devastated social structures. This situation poses new challenges for donor countries. New approaches have to be identified and gaps in existing responses bridged.

9.17 The availability of conventional arms is the strongest external factor inhibiting the achievement of peace in many situations. Landmines are a particularly vicious instrument of death and injury which have wrought havoc in many developing countries. The Government's policy on arms sales, and especially landmines, is set out in detail in Chapter Six.

Ireland's Response

9.18 In response to these challenges the Government will give renewed focus in its development policy to –

- prevention of violent conflict and the promotion of human rights and the rule of law;

233

- improving the effectiveness of aid response to humanitarian crises and natural disasters;

- assisting war-ravaged societies to recover from the effects of war;

- responding to the growing number of refugees and displaced people.

Preventing Violent Conflict

9.19   The Government recognise the importance of supporting the efforts of regional and international organisations to prevent and resolve violent conflicts by peaceful means. To date they have financially supported a number of initiatives in Africa in the context of regional conflict-prevention activities.

9.20   In recognition of the importance of addressing conflicts before they escalate into violence, the Government are committed to allocating significant funding over the coming years to conflict-prevention measures e.g. support for institutions of civil society, which have a key role in both preventing crises and in the peaceful and constructive resolution of conflicts.

Human Rights

9.21   The promotion of democracy and respect for human rights has been implicit in the Irish Aid programme since its inception. It was only in 1993, however, when the Government decided to make a commitment to increase ODA, that it was possible to establish a specific democratisation and human rights programme.

9.22   The Government will ensure that all aspects of human rights are an integral and indispensable part of policy dialogue with developing countries, including the priority countries. Recent agreements which Ireland has signed establishing aid programmes have included explicit references to democracy and human rights and this will be the standard for all future technical cooperation agreements.

9.23 Specific initiatives are spelled out in Chapter Eight which deals with Human Rights. There is no wish on the Government's part to contribute to the imposition on developing countries of preconceived western models of political and social development. At the same time, the Government will hold to the fundamental standards enunciated in the UN Charter in the belief that there are certain irreducible human rights to which all people are entitled, wherever they live.

Responding to Humanitarian Crises

9.24 There is likely to be a continuing need for sustained and well co-ordinated support for the victims of humanitarian crises arising from conflicts and natural disasters. The NGOs, the *International Committee of the Red Cross (ICRC)* and UN agencies such as the *Office of the UN High Commissioner for Refugees (UNHCR)*, the *UN Children's Fund (UNICEF)* and the *World Food Programme (WFP)* all have a vital role to play in protecting and bringing relief to victims of disaster and in assisting them to regain control over their lives. Irish NGOs have a distinguished record of service in emergency relief spanning the last three decades.

9.25 The delivery of emergency assistance in situations of political instability and violence poses threats to the security of aid workers. The new environment has seen abuses of humanitarian aid by warring parties and threats to the integrity and independence of humanitarian assistance.

9.26 In order to maximise Ireland's support for humanitarian activities, the Government intend to ensure substantial funding of the *Emergency Humanitarian Assistance Fund.*

9.27 Furthermore, in recognition of the difficulty of humanitarian agencies in mobilising personnel and organisational/logistical capacity to deal with emergencies, the Government will establish a *humanitarian liaison group* to ensure that the response of all relevant Government Departments and agencies is as fully coordinated as possible.

9.28   The humanitarian liaison group will
work to identify personnel from the public service and elsewhere who
would be available for speedy deployment for emergency relief activities in
response to requests received from the humanitarian agencies and the Red
Cross movement. A register will be established with the names and skills of
such persons with a view to maximising Ireland's capacity to respond to
humanitarian crises.

9.29   The aim will be to establish a "Rapid
Response Register" of personnel drawn from all aspects of the caring
services. Individuals working in the private sector who wish to be placed on
the Register will be encouraged and facilitated. The existence of this register
of people willing and able to be deployed on an emergency basis wherever
needed will help to ensure that Ireland's response, official and voluntary, to
such emergencies takes into account all possible contributions and skills.
Persons whose names are on the Register may be expected to participate in
occasional training and orientation programmes.

Rehabilitation Assistance

9.30   Traditionally, emergency relief and
economic development assistance have been seen and treated as separate
activities. This arose from the notion that emergencies were temporary
interruptions to what was otherwise peaceful socio-economic development.
This approach may hold true for natural disasters, but it has proved
inadequate as an approach for societies which suffer from recurring and
protracted man-made disasters.

9.31   The concept of the *relief-
rehabilitation-development* continuum takes account of the critical need to
develop a sustained, integrated approach which will help societies break out
of the cycle of recurring emergency. Central to this is the idea of an
intermediate stage, the rehabilitation phase, lying between emergency relief
and long-term development.

9.32 The continuum approach emphasises the need for aid to provide a more systematic response to the needs of societies in pre-conflict, conflict and post-conflict phases. Making this concept work in practice is an immense challenge to the aid community.

9.33 The Government will continue to provide funds for rehabilitation projects in countries emerging from crises. Their approach will focus on rebuilding devastated administrative structures and social services and improving the food security of local populations. The aim will be both to alleviate the material consequences of the crises and to contribute to political reconciliation.

Refugee Emergencies

9.34 The political instability caused by violent conflict in recent years has provoked massive population movements and the displacement of people from their homes. The UNHCR estimates that there are some 27 million refugees in the world and a further 20 million internally displaced people. Ireland is committed to working closely with UNHCR, which is legally mandated to offer protection for refugees. The UNHCR is also a 'lead agency' for many refugee emergencies and has received considerable Irish Government support for its emergency humanitarian work.

9.35 The Government will maintain support for UNHCR's protection and humanitarian roles in the coming years. In addition, they have decided that our close relationship with UNHCR will be strengthened and that Ireland will seek to join the UNHCR Executive Committee. Membership of the Board would enhance Ireland's influence on the future direction of UN refugee policy and protection.

9.36 In the domestic context, the Government have admitted groups of people into Ireland who have been displaced from their homes as a consequence of war. The Refugee Agency was established in 1991 to help with integration of such refugees in Ireland. The resources of the Refugee Agency have been strengthened to ensure that Ireland's resettlement programme complies with best international practice.

Bilateral Aid Programme: Effectiveness and Quality

9.37   The Bilateral Aid Programme is the channel through which the Government provide long-term assistance with the objective of reducing poverty and promoting sustainable development in the developing world. The main features, aims and objectives of the Bilateral Aid Programme have been described in detail in *Irish Aid: Consolidation and Growth — A Strategy Plan.*

9.38   In the continuing effort to ensure that long-term development is as effective as possible, there are a number of important issues, many of which were highlighted in submissions on the White Paper.

9.39   They include –

•   Poverty Reduction

•   Self-reliant Development

•   Partnership

•   Sustainability

•   Human Resources

•   Gender

•   Food Security

Poverty Reduction: Addressing Basic Needs

9.40   The target of reducing poverty is reflected both in the choice of Irish Aid priority countries, all of which are among the poorest in the world, and in a heavy concentration of the Bilateral Aid Programme on basic needs such as water supply, primary education, health-care and sanitation.

9.41   The motivation is two-fold: first, to support the intrinsic human right to access to the basics of life — food, safe water, basic education, health, shelter and security; secondly, in the conviction that truly sustainable development — economic and environmental as well as human — cannot be achieved without poverty reduction, improved standards of living and human resource development.

9.42   At the Social Summit in Copenhagen in 1995, Ireland supported the Twenty-Twenty concept, a formula whereby 20% of developed countries' ODA and a matching 20% of developing countries' national budgets would be devoted to basic social programmes. The Government will pursue the application of these principles in the Irish Aid programme and will work at international level to generate broader support for them.

Self-Reliant Development: Capacity Building

9.43   Progress towards sustained, more equitable and self-reliant development depends critically on the strength and quality of a country's institutional and human capacity. Contributing to this objective is a priority objective of the Irish Aid programme.

9.44   Specific capacity-building programmes are in place to increase the management capacity of decision makers at various levels, including senior civil servants, regional and district representatives. Secondly, in all general programmes and projects, most notably in the many district-based rural development programmes, priority is increasingly accorded to ensuring that partner authorities, institutions and communities, right through to grassroots level, are fully involved in planning and implementation and that their capacity to plan and manage available resources is enhanced in the process.

9.45   Where possible, capacity-building training is provided locally, in the form of on-the-job, task-related training and even greater emphasis will be placed on such local training in the coming years. In cases where such training or more formal studies are not feasible or effective locally, fellowships and training courses in Ireland will continue to be provided.

9.46 Greater attention will also be given to supporting, and utilising, courses and training programmes in-country and in the region, as well as to encouraging links between third level institutions in Ireland and developing countries, including scholarship exchanges.

Partnership

9.47 There is growing consensus among recipients and donors on the need for strong, equal partnership, based on mutual respect. The focal point for the partnership should be a broad policy framework, setting out in a realistic and focused manner national development objectives, priorities and strategies — as agreed with the partner government.

9.48 Ireland has based its development programmes on cooperation with the governments of partner countries, both at central and local level, to ensure that they are based on the host countries' priority needs and their development strategies. Such cooperation also involves local communities.

9.49 With a view to achieving greater coherence in the country programmes, a more programmatic approach is being adopted. This involves a broader approach to programme and project planning, with particular priority sectors in each country targeted for support, greater integration between and within projects and, most recently, a country review and planning process which maps out a coherent country programme on a sectoral and geographic basis for a three-year period. These country programmes will be developed in close cooperation with the host governments and communities and they are intended to lead to greater effectiveness in aid coordination and delivery for both partners.

Sustainability

9.50 One of the main lessons of development cooperation experience is that aid-supported activities must be capable of being absorbed and sustained in the environment in which they exist. Viability in the long run without external support must be guaranteed by ensuring that development activities –

- are at an appropriate level of technology and not too sophisticated for the environment in which they take place;

- are realistic in terms of their need for ongoing budget support;

- rely only on the level of institutional and administrative support that is likely to be available locally;

- ensure efficient use of resources so as not to damage or degrade the environment;

- involve local communities in the process of identifying needs and deciding on the actions to be taken;

- take full account of the important role of women in development;

- are culturally sensitive.

The aim is to put people at the centre of the development process and to ensure a sense of ownership of the activities by those who are affected by them. This approach will increasingly inform Irish Aid's work in the coming years.

9.51 The United Nations *Conference on Environment and Development*, held in Rio de Janeiro from 3-14 June 1992, agreed a global plan of action to address the challenge of sustainable development. The Government believe that the agreements and commitments on sustainable human development reached at recent UN Conferences from Rio to Beijing require closely coordinated follow up and Ireland will play its full part in seeking to ensure effective international implementation of these agreements. (For further detail on the Government's policy on the environment, see Chapter Thirteen.)

Human Resources/Technical Cooperation

9.52 Technical cooperation including the sending of experts from Ireland to developing countries has been a central element of the Irish Aid programme. As a result of a close partnership

241

arrangement with recipient governments, institutions and communities, together with the strong calibre and motivation of the advisers recruited, our technical cooperation has been acknowledged as being of high quality and a successful vehicle for skills transfer.

9.53 As such, technical cooperation will continue to play a key role in Irish ODA activities. However, in line with international reappraisal of the role of technical cooperation and the increasing emphasis justifiably being placed on the development and use of local human resources, it is intended to make greater efforts to maximise partner countries' input into, and management of, programmes. This is already under way in a very effective manner in the new country programme in Ethiopia.

9.54 The Agency for Personal Service Overseas (APSO), the Government agency for recruiting and placing Irish volunteers in developing countries, currently sponsors over 1,000 volunteers in the field each year, ranging from young graduates through qualified professionals to retired professionals recruited under the Senior Service Overseas programme.

9.55 Given the track record of the APSO volunteers, their high calibre and dedication and the strong commitment evident in Irish society to the developing world, the Government have suggested that the number of APSO volunteer placements could be increased towards a target figure of 2,000. This figure is, however, subject to the established needs of developing countries, to the availability of qualified nationals and to the interests of sustainability including increased emphasis on local capacity.

9.56 Coordination between Irish Aid and APSO will be strengthened to ensure greater cohesion on sustainable technical cooperation policies and practices.

Gender

9.57 Gender issues are increasingly taking centre stage as the donor community and developing countries alike evaluate their gender policies and programmes. The Beijing *Women's Conference* in September 1995 reviewed progress over the past decade and agreed a comprehensive Platform of Action for the coming decade.

9.58 The issue of gender in the development context is one of basic human rights and equality, but it also has far-reaching social and economic implications. It is now generally acknowledged that sustainable development cannot be achieved without the active involvement and participation of both women and men on a basis of full equality.

9.59 Since the adoption in 1986 of a Women in Development mandate and outline strategy, gender has become a significant focus of the Irish Aid programme, both bilateral and multilateral. A recent review of its gender policy and programme will serve as the basis for a more systematic gender strategy with comprehensive operational guidelines to cover all aspects of the official aid programme.

Food Security

9.60 Food security — access for all to adequate food — is an issue which concerns everyone in the developing world and is a priority sector for Irish Aid. There are two important factors involved, production of food and access to food.

9.61 To promote greater access to food in urban areas and other areas where food production opportunities are limited, Irish Aid will continue to support income-generation projects to enhance the capacity of people without sufficient resources to purchase food.

9.62 As regards food production, the broad principles for Irish Aid will be –

- the promotion of strategies that involve farmers in the identification of their own needs and possible solutions;

- the promotion of appropriate low cost, low-risk technologies to overcome bottlenecks in food production, utilisation and storage;

- the empowerment of rural women;

- support for programmes that increase access to information and technology.

9.63 Food security is an issue with particular resonance in view of the commemoration of the Irish Famine, the 50th anniversary of the founding of the UN Food and Agriculture Organisation, and the World Food Summit to be held in November 1996. In international fora, and particularly in the European Union, Ireland will promote food security as an urgent priority requiring a concerted international response.

Non-Governmental Organisations

9.64 Irish Aid works in collaboration with non-governmental development organisations in a variety of ways: in the provision of emergency humanitarian assistance, in the implementation of reconstruction and rehabilitation programmes, and through a scheme of co-financing development projects. The funding provided for these activities has been increased significantly in recent years. This is a reflection of the capacity of the organisations concerned to provide aid in an efficient and cost-effective way to meet the priority needs of developing countries.

9.65 The Government value their relationship with NGOs, not only in relation to the implementation of aid programmes but also for the contribution they can make to public debate and understanding in Ireland of development issues. For that reason, arrangements have been put in place to facilitate strong links between Irish Aid and the NGOs, for example through the participation of NGO representatives in the work of the Irish Aid Advisory Committee and in the annual Forum on Development Aid.

Multilateral Aid

9.66 Multilateral development agencies have the capacity to act on a global scale and are an indispensable source of assistance for developing countries. Ireland takes an active interest in the activities of these agencies with a view to ensuring that their programmes are as effective as possible. A significant part of Ireland's ODA takes the form of mandatory contributions to multilateral development and finance organisations, notably the World Bank Group and EU bodies. The contributions are mandatory in the sense that Ireland's membership of the bodies in question entails payments related to GNP. They are an integral part of Ireland's development assistance.

9.67 The Government will seek to ensure that, insofar as possible, Ireland's multilateral contributions are used to further the aims of our development policy and in a way that is consistent with our relationship with the developing world.

9.68 It was clear from the White Paper consultation process that there is some unease among NGOs and interested individuals that the funds allocated under Irish Development Assistance to multilateral agencies is being absorbed in large institutional budgets with limited Irish influence over the policy objectives which that funding serves.

9.69 An important challenge, therefore, is to increase the degree of influence Ireland can bring to bear over how our multilateral contributions are used. Ireland's contributions are only a small part of the overall budgets of these organisations but this will not prevent the Government from seeking to maximise our input into the policies of the agencies in question.

The European Union's Development Policy

9.70 The Treaty on European Union established an EU Development Cooperation Policy, by providing for the insertion of a specific Title (Title XVII) in the revised EC Treaty. Subject to the general objective of promoting democracy, the rule of law and respect for human rights and fundamental freedoms, the Union's aim is to bring about the sustainable economic and social development of the developing countries, and especially the most disadvantaged among them, as well as the smooth and gradual integration of developing countries into the world economy.

9.71　　　　　　　　　　There are a number of important requirements on which attention is increasingly focusing to ensure that these policy objectives are achieved –

- *coherence* between development cooperation and other policies which may affect it;

- *complementarity* between Community policy and the policies pursued by the member states; and

- intensified *coordination* within the Union, both in individual developing countries and internationally, at conferences and in multilateral organisations.

European Development Fund (Lomé Convention)

9.72　　　　　　　　　　EU aid to the developing countries of Africa, the Caribbean and the Pacific (ACP countries) is funded under the Fourth Lomé Convention by a system of national contributions administered by the Commission. The present Convention expires in the year 2000 and attention is now beginning to focus on future arrangements.

9.73　　　　　　　　　　The ACP countries have benefitted greatly from the Lomé Convention, but EU development policy is evolving. The concept of a single, comprehensive and coherent EU policy on development cooperation with all partner countries, and a renewed emphasis on the poorest countries and populations, merits serious examination. Ireland will play a constructive role in that debate, in consultation with the developing countries themselves and with the NGO community.

Voluntary Contributions to the United Nations

9.74 As with other donor countries, Ireland makes voluntary contributions to a variety of UN development agencies and programmes. Our contributions to these agencies have expanded considerably in recent years in line with the expansion of our aid programme.

9.75 The largest share of funds goes to three main agencies involved in development and relief work: the *United Nations Development Programme (UNDP), UNICEF* and *UNHCR*. Other UN agencies to which Ireland contributes on a voluntary basis include the *UN Relief and Works Agency for Palestinian Refugees (UNRWA)*, the *UN Population Fund (UNFPA)* and the *UN Volunteers (UNV)*.

9.76 Ireland will play its full part along with other donor countries in the financing of these agencies, which are the principal channel of the UN's development cooperation policy. It is intended to increase our contributions until they are comparable, as a percentage of GNP, with the average of the other donor countries.

9.77 At the same time, there is a need to ensure that the agencies perform effectively and that the funds are used in the most efficient manner possible. The UN Funds and Programmes are undergoing a process of reform designed to streamline their activities and to ensure that they respond to real needs.

9.78 One way of monitoring the effectiveness of the UN agencies is through membership of their Executive Boards. At present Ireland enjoys observer status on the Boards of both UNDP and UNICEF. In accordance with a rotation scheme for seats, Ireland will be assured of a place on the Board of both bodies over the next decade. As presently envisaged, Ireland will be a member of the Board of UNDP for the years 1998-2000 and of UNICEF for the years 2002–2003. Ireland has also recently applied for membership of the UNHCR Executive Committee.

9.79 While some criticism of the performance of the UN agencies in the field may be valid, there is no equivalent to the UN system in terms of capacity and size. The UN has established a global network of offices at country and regional level to which we have access when necessary and which we could not replicate. It operates on the basic premise of neutrality in relation to national and commercial interests and provides recipients with resources which do not tie them to any particular donor. Finally, the UN plays a very important coordination role in the field, particularly with regard to the effective delivery of humanitarian aid. The Government will continue to work actively to ensure that these agencies perform more effectively as envisaged under the UN reform process.

Trade

9.80 The point was made at several of the White Paper seminars that Ireland should, in its own policies, promote the economic development of less well-off countries and adopt an advocacy role in favour of the trade interests of these countries in international meetings and organisations. The development aid effort in poorer countries can be either facilitated or undermined by donor-country activities in the broader macro-economic context.

9.81 Access to markets, it is often argued, is more important to developing countries than resource transfers. This calls for a positive spirit of fair trade and fair play on the part of the developed countries. It requires a readiness to strike a fair balance between the interests of domestic producers and the opening of markets to imports from developing countries. Ireland will use its membership of the EU and other international bodies to promote a coherent strategy on trade/development issues.

Debt

9.82 The heavy burden of debt carried by many developing countries is a major issue for the international community which needs to be tackled at global level. The Government will support the efforts being made by the international financial institutions to resolve the problem through our membership of the World Bank and the International Monetary Fund.

9.83 The Government acknowledge that progress has been made in recent years to alleviate the debt burden but much more remains to be done. This is particularly so in the case of low-income countries which are often struggling to implement Structural Adjustment Programmes, frequently involving painful adjustments in public expenditure.

9.84 International initiatives have focused mainly on the problem of bilateral debt. Ireland has consistently supported such initiatives in international fora. The *World Summit for Social Development* held in Copenhagen in March 1995 provided a further impetus towards the alleviation of the debt problem.

9.85 The Declaration adopted by the Summit included a commitment calling for immediate implementation of the terms of forgiveness agreed upon by the Paris Club decision of December 1994, and a clear reference to debt cancellation. In addition, the international financial institutions were invited to examine innovative approaches to assist low-income countries with a high proportion of multilateral debt.

9.86 There is a need to examine all options, including debt cancellation. These measures should be so designed as not to undermine the effectiveness of the institutions nor add disproportionately to the cost to other borrowers. The Government will press for international action on debt to build on the momentum established by the World Summit for Social Development, and are ready to play their full part in international fora in the search for a just solution to this urgent problem.

Management and Accountability

9.87   The Government are conscious of the need to ensure that the greatly expanded aid programme is effectively managed. Staff numbers in the Department of Foreign Affairs' Development Cooperation Division and in Development Cooperation Offices abroad have been substantially increased since 1993 so as to provide the necessary management resources. A new post of Programme Officer has been created in each of the priority countries to assist in the planning and implementation of development programmes. The Planning and Evaluation Unit now includes experts on management, rural development, health and education as well as an internal auditor.

9.88   To meet the challenges of an expanded Irish Aid programme, the Government will ensure the continued availability of appropriately qualified staff and will take account of the need to maintain continuity. A programme of staff development and training has been initiated.

9.89   There are inextricable links between development cooperation and the other pillars of foreign policy, notably human rights, conflict prevention and resolution, and commercial and financial policies. This, as well as the fact that cooperation takes place on a government-to- government basis, involves close coordination within and between the different Divisions of the Department of Foreign Affairs. In addition, consultation takes place between Government Departments on the various policy issues which affect development. These have been carried out, for the most part, on an ad-hoc basis. Given the increasing complexity of the issues involved, the obligation arising from the EU Treaty to ensure consistency across the whole spectrum of the European Union's external activities, and the desirability of developing as coherent a policy as possible, it is intended to institute more formal liaison arrangements between the Departments concerned.

9.90   The *Interdepartmental Committee on Development Cooperation*, which currently concerns itself with the annual

ODA budget, will have its remit expanded to consider development policy issues and will meet more frequently to carry out this new function.

9.91   The Department of Foreign Affairs reports on its development policy directly to both the Government and the Oireachtas. Irish Aid expenditure is approved by the Joint Oireachtas Committee on Foreign Affairs and is subject to scrutiny by the Public Accounts Committee and normal government audits. The Joint Committee on Foreign Affairs has established a sub-committee on development cooperation, which is regularly briefed by the Department. In addition, the *Development Assistance Committee (DAC)* of the OECD regularly reviews the aid programmes of its member countries and is a source of valuable information and guidance. The 1994 DAC review of Irish Aid produced a favourable report.

9.92   Public support for development cooperation policy is high in Ireland. It is desirable that a wide range of citizens and organisations continue to engage in debate about aid and development. The Government will continue to facilitate such dialogue, for example through the *NGO Forum* organised annually by the *Irish Aid Advisory Committee* which has been set up to advise the Government on development issues. The *National Council for Development Education* and Irish Aid will promote public knowledge and understanding of development issues and of the Irish Aid programme through, respectively, development education in schools and community bodies and through public debates and publications.

Chapter 10

REGIONAL ISSUES

10.1   In this chapter, regional issues and conflicts are considered in greater depth. The process of consultation which accompanied the preparation of the White Paper demonstrated the extent of the interest and concern felt by Irish people about issues involving human suffering.

10.2   The range of issues addressed was wide, covering, in addition to the highly-publicised crises in former Yugoslavia and Rwanda, developments in many other regions which may be less well-known.

10.3   Concern was expressed about the human rights situation in many areas — East Timor, Iran, Iraq, Myanmar, Nigeria and Tibet, as well as many others. The principles which the Government are following in its approach to regional issues are set out in the chapters on International Security, Peacekeeping, Human Rights and Development Cooperation. However, the practical implementation of this

15. President Robinson in Rwanda, October 1995, inspecting an Irish supported project to provide housing for survivors of the genocide.

approach represents a major part of the work of the Irish foreign service, both at home and abroad.

10.4   For the purposes of this White Paper, a comprehensive survey of regional issues and conflicts, and description of the Government's policy in each instance, would be beyond the scope of a single chapter. Instead, illustrative examples of three major current crises in three different regions have been selected.

10.5   It is envisaged that these examples will help to demonstrate the manner in which the different strands of Irish foreign policy — conflict prevention and crisis management, peacekeeping, human rights, humanitarian assistance, development cooperation, economic reconstruction, protection of Irish citizens' interests — are implemented in a coherent and consistent way to ensure the policy's maximum overall effectiveness.

10.6   The three examples selected are the conflict in former Yugoslavia, the long-standing dispute between Israel and its neighbours, and the crisis in Rwanda. In all of these there has been considerable Irish involvement, bilaterally and through the UN and the EU. Peacekeepers, aid workers, diplomats, non-governmental organisations and individual citizens have all contributed to efforts to resolve these conflicts or ameliorate their effects.

10.7   These examples show not only the potential but also the limitations and the problems that arise in attempting to make a meaningful contribution to the resolution of regional issues and conflicts.

Former Yugoslavia

10.8   The violent dissolution of the Socialist Federal Republic of Yugoslavia in 1991 and 1992 has resulted in an appalling tragedy in the region. While estimates vary considerably, perhaps more than 250,000 people have been killed in Bosnia-Herzegovina and some 10,000 in Croatia. Population movements on a scale not seen in Europe since the Second World War have occurred.

10.9　　　　　　　　The situation in former Yugoslavia continues to pose a serious threat to peace and stability in Europe. It also poses a serious challenge for the upholding of internationally-agreed standards for the observance and safeguarding of human rights.

10.10　　　　　　　　The crisis has underlined that, notwithstanding the democratic revolutions in central and eastern Europe, the end of the Cold War and the consequent improvement in the security situation of Ireland and Europe generally, devastating ethnic conflicts and territorial disputes of such a profound magnitude can arise that they are beyond the capacity of individual states to deal with effectively.

10.11　　　　　　　　All of the bodies involved in international and European security — the United Nations, the European Union, the OSCE, NATO and the WEU — have been engaged in the search for peace in former Yugoslavia.

10.12　　　　　　　　This collective effort involving virtually all the states of Europe, including Ireland, and of North America and the wider membership of the UN, has constituted one of the largest and most sustained political, diplomatic, peacekeeping and humanitarian operations in recent times. The United Nations peacekeeping presence in Bosnia-Herzegovina, Croatia and the Former Yugoslav Republic of Macedonia has been the largest UN peacekeeping mission ever deployed.

10.13　　　　　　　　The presence of these peacekeeping forces, together with that of UNHCR, the lead humanitarian agency, has helped save many thousands of lives. Notwithstanding these efforts and the operational limitations arising from the peacekeeping mandate of the *United Nations Protection Force (UNPROFOR)*, public opinion in Ireland and internationally was concerned at the seeming inability of the security bodies, particularly the United Nations, to bring an end to the violent conflict in Bosnia-Herzegovina and to prevent large-scale tragedies such as Srebrenica.

10.14 More recent developments give grounds for hope that the war in Bosnia-Herzegovina may, at last, be at an end. A comprehensive Agreement for peace in Bosnia-Hercegovina was concluded on 21 November, 1995 by the parties at the proximity talks which were held in Dayton, Ohio, under the co-chairmanship of the European Union, the United States and the Russian Federation.

Ireland's contribution

10.15 Ireland is making a significant practical contribution in terms of personnel to the international missions engaged in efforts to promote peace on the ground in former Yugoslavia. At present, some 60 Irish Government personnel are serving with peacekeeping, monitoring and humanitarian bodies, including a contingent of 30 Garda personnel with the *International Police Task Force* in Bosnia-Herzegovina. Ireland has a strong presence with the *European Community Monitor Mission (ECMM)* and this will be increased significantly for Ireland's EU Presidency when we will provide some 80 personnel to this mission, including some 70 Permanent Defence Force personnel and a number of diplomatic staff of the Department of Foreign Affairs.

Ireland is also providing military observers for the remaining UN missions in the region, as well as staff for the *European Community Humanitarian Assistance Task Force (ECTF)*, the OSCE's mission in Bosnia-Herzegovina, the OSCE's *Sanctions Assistance Mission* in the former Yugoslav Republic of Macedonia, and the border-monitoring mission of the *International Conference on former Yugoslavia (ICFY)* in the Federal

Republic of Yugoslavia (Serbia and Montenegro).

10.16   The Government have also given
financial support to these bodies, as well as to the *International Criminal
Tribunal for the former Yugoslavia* and the European Union's Administration
of Mostar.

10.17   The Government's contribution to
emergency humanitarian and rehabilitation programmes in former
Yugoslavia has amounted to more than £4.5 million between 1991 and
1995. This assistance has been channelled for the most part through
UNHCR. Ireland has given refuge to a total of 530 refugees from former
Yugoslavia and a further 170 will have been admitted by the end of 1996.
The Government remain open to considering the admission of further
refugees in light of the requirements identified by the UNHCR and our
ability to cope in this regard.

10.18   Diplomatic relations have been
established with Bosnia-Herzegovina, Croatia, Slovenia and the former
Yugoslav Republic of Macedonia.

10.19   Key principles underpinning the
Government's approach to former Yugoslavia are that all of the states in the
region should be able to live in peace within their internationally-
recognised boundaries and that there should, within these states, be
comprehensive provisions to ensure the protection of human rights and the
rights of minorities.

10.20   The Government have worked, both
nationally and through their contribution to the formulation of European
Union policy, to promote the resolution of the conflicts in Bosnia-
Herzegovina and Croatia by peaceful means, in line with the underlying
principles of Ireland's foreign policy. Ireland has also supported the

257

collective effort to prevent the spread of the conflict throughout a complex and unstable region.

Paramount importance has been attached to ensuring the supply and delivery of humanitarian assistance to the victims of conflict.

10.21   The Government consider that, ultimately, there can be no military solution to the conflict in former Yugoslavia. Its efforts have, therefore, been geared towards promoting a permanent peaceful settlement.

10.22   In this respect the priority objectives which in the Government's view should be followed at this stage are –

• to support the full implementation of the Peace Agreement for Bosnia-Herzegovina which ensures its existence as a democratic multi-ethnic state within its internationally recognised boundaries;

• to support the full implementation of the Basic Agreement between the Croatian Government and the Croatian Serbs on Eastern Slavonia and also respect for the rights of Croatia's Serb population;

• to work to ensure respect for human rights and the rights of minorities not only in Bosnia-Herzegovina and Croatia but also in all of the areas of former Yugoslavia including the Kosovo region in Serbia;

• to alleviate the suffering of all refugees and displaced persons and to ensure respect for their right to return voluntarily to their homes; and

• to support the process of mutual recognition of the states of former Yugoslavia within their internationally-recognised borders.

Current perspectives

10.23   The Peace Agreement which was initialled at Dayton, Ohio on 21 November, and signed in Paris on 14 December, 1995 builds upon the broad approach which had been developed by the European Union and the International Contact Group. It is essential that the military and civil aspects of the Peace Agreement be implemented in full. With support from the UN, EU, OSCE, NATO and other international organisations, implementation of the Agreement is proceeding.

10.24 At the peace implementation conference in London in December, 1995 new structures were established to coordinate the implementation of the civil aspects of the Agreement. These include a *Peace Implementation Council*, of which Ireland is a member. A *Steering Board* of the Peace Implementation Council will meet regularly and give political guidance to the implementation effort. At the centre of these structures is the High Representative, Mr Carl Bildt, who has been entrusted by the United Nations Security council with the task of monitoring and coordinating the implementation of the Peace Agreement.

10.25 Under the authority of the UN Security Council, NATO has established a multi-national *implementation force (IFOR)* to implement the military aspects of the Peace Agreement. The Government welcome the deployment of the implementation force.

10.26 The Government also consider it desirable that effective confidence- building and arms control measures, together with regional security and stability arrangements, be put in place in order to reduce the risk of further conflict. In this regard, the Government support the efforts to promote these objectives which were launched at Conferences in Paris and Bonn in December, 1995.

10.27 The humanitarian consequences and human suffering which have resulted from the conflict must also be addressed. Massive population movements have taken place — for example, some 300,000 people were displaced between May and September 1995. Vast numbers of refugees and displaced persons will continue to require emergency assistance in the medium term. This assistance should continue to be impartial and without conditionality. Substantial financial support will be necessary from the international community to meet on-going humanitarian needs.

10.28   The Government are committed to playing their full part in this regard. Such assistance will be essential to help facilitate the successful return of refugees and displaced persons to their homes.

10.29   In the context of the peace settlement in Bosnia-Herzegovina, it is important that the international community should assist in the arrangements for, and monitoring of, free and fair elections. The European Union and the OSCE are well positioned to make a contribution to this end.

10.30   An enormous and well-coordinated reconstruction effort will be required for Bosnia-Herzegovina and the war-affected areas in Croatia. In addition to infrastructural work, priority should be given to developing democratic political institutions which guarantee the rule of law, human rights and fundamental freedoms, and also the reinforcement of civil society.

10.31   Also, it is important that economic development be promoted, together with the normalisation of relations between all of the states of the region. The EU is strongly committed to playing its part in the process of reconstruction together with the United States and other members of the international community.

10.32   To facilitate reconstruction, active support for economic development and, when conditions permit, the development of contractual relations with the European Union, it is essential that the peace plan be comprehensively implemented in Bosnia-

Herzegovina. It is also essential that all of the states of the region respect the right of return of all refugees and displaced persons and fully respect human and minority rights. For example, contractual relations with the Federal Republic of Yugoslavia (Serbia and Montenegro) could not be envisaged before the granting of a large degree of autonomy to the province of Kosovo.

10.33 The international community must continue its efforts to bring to justice those responsible for war crimes. The Government consider that the work to this end of the International Criminal Tribunal for the former Yugoslavia should be fully supported.

The Middle East Conflict

10.34 The conflict between Israel and its Arab neighbours has been one of the greatest challenges to regional and world peace for the past half-century. It has been characterised throughout that period either by outright war or by insurgency and the threat of war. For many years the conflict had the potential to escalate into a confrontation between the two Superpowers. It also led to a series of international terrorist incidents and to the assassination of a number of leading political figures, most recently the Prime Minister of Israel, Mr Yitzak Rabin.

10.35 The human cost of the conflict has been immense in a number of ways. Apart from the loss of life, the conflict has bequeathed a huge refugee population. The lack of a resolution to the refugee problem has further destabilised the region.

10.36 As a result of the strategic importance of the Middle East, with its heavy concentration of oil resources, conflict in the region has, at times of heightened tension, had wider consequences including severe disruption of the world economy.

Ireland's contribution

10.37　　　　　　　　　In recent years Ireland's involvement in the search for a just and lasting solution to the Middle East conflict has been pursued within the framework of the European Union and the UN. Ireland has, from the early days of EU membership, played a significant role in the development of the EU's Middle East policy, notably by our contribution to the 1980 Venice Declaration, which remains a corner-stone of the Union's policy.

10.38　　　　　　　　　The Venice Declaration is based on two fundamental principles: first, the right of all states in the Middle East, including Israel, to exist in peace and security; and secondly, the right of the Palestinian people to exercise fully their right to self-determination.

10.39　　　　　　　　　For decades Ireland has provided financial support to the *UN Relief and Works Agency (UNWRA)* which supplies relief, health and education services to Palestinian refugees in Lebanon, Syria, Jordan, the West Bank and Gaza. The Government have also had a small programme of bilateral assistance in the Occupied Territories since the 1970s, which was substantially increased following the conclusion of the agreements between Israel and the Palestinians.

10.40　　　　　　　　　Ireland has made a direct and substantial contribution to the achievement of peace through its participation in UN peacekeeping forces in the region, starting with the first contingent of Irish peacekeeping forces in the UN Observer Group in Lebanon in 1958, and continuing to the present day.

10.41　　　　　　　　　Most Irish troops serving with the UN are in UNIFIL which was set up under Security Council Resolution 425 in 1978 to maintain the sovereignty and territorial integrity of Lebanon and thereby the stability of the neighbouring region. Our troop commitment to UNIFIL has consistently been among the highest of the participating countries and Ireland is the only EU member state to have contributed to UNIFIL continuously since its establishment. UNIFIL has played a fundamental role in maintaining the stability and integrity of Lebanon.

10.42 UNTSO, in which Irish troops are also serving, maintains a force of military observers to monitor ceasefire arrangements on the Golan Heights, the Israel-Lebanon border and the Egypt-Israel border.

10.43 Ireland participates, through the EU, in international efforts to develop the full potential of the Middle East Peace Process. The Government are of the view that the EU has a particular contribution to make to fostering peace in the region.

10.44 The Union's policies have focused on the multilateral track of the Peace Process, which involves both Middle Eastern and other states addressing concrete social and economic issues of general regional concern. A major EU objective in this undertaking (advanced, for example, at the Euro-Mediterranean Conference in Barcelona in November, 1995) is to promote amongst the countries of the Middle East the Union's own vision of a system of regional cooperation and economic interdependence held together by appropriate institutional arrangements. The EU presides over the key working group within the multilateral track of the Peace Process, namely, that on regional and economic development.

10.45 In the Government's view, the EU's role in the coordination of economic development and regional cooperation must be based on the principle that it is for the states of the region to define their own objectives in these areas, and to decide themselves on the mechanisms they will establish in order to achieve them. The Government will continue to encourage the increasing willingness of the regional states to take on a larger role in the relevant fora in charting the course of regional and economic development in the Middle East.

10.46   The EU has also made its participation in the Middle East Peace Process the subject of a *Joint Action* under the Treaty on European Union; this was decided by the EU Council of Ministers in April 1994 in response to the historic 1993 agreements between Israel and the Palestinians.

10.47   A central aim of the Joint Action is to provide political, economic and practical support to the new *Palestinian National Administration*. The EU has pledged a total of 500 million ecus to the Palestinian Administration over the period 1994–98, making it by far the largest international aid donor to the Palestinians. In addition, Ireland has its own bilateral aid programme which has been mentioned above.

10.48   The EU played an important role in monitoring the Palestinian elections in January 1996. Under the *Interim Agreement* the EU was given responsibility for organising the entire international observation of the elections. It established a 32-strong Electoral Unit, consisting of experts in various aspects of election organisation, which oversaw the organisation of the international observation of the elections; 3 Irish nominees were appointed to this Unit. In addition, the Union fielded 300 of its own observers, consisting of eighteen observers from each member state, both parliamentarians and non-parliamentarians, and members of the European Parliament. Ireland's complement of observers was deployed in the West Bank and Gaza.

10.49   The Government will continue to work towards a peaceful and just solution to the Middle East conflict, both bilaterally and within the framework of their EU and UN commitments.

Current perspectives

10.50   The present stage of the *Middle East Peace Process* was launched in Madrid in October 1991. The Peace Process represents a radically new framework for international negotiation on the Middle East conflict. For the first time the parties involved have undertaken to engage in face-to-face negotiations, based on the principles enshrined in Security Council Resolutions 242 (1967) and 338 (1973).

10.51   The Peace Process is intended to conclude with a comprehensive peace settlement, not only between Israel and the Palestinians, but between Israel and the neighbouring Arab states of Jordan, Syria and Lebanon.

10.52   Since the *Declaration of Principles* between Israel and the Palestinians of September 1993, Israel has concluded two agreements with the Palestinians, providing for territorial autonomy in Gaza and the West Bank. The latter agreement provides the Palestinians with extensive autonomy in the West Bank for the first time.

10.53   The Government warmly commend Israel and the Palestinians for the courage and foresight which they have shown in concluding these agreements. The two parties have agreed to leave over the question of Jerusalem until the final status negotiations; in common with its EU partners Ireland does not recognise Israeli control over East Jerusalem. Israel also signed a formal peace treaty with Jordan in October 1994.

Rwanda

10.54   There have been many catastrophes in Africa in recent years, some resulting from natural causes, some the result of human conflict. However, the disaster which befell Rwanda in 1994 was of a scale and intensity that shocked world opinion and challenged the

265

ability of the international community to make an adequate response.

10.55 It is estimated that well over half a million people were killed and that close to two million others have been displaced in the genocide and civil war. More than a year after the massacres, the situation in Rwanda, and in the African Great Lakes region generally, continues to be critical. The humanitarian problem remains acute with up to a quarter of a million people displaced within the country and two million Rwandan refugees living in camps along the borders of Zaire and Tanzania, and in Burundi; there is also severe overcrowding in Rwandan prisons.

10.56 The major issue, which is both political and humanitarian, remains the repatriation of the refugees. It is essential that the refugees return home, but it is necessary to create the conditions on the ground in Rwanda which would provide them with sufficient confidence to return voluntarily. At the same time, the underlying political causes of the refugee problem must be addressed in a process of national reconciliation.

10.57 Genuine peace and stability can be brought about only if those responsible for atrocities are brought to justice and the culture of impunity ended. Measures such as the re-establishment of the justice system, the rehabilitation of other civil institutions and improvement in the conditions of those in prison are all essential to the process of recovery. The involvement of the neighbouring countries in the crisis, especially Zaire, Burundi and Tanzania, and Rwanda's relations with these countries, is a major part of any solution. Ireland strongly favours the holding of an international conference, organised by the UN and OAU, to address the fundamental problems in the Great Lakes Region, while recognising that to be effective, such a conference would be a major undertaking for the countries directly involved as well as for the wider international community.

Ireland's contribution

10.58   Ireland has been closely involved in the crisis in Rwanda both through the provision of emergency assistance and also through the dedicated commitment of Irish NGO personnel. This engagement has been reflected in the efforts made by the President and by Government Ministers to focus international attention on the crisis with a view to securing an adequate response from the international community as a whole.

10.59   President Robinson visited Rwanda in October 1994 — the first visit by a Head of State following the genocide — and from 9 to 13 October 1995. These visits helped focus attention at the United Nations and internationally on the humanitarian aspects of the refugee situation, the issue of justice and the *International Tribunal,* and the humanitarian aspects of the prison and judicial systems. The President's visits have symbolised the concern felt by the people of Ireland and their appreciation of Rwanda's urgent needs.

10.60   Since 1994 the Government have disbursed £6.9 million in emergency humanitarian assistance to the African Great Lakes Region. In addition, the Government have provided £350,000 to the *UN Human Rights Monitors Team,* the *International Tribunal* and others. A further £1 million pledged by the Government at the January 1995 *Round Table Conference* in Geneva for rehabilitation in Rwanda has been fully allocated.

10.61   Irish personnel are serving with the *UN Human Rights Field Operation (HRFOR)* in Rwanda whose mandate includes the whole range of human rights violations. HRFOR is also assisting in the efforts to rebuild the national judicial system. Irish volunteers working with Irish and international aid agencies are engaged in relief efforts within Rwanda and in neighbouring countries, especially Zaire.

10.62   The Government's approach to African issues generally, and Rwanda in particular, is informed by two overriding policy objectives. These two objectives, which also underpin the Government's development aid policy, are –

•   the prevention and resolution of conflicts, and

•   support for democracy and human rights.

10.63   As regards Rwanda, the Government will continue to pursue the following aims –

•   to encourage a concerted international approach to help bring about national reconciliation, reconstruction and rehabilitation;

•   to work towards the holding of an international conference on the Great Lakes region to determine and implement concerted action on the underlying problems of the region;

•   to encourage the efforts of the International Tribunal to try those responsible for genocide;

•   to encourage the return of the refugees and the provision of adequate conditions for them to return in safety and dignity;

•   to provide financial and other forms of assistance to address the humanitarian problems.

Current perspectives

10.64   The on-going crisis in Rwanda demonstrates the need for intensified efforts to improve international arrangements for conflict prevention. It is clear that Africans themselves will have the major responsibility in this regard. The Government will play an active role in encouraging conflict prevention in Africa and are committed to the provision of substantially increased funding for conflict resolution in coming years.

10.65   The Government will encourage further cooperation between the EU and the *Organisation for African Unity (OAU)* aimed at developing African capabilities in the prevention, management and resolution of disputes. Ireland will contribute financially to the strengthening of the OAU mechanisms for this work and, with our EU partners, will assist the OAU in areas such as the development of early warning systems, preventive diplomacy, peacekeeping capabilities and the emergency deployment, where necessary, of peacekeeping forces.

10.66   The Government will continue to provide support for democratisation and the protection of human rights in Africa, including, where appropriate, through the provision of human rights and election monitors. Additional funding will be allocated for a democratisation and human rights programme. Cases where democracy is threatened or where there are human rights violations will be actively pursued by Ireland in international fora, such as the UN.

Burundi

10.67   The Government are equally concerned about the very serious situation in Burundi and welcome the recent appointment of an EU Special Envoy to the Great Lakes region. His mission will have a particular focus on Burundi. Together with their EU partners the Government will do what they can to assist in preventing a repetition there of what happened in Rwanda. Burundi is of major importance to the security and stability of the region and the international conference would address the situation there also.

BORD TRÁCHTÁLA/IRISH TRADE BOARD

WINNING BUSINESS FOR IRELAN

Chapter 11

TRADE AND INTERNATIONAL ECONOMIC COOPERATION

11.1 It would not be possible to address Ireland's foreign policy adequately without reflecting the extent to which trade and investment concerns influence its formulation and conduct. The Minister for Tourism and Trade has primary responsibility for trade policy and the Minister for Enterprise and Employment for the promotion of overseas investment into Ireland. It is clear however that if the purpose of Ireland's foreign policy is to promote and protect Ireland's interests and concerns in the external environment, then foreign policy must take full account of the vital importance of foreign trade and investment to the prosperity of the Irish people. The Government are determined to ensure that our political and economic policies are conducted in a coherent and complementary manner in the overall interests of the economy.

11.2 The crucial importance of foreign trade and investment to the Irish economy is a result of our small home market and a deficit of domestic investment capital.

16. *Bord Tráchtála "Winning Business for Ireland".*

11.3 Within the European Union, Ireland has the heaviest dependence on exports, which account for over 70% of the goods we produce and two out of three jobs in manufacturing industry depend on exports.

11.4 Foreign investment plays a significant part in the creation of employment in Ireland. There are now a thousand foreign companies located here employing 40% of Ireland's manufacturing workforce and supporting a further 95,000 jobs in service and supplier companies in the economy. The value of exports by such companies is essential to Ireland's export performance.

11.5 The Government are committed to attracting further inward investment as well as to increasing sales of Irish goods and services. In particular, the Government are committed to doubling exports by indigenous business in real terms between 1994 and 1999.

The role of foreign policy in promoting trade and investment

11.6 Through its foreign policy, Ireland seeks both to secure an international environment within which trade and investment can flourish, and to build relations with other nations as a basis for the development of mutually beneficial commercial exchange. This is currently being done in a number of ways, including by –

- contributing to the maintenance of a just and stable international order conducive to the growth of trade and investment;

- encouraging less-developed countries along the path to sustainable development;

- supporting the establishment of international bodies aimed at the liberalisation of trade on the basis of agreed rules and safeguards;

- seeking to develop bilateral relations with countries with which Ireland can develop business and investment.

11.7   The first two of these aspects of our
foreign policy are dealt with elsewhere in the White Paper. This Chapter
will concentrate on international economic cooperation and the facilitation
of bilateral trade and investment.

International Economic Cooperation

11.8   Ireland was involved in the very first
move towards multilateral economic cooperation in post-war Europe when,
in June 1947, it became a founder member of the Committee for European
Economic Cooperation, the forerunner of what is now the *Organisation for
Economic Cooperation and Development (OECD)*. Ireland subsequently
became a member of a series of international institutions whose purpose
was, wholly or partly, to stimulate and regulate economic cooperation on a
global scale. The most significant of these were the *United Nations* (1955),
the *World Bank* (1957), the *International Monetary Fund (IMF)* (1957), the
General Agreement on Tariffs and Trade (GATT) (1967) and, most recently,
the *World Trade Organisation* (1994).

11.9   Ireland has sought to use its
membership of these organisations to achieve a liberalised, rule-based,
international trading environment, featuring safeguards against unilateral
protectionist actions which would be particularly damaging to a highly
trade-dependent country such as ours. Significant progress in this direction
was achieved with the completion of the Uruguay Round negotiations,
which provide for a substantial further liberalisation of world trade, while
catering for the special needs of sensitive sectors like agriculture and
textiles, and which also provide for the replacement of the GATT by the
more powerful World Trade Organisation (WTO).

The European Union

11.10   Important as these organisations are,
however, there is no doubt that Ireland's entry into the European
Community in 1973 has had the greatest impact on our economic and

trade performance. Not only did membership of the Community stimulate a substantial diversification of our trade away from a traditional over-reliance on the UK market, it also served to increase significantly the attractiveness of Ireland as a location for foreign investment in manufacturing and services.

11.11	Membership of the Community has had a fundamental impact on the way in which Ireland's trade is governed. The on-going process of integration on which the Community was engaged, and which led to the creation of the European Union in 1993, involved the establishment of a common commercial policy, a common tariff structure, a common external frontier and the establishment of an internal market by the removal of internal barriers to the movement of goods, capital and services.

11.12	This has meant that the regulation of commercial relations between EU partners and third countries is largely a Union competence under which the European Commission plays a central role, particularly when acting as negotiator on behalf of the Union in close consultation with the member states. The Commission also plays a central role in setting the policy for state aid regimes in the Union and in monitoring levels of aid throughout the member states.

11.13	Successive Governments have sought to ensure that Irish interests are fully reflected in the operation of the common commercial policy, in the development of trade agreements between the EU and third countries and in the development of industrial policy. This has been achieved through effective representation at the Council of Ministers and cooperation with the Commission, which has exclusive competence in the area of state aids and substantial independent competence in commercial policy. The Government are determined to ensure that Irish interests continue to be effectively promoted within the EU institutions.

11.14　　　　　　　　An important aspect of the work of Ireland's Permanent Representation to the European Union, and of our Permanent Missions to the UN and other organisations, is to assist in monitoring contracts funded by the European Union and other international agencies in developing countries and in supporting Irish companies seeking such contracts.

11.15　　　　　　　　Consultancy and transfer of expertise under EU programmes is an important activity of Irish companies in developing countries, as well as in the countries of central and eastern Europe and the former Soviet Union, and our overseas missions actively support their efforts.

Facilitating Bilateral Trade and Investment

11.16　　　　　　　　Given Ireland's heavy dependence on trade and overseas investment, it is essential that the promotion of trade and investment be taken fully into account in the shaping of our foreign policy, particularly as regards the development of bilateral relations.

11.17　　　　　　　　This raises questions about –

(a)　how trade issues are factored into our relations with other countries;

(b)　the means by which the foreign service can assist in the promotion of trade and investment;

(c)　the development of our network of overseas missions; and

(d)　cooperation between diplomatic and consular missions and representatives of the state agencies.

Factoring trade and investment into our bilateral relations

11.18　　　　　　　　Primary responsibility for the conduct of foreign policy is vested in the Minister for Foreign Affairs. The Minister for Tourism and Trade is responsible for trade policy and the Minister for Enterprise and Employment for the promotion of overseas investment in Ireland. There is close cooperation between these Ministers and their Departments on the question of the external promotion of trade and investment. This cooperation extends to a number of other Government Departments, including the Department of Agriculture, Food and Forestry, and to those state bodies actively engaged in overseas promotion, such as *An Bord Tráchtála, IDA Ireland, Bord Fáilte, An Bord Bia*, and *Bord Iascaigh Mhara*. There is also frequent contact with business and exporter groups as well as with individual companies.

The remit of the Department of Tourism and Trade is to maximise Ireland's foreign earnings potential. That Department was established by amalgamating the respective trade functions of the Departments of Foreign Affairs and of Industry and Commerce, thereby establishing clear ministerial responsibility and focus. At present, there is an arrangement whereby a number of officials from the Department of Foreign Affairs are seconded to the Department of Tourism and Trade on a rotating basis.

11.19 The relevant Government Departments and the promotional semi-state bodies are represented on the *Foreign Earnings Committee*, which is chaired by the Minister for Tourism and Trade. The Committee monitors the combined Irish promotional effort abroad, ensures coordination of that effort to best effect, and advises on the trade and investment implications for the conduct of our bilateral relations.

The contribution of the foreign service to the promotion of trade and investment

11.20 Ireland's overseas missions are charged with protecting and promoting our interests and concerns abroad. These interests and concerns vary in scope according to location. However, the promotion of trade and investment in conjunction with the trade and industry development agencies is a major obligation of our overseas missions.

11.21 In *developed countries* where trade and investment is liberalised, diplomatic and consular missions have three main functions in the area of the protection of Irish economic interests.

First, they inform the home administration of economic and political developments likely to affect Irish interests, including those of Irish-based companies.

Second, they represent Irish concerns and those of individual Irish- based companies to the host government.

Third, they act in support of the trade and investment activities of the state bodies and of companies, particularly in terms of access to public and private sector decision-makers.

11.22 In countries where government has a major say in commercial decisions, diplomatic and consular missions play a direct role in support of Irish state agencies and Irish-based companies in representing their interests with host governments.

11.23 In most countries, diplomatic personnel, particularly Ambassadors, enjoy privileged access to government decision makers and senior business managers. This access can be of invaluable assistance to individual companies and state agencies in terms of providing contacts and removing obstacles to business. It is a major responsibility of our overseas missions to ensure that these opportunities are exploited to their maximum potential in the interest of generating increased trade and investment.

Irish missions play a role in the promotion of *tourism;* diplomatic staff support Bord Fáilte's promotional efforts and cooperate with the tourist industry in encouraging tourism to Ireland.

11.24 The limited resources of the foreign service and the small size of most overseas missions mean that all Irish diplomats are required to take an interest in the promotion of Ireland's economic interests. There is a clear need, under the circumstances, for in-career training of diplomats in relation to the promotion of trade and investment.

11.25 The Minister for Foreign Affairs, in conjunction with other relevant Ministers, intends to develop further cooperation with the state agencies especially with regard to training and to the possibilities for the temporary exchange of staff between the Department of Foreign Affairs, state agencies and the private sector. Cooperation with the representative bodies in the export field will continue to be a priority.

Involving the Irish Abroad

11.26 Another dimension to the promotional effort in trade and foreign investment is the development of a close liaison with Irish business people living and working abroad. For example, in the United States, cooperation fostered by the Embassy and the state agencies with people of Irish origin plays a significant role in the marketing strategy of the promotional state agencies. The *Ireland-America Economic Advisory Board*, of which the Taoiseach is Chairman, brings together senior US business figures with Irish ties to provide advice and assistance to the Irish Government and to business.

11.27 Cooperation and close involvement of foreign service personnel with Irish communities abroad helps to maintain links with people of Irish origin who are active in business. The potential for further developing these links will be kept under review, especially in the light of experience in the United States.

The development of Ireland's network of overseas missions

11.28 Trade and investment are factors of primary importance in determining the development of Ireland's network of overseas missions. All proposals for new missions are referred for the views of the Foreign Earnings Committee prior to consideration by the Government.

11.29 Ireland already has an extensive network of missions in those areas with which we conduct most of our trade. 72% of Ireland's exports go to the enlarged European Union market (including the 27.5% of total exports which go to the United Kingdom) and another 8.5% go to the United States. Ireland has Embassies in all EU member states and an Embassy and four Consulates-General in the US.

11.30 While the major emphasis of our trade promotion activity is centred on our main and established markets, we should not ignore the potential of new and emerging markets where governments may still play an important role in individual business decisions. In such markets, overseas missions can play an important role in assisting Irish exporters. Over the past decade, the collapse of the old regime in central and eastern Europe and the rise of the Asian economies have presented new challenges and opportunities to Ireland.

11.31 Ireland must pay particular attention to the development of *central and eastern Europe*. Quite apart from the fact that countries in the region will become members of the European Union, the large measure of trade liberalisation introduced since 1990, their location in close proximity to lucrative markets in the Union and their low cost base means that they are likely to be formidable competitors for Irish industry. The Government therefore decided in 1995 to strengthen our network of representation in the region. In addition to the Embassy in Warsaw, which was opened in 1990, Embassies in Budapest and Prague have now been opened.

11.32 The economies of the countries of *East and South Asia* are growing very rapidly and present a challenge to the economies of Europe and North America. The economies of the ASEAN region grew by 7% in 1993. India has a middle-class market of upwards of 30 million people and an increasingly liberalised economy. Clearly, involvement in these countries will have to be selective and carefully planned. Embassies are already established in Tokyo, Beijing, Seoul and New Delhi. A new Embassy opened in Kuala Lumpur, Malaysia, in 1995.

11.33 The development of trade and investment opportunities in close cooperation with the other Government Departments, state agencies and Irish companies will be a major priority for all of these missions.

Cooperation between diplomatic and consular missions and representatives of the state agencies

11.34　　　　　　　　　Cooperation between Embassies and Consulates and the overseas representatives of the state agencies plays a fundamental part in Ireland's approach to trade and investment promotion. In our nine largest markets, representatives of the state bodies meet regularly under the chairmanship of the Ambassador in order to monitor developments of interest and to ensure that their activities are effectively coordinated. The level of cooperation between the agencies and missions is subject to regular review by the Foreign Earnings Committee.

11.35　　　　　　　　　The Government are concerned to ensure the optimum use of the State's limited resources and to maximise the potential impact of Ireland's various overseas representatives.

11.36　　　　　　　　　One possibility receiving close attention is that of bringing diplomatic and state agency staff under the same roof, thereby encouraging cooperation in the promotion of Irish interests and establishing a significant Irish presence in a particular location.

11.37　　　　　　　　　The most developed form of this arrangement is the "Ireland House" concept, according to which the diplomatic mission and the offices of the state agencies are brought together physically in one building. Ireland Houses have so far been inaugurated in New York (1993) and in Tokyo (1995).

11.38　　　　　　　　　In a number of capital cities, staff representing state agencies have been accommodated in Embassies from which, due to local conditions, they are able to operate more effectively. Bord Tráchtála representatives are already based in the Embassies in Riyadh, Beijing and Moscow, and the Government have decided that the Deputy Heads of Mission in the new Embassies in Prague and Budapest will be Bord Tráchtála officials. The IDA representative in Seoul is based in the Embassy there.

11.39 The Government, in liaison with the state agencies through the Foreign Earnings Committee, will examine the possibilities of expanding the Ireland House concept to other locations. A flexible approach will be adopted to the inclusion of representatives of the promotional semi-state bodies as members of the Embassy staff. Any such arrangements must obviously be shown to be both cost-effective and conducive to the more effective representation of Ireland's interests.

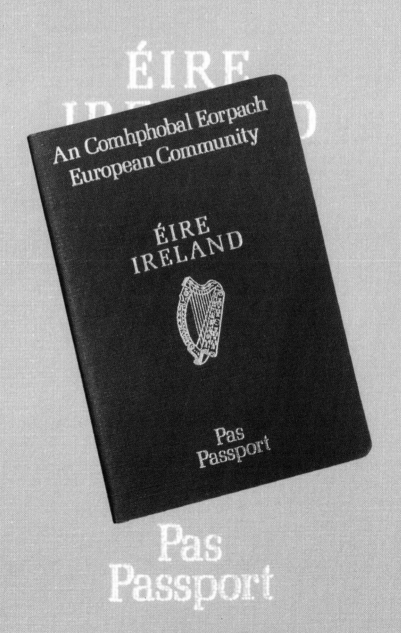

Chapter 12

THE IRISH ABROAD

12.1   It has been suggested that as many as 70 million people throughout the world can claim Irish descent. The existence of this vast extended Irish family creates an immense reservoir of goodwill towards Ireland and is one of our most important assets as a nation.

12.2   Ensuring that the relationship between Irish people at home and abroad is characterised by realism and mutual respect, and that the reciprocal pride and affection is channelled in the most constructive possible way, will remain an important Government priority.

12.3   Among the tens of millions who can claim Irish descent, there is a much smaller but still very significant number of Irish citizens. The entitlement to citizenship conferred under Irish law is relatively generous by comparison with the practice in many other countries: it extends to people born in Ireland, their children born abroad and, in some cases, their grandchildren and great-grandchildren.

17. *The European format passport has been issued by the Irish passport authorities since 1985.*

12.4   It is estimated that there may be almost three million Irish citizens living outside Ireland. Of that total, around two million are in Britain, half a million in the US, sizeable numbers in Australia (213,000), Canada (74,000), New Zealand (38,000), EU countries other than Britain (36,000) and South Africa (35,000), and a scattering of some thousands in other countries. About 1.2 million of the total number of our citizens abroad were born in Ireland.

12.5   Emigration patterns have fluctuated considerably over the past couple of decades. Following low levels of emigration in the 1970s, the numbers crept upwards in the early 1980s (net emigration of 20,000 in the first five years of the decade) and became very significant in the late 1980s (net emigration of 137,000 in the latter five years of the decade). In the early 1990s, the tide has receded considerably and the total net outflow over the past five years has been just under 40,000.

12.6   Irish people are also enthusiastic holiday and business travellers. Over two million trips are made out of the country each year and the number is on the increase. In 1995, for example, there were over 2.5 million such trips.

Outreach

12.7   These patterns of historic and contemporary emigration have shaped the evolution of the Irish foreign service. Reaching out to the millions of Irish around the world and particularly to our citizens abroad will continue to rank among the priorities of the service. The various steps being taken to draw on the goodwill and talents of Irish people abroad to help advance our national political and economic objectives are described in other chapters. This chapter looks in particular at consular and welfare issues and indicates how the Government envisage those services will be maintained and extended in the future.

Consular Services

12.8   A broad range of consular services is provided by the Department of Foreign Affairs to protect the rights and interests of Irish citizens abroad, whether as visitors or residents. The aim is to provide a caring, efficient and consistent service with the widest possible international coverage.

12.9   For many Irish people, the consular area is their most immediate and practical point of contact with the foreign service; their sense of the relevance and effectiveness of foreign policy will inevitably be influenced by the quality of service they encounter. The Minister for Foreign Affairs intends to ensure that their experience is a positive one and that travelling or living abroad is as trouble-free as possible for Irish citizens.

12.10   Together with significant increases in the volume of business and holiday travel, the range of destinations is becoming more diverse. Ireland's inclusion in the US Visa Waiver Programme from April 1995 has made holiday travel to the US easier than ever before. Freedom of movement within the European Union and the ending of restrictions in Eastern Europe are also affecting trends.

12.11   In terms of emigration, while the traditional destinations — Britain, the US, Australia, Canada, South Africa and New Zealand — remain popular, a higher proportion of emigrants now go to live and work in other countries in Europe and elsewhere.

Extending Coverage

12.12   The extent of Ireland's network of resident diplomatic missions is such that it cannot, on its own, provide a consular service sufficient to meet the requirements of our citizens. While the Government envisage a continued selective strengthening of the residential network, supplementary methods of extending consular coverage will continue to be developed.

Honorary Consuls

12.13   Traditionally, Ireland has relied heavily on the work of Honorary Consuls in many overseas locations where we do not have resident missions. As the title implies, these are honorary appointments. The Government envisage a continuing dynamic role for Honorary Consuls and will seek to ensure that their potential contribution in the economic and trade area is developed to the full. However, their core consular work will remain crucially important in maximising the spread and effectiveness of our services abroad.

12.14   There are currently 58 Honorary Consuls, a number of whom have been appointed in the past few years. The Government will continue to extend the service; with the approval of the authorities of the countries concerned, they propose shortly to appoint Honorary Consuls for the first time in a number of Eastern European and other countries.

Arrangements with Britain

12.15   Since 1967 there has been a bilateral agreement with the British authorities for the provision by their missions abroad of consular services to Irish citizens in countries where we are not represented. That agreement now applies in some forty countries. The Government greatly appreciate this assistance from the British authorities, as do the Irish people abroad who avail themselves of it, and it will continue to form a valued part of our consular coverage.

EU Consular Cooperation

12.16   The Solemn Declaration on European Union of 1983 provided for closer co-operation in a number of areas, including consular matters, between representatives of the EU member states in countries outside the EC; in subsequent years, a modest amount of cooperation was established on that basis. However, the Maastricht Treaty went considerably further by introducing provisions in the European Community Treaty on common citizenship of the European Union which is, of course, a supplement to rather than an alternative to national citizenship.

12.17 The provision states that: *"Every citizen of the Union shall, in the territory of a third country in which the member state of which he is a national is not represented, be entitled to protection by the diplomatic or consular authorities of any member state on the same conditions as the nationals of that State . . . ".*

12.18 Since the entry into force of the Maastricht Treaty, therefore, co- operation has been extended to include the protection of unrepresented EU nationals by Embassies and Consulates of EU countries other than their own. The kinds of protection available in this way include assistance in cases of death, serious accident or illness, arrest or detention.

12.19 Help is also available to victims of violent crime and for relief and repatriation of distressed nationals. Citizens of many EU member states are benefiting from these forms of co-operation. They also benefit from informal cooperation; for example, in 1994 Irish and other EU nationals were assisted in being evacuated from Rwanda and Yemen by the Belgian, British, French and German Embassies.

12.20 The Government are conscious of the particular benefits for smaller member states of EU consular cooperation in countries outside the EU, and are actively participating in current moves to give clearer and more legally-binding expression to such cooperation. The Government will seek to expand the scope of cooperation to include matters such as the emergency evacuation of EU nationals and the welfare of abducted minors and of people with a disability.

Passport Services

12.21 The increase in numbers of people travelling abroad is reflected in the sharp rise in demand for passports in recent years. Demand rose over 30% in the early years of this decade, from 161,000 applications in 1991 to 223,000 in 1995.

12.22 The strains created by the volume and seasonality of demand led to unacceptable peak season delays; however, steps have now been taken which have put the service on a far more satisfactory footing. Staff increases, upgrading of computer and telephone systems, and expansion of premises have all helped to significantly improve the quality of service to the public.

12.23 The single most important step forward was the introduction in early 1995 of a new service operated jointly with An Post: *"Passport Express"*. This service, which makes passports available quickly and conveniently through the extensive post office network, has proved extremely popular and over 50% of all passport applications are now being routed through this channel. The consequent reduction in numbers of personal callers to the Passport Office means that lengthy delays are no longer encountered.

12.24 The most recent step has been the upgrading of the Passport Office in Cork to provide a full passport service for the people of Munster. The Government will keep the overall development of the passport service under careful review; they recognise the public entitlement to an efficient passport service and are determined that the present high standard of service will be maintained.

Emigration

12.25　　　　　　　　　Recent emigration trends are outlined at the beginning of this chapter. The Government accept that many of those who go are well-qualified young people wishing to get valuable experience abroad and to advance their career prospects there or on return to Ireland. However, they also know that many leave unwillingly simply because they cannot get employment at home, and many are not sufficiently equipped for the demands they will meet.

12.26　　　　　　　　　The reduction or ending of involuntary emigration has long been a policy objective of Irish Governments. The only effective solution is the creation of job opportunities in Ireland through the promotion of economic growth and this will remain at the top of Government priorities. At the same time, the Government are determined to reinforce the continuing ties with Ireland which so many of our emigrants maintain.

12.27　　　　　　　　　As an important step in this direction, it has been decided to put proposals to give emigrants the right to elect three members of the Seanad to a referendum and the necessary Constitution Amendment Bill is being prepared. If the proposal is approved by the people, detailed legislation will be required covering such matters as entitlement to vote, registration of electors and the conduct of elections.

12.28　　　　　　　　　The Government will also continue to monitor the welfare of Irish emigrants abroad and, in cases of particular need, provide assistance to support organisations in the host country. With a view to better coordinating the activities of all relevant Government Departments and agencies, the Interdepartmental Committee on Emigration, chaired by the Department of Foreign Affairs, was established in 1989.

289

This Committee acts as a clearing house for information and, in the recent past, has particularly concentrated its attention on the need for pre-departure advice for intending emigrants, particularly those who are most vulnerable.

12.29 The Government will maintain a special focus on our largest emigrant communities in Britain, the United States and Australia.

Emigrants in Britain

12.30 Large-scale emigration to Britain has been taking place in waves for at least 150 years, in most cases prompted by a search for improved job prospects. For up to 85% of emigrants (NESC 1991), this search is successful. Irish migrants and their descendants have played an enormous part in the social and economic development of British society.

12.31 Currently, Irish-born migrants make up more than a quarter of all non-nationals working in Britain. Many of them do extremely well; indeed, 25% of Irish nationals are in the top socio-economic group as opposed to 23% of British nationals. However, there is also a marginally higher representation (44%) of Irish people in the semi- and un-skilled work categories compared to British nationals (42%).

12.32 A minority of Irish people emigrating to Britain fail to find a foothold and their situation can be very difficult, with long-term persistent disadvantage in housing, employment and health; their problems tend to be complex and require multiple long-term interventions.

12.33 However, this is not a typical emigrant profile. A recent sample survey of clients of eleven of the major Irish-run welfare organisations indicated that fewer than 100 new arrivals a month were seeking help from these agencies and that the majority of their

Irish clients were long-term residents in Britain. Although this cannot be regarded as a comprehensive record of the difficulties of new arrivals in Britain, it is a significant signpost.

12.34   The British social services assist to Irish citizens who qualify for and seek support under EU and national arrangements. The Government are committed to continuing the present close cooperation between the Irish and British social services. Since 1984, Irish Government funds have also been made available to voluntary organisations in Britain providing advisory and welfare services for Irish emigrants.

12.35   £500,000 a year is allocated by the Minister for Enterprise and Employment on the basis of recommendations from the *Díon Committee*, a body comprising representatives of voluntary groups and chaired by a member of the London Embassy staff. The Government are committed to continuing to assist voluntary bodies through Díon and to promoting high standards of service as well as cooperation among them. The Government will also continue to encourage research that is relevant to the Irish community in Britain as a whole, and into the needs of particular "at risk" groups within that community.

12.36   Given the employment mobility between Britain and Ireland, it is important to provide as much support as possible to those wishing to move to or from either country. The Irish and British Governments have jointly established a *Trans-frontier Committee (TFC)* comprising representatives of FÁS, the Training and Employment Authority, the British Employment Service and voluntary agencies in both countries. The purpose of the TFC is to cooperate in providing appropriate support to workers seeking to move between the two countries and to minimise difficulties of entry to training and employment in either.

The Government will examine the possibility of extending further the range of consular services available to our citizens, especially in Britain.

Emigrants in the US

12.37   Reflecting a long tradition of emigration to the United States, there are today, according to the most recent census, some 40 million Americans of Irish origin. While large-scale emigration had effectively ended by the mid-1960s, considerable numbers, particularly of young people, have continued to seek opportunities to work and live in the US. The vast majority of them quickly establish themselves in productive employment and are widely recognised as making a valuable contribution to their country of adoption.

12.38   In the late 1970s and in the 1980s concern at the number of "undocumented" Irish immigrants prompted the Government and Irish organisations in the US to press Congress for legislation to alleviate the problem. As a result, and with bipartisan support from members of both Houses, a number of programmes sponsored by Congressmen Morrison, Berman and Donnelly and by Senators Kennedy and Simpson were introduced and played a very significant part in effectively resolving the problem. A little more than 2,000 Irish people a year currently emigrate to the US.

12.39   The vast majority of Irish immigrants to the US are single and about half are aged 24 or under. On arrival, they can get advice and guidance from voluntary Irish organisations throughout the country. The Embassy and Consulates cooperate closely with those organisations to ensure the best possible service for existing and newly-arriving immigrants. The Government give grants amounting to £150,000 a year (totalling £900,000 since 1990) to assist them.

Emigrants in Australia

12.40   Irish people have emigrated to Australia since the beginning of European settlement and although strict immigration requirements have reduced the numbers currently travelling, there are about 100,000 Irish-born Australian residents. Up to 40% of

Australians claim Irish ancestry and their sense of Irishness has manifested itself in all areas of Australian life including politics, the churches, trade unions, sport, and culture.

12.41 In part as a result of strict immigration requirements, the majority of current Irish emigrants to Australia are highly skilled and well educated. They have established a network of business associations which are of considerable assistance in advancing Ireland's economic objectives in the region. Some emigrants do encounter difficulties and require assistance. Consular work is a high priority of the Embassy in Canberra.

Social Security and Health Agreements

12.42 The Government are conscious that entitlement to the social-security and health benefits of the foreign countries in which they reside or are visiting is an important issue for Irish people abroad and this is an area to which they will continue to give attention.

12.43 Irish people residing in or visiting the seventeen other countries of the European Economic Area are covered for social-security and health purposes on the same basis as the nationals of the country concerned. In recent years reciprocal bilateral agreements according to which social insurance paid in Ireland is treated for pensions purposes as if paid in the other countries have come into operation between Ireland and Australia, Canada, New Zealand and the United States. A similar agreement with Switzerland is under negotiation.

12.44 An agreement with Australia under which Irish visitors can get emergency medical attention on the same basis as Australians will be signed soon. The possibility of similar agreements with other non-EEA countries to which Irish people travel frequently such as Canada, New Zealand and the US is being actively explored.

Prisoners

12.45 Special attention will continue to be paid to the welfare of Irish prisoners abroad. There are currently about 800 Irish citizens in prison in other countries, 675 of them in Britain. Around 600 of the total (about 500 in Britain) are serving sentences and the remainder have not yet been tried. Our Embassies and Consulates seek to keep in touch with prisoners and their legal representatives and regularly visit many of them; there is also liaison between the Department of Foreign Affairs and the Catholic Church's Irish Commission for Prisoners Overseas.

12.46 Ireland's recent ratification of the *European Convention on the Transfer of Sentenced Persons* will, with the agreement of the authorities of the countries concerned, enable Irish prisoners abroad who wish to do so to complete their sentences in Ireland.

Working Holidays

12.47 There are exchange schemes with a number of countries which enable students and other young Irish people to spend some time getting to know those countries and to cover their expenses by taking temporary jobs. Schemes for students going to the US and Canada for the summer months are managed by USIT (Union of Students in Ireland Travel) in cooperation with the Council for International Education Exchange in the US and the Canadian Federation of Students.

12.48 About 6,300 Irish students availed themselves of these schemes in 1995. Under a similar exchange scheme agreed with the Australian Government, Irish students and recent graduates may spend up to a year in Australia on the basis of temporary employment; in 1995 about 3,500 Irish people did so. Agreement on a similar scheme has recently been reached with the New Zealand authorities; it allows up to

250 Irish people (not necessarily students, in this case) to spend up to a year in that country.

12.49 The Government will seek to maintain and, when possible, to extend such schemes. 70 million people throughout the world can claim Irish descent. The existence of this vast extended Irish family creates an immense reservoir of goodwill towards Ireland and is one of our most important assets as a nation.

MOVING TOWARDS
SUSTAINABILITY

DEPARTMENT OF THE
ENVIRONMENT

Printed on recycled paper

Chapter 13

THE ENVIRONMENT

Introduction

13.1   Over the past 25 years, international cooperation to address global and regional environmental problems, including the degradation of natural resources, has grown dramatically. This is reflected in the adoption of a large number (approximately 180) of international conventions. Environmental issues now figure prominently in the work programmes of the European Union and all the major multilateral organisations such as the United Nations, the Organisation for Economic Cooperation and Development and the World Trade Organisation.

13.2   This international cooperation has grown from initial efforts to combat trans-boundary pollution at the regional level to global efforts to deal with problems that are seriously threatening the ecological balance of the planet as a whole, such as ozone layer depletion, global warming, biodiversity loss and deforestation.

18. "Moving Towards Sustainability", *report on progress in the preparation of a national sustainable development strategy, issued by the Department of the Environment.*

13.3   There is now international consensus that degradation of natural resources, poverty and unsustainable patterns of production and consumption are not separate issues but are in fact closely interconnected and can be contributory factors to conflict within and between nations.

13.4   In addition, collective action in these areas is necessary not only because many environmental problems require concerted action to achieve a satisfactory resolution, but also to avoid market and competitive distortion that might result from unilateral actions.

13.5   The *Earth Summit* in Rio de Janeiro in June 1992 recognised the need to deal with the complex inter-relationship of these issues in a comprehensive and balanced manner. The Summit adopted *Agenda 21* as a guide for government and for the private and voluntary sectors in their pursuit of sustainable development.

13.6   This "globalisation" of environmental concerns has resulted in the development of a substantial body of international policy and legislation on a range of environmental issues which has had to date, and will continue to have in the future, a major impact on our environment policy, legislation and practice.

13.7   Ireland, in accordance with the *Declaration on the Environment* adopted by the European Council in Dublin in June 1990 will continue to participate actively in efforts in the United Nations and in the European Union to combat regional and global environmental problems and to advance international efforts to promote sustainable development and respect for our common global environment.

13.8   Due to the diversity of the issues on the environmental agenda, a range of Government Departments is involved with international environmental issues including the Departments of the Environment, Tourism and Trade, Marine, Arts, Culture and the Gaeltacht and Transport, Energy and Communications.

The United Nations

13.9   The United Nations *Conference on Environment and Development (UNCED)*, held in Rio de Janeiro in June 1992 involving the participation of some 130 Heads of State or Government resulted in the adoption of –

- the *Rio Declaration*, which is a charter of basic principles on environment and development;

- two new major *Conventions on Climate Change and Biodiversity*;

- Agenda 21 which establishes a set of practical action programmes in all relevant areas (e.g. water management, atmosphere, waste) to be followed by countries in their environment and development policies towards the 21st century;

- agreement on a statement of principles on forests as a precursor to a more comprehensive international convention;

- agreement on the commencement of negotiations for a Convention on desertification which has since been concluded.

13.10   The *UN Commission for Sustainable Development (CSD)* was set up to monitor the implementation of UNCED agreements. It meets annually to discuss sustainable development and the implementation of Agenda 21 based on national reports. CSD discussions have focused to date on national sustainable development strategies, and on sectoral issues such as health, human settlement, freshwater, chemicals, waste, land management, deforestation, desertification and sustainable agriculture.

13.11   The *Global Environment Facility (GEF)* funds projects in the following areas having global environmental benefits –

- climate change

- biological diversity

- international waters

- ozone depletion.

13.12   The GEF will act as the interim financial mechanism for the Climate Change and Biodiversity Conventions. The GEF is the primary funding mechanism for environmental measures having global benefits. Ireland will subscribe some £1.64 million to it over four years, beginning in 1996.

Policy Response

13.13   Ireland has co-operated substantially in international action to take forward the UNCED process and has actively implemented relevant UNCED conclusions at national level. Since 1992, the Climate Change and Biodiversity Conventions have come into force, the UN Commission for Sustainable Development and an intergovernmental panel on forests have been established and the Global Environment Facility has been restructured. Ireland has ratified the UN Framework Convention on Climate Change, and has presented a national communication which was recently reviewed by the Convention Secretariat. Ireland proposes to ratify the Biodiversity Convention shortly and has signed and the Desertification Convention. Ireland reports to the Commission on Sustainable Development and attends meetings as an observer.

13.14   The European Union, with Irish participation, has provided strong support for the work of the Commission on Sustainable Development in reporting progress on UNCED and in identifying further action required. Successive meetings of the EU Councils of Environment and Development Aid Ministers have also sought to maintain the momentum of follow-up to UNCED in regular policy discussions.The EU, with Irish support, has played a leading part in the adoption of the Berlin mandate, under which a binding protocol to the Climate Change Convention is now being negotiated.

13.15   At national level, the Government have undertaken to prepare and publish a national sustainable development strategy by mid-1996. A related progress report *"Moving Towards Sustainability"* was published by the Department of the Environment in May 1995. A joint Oireachtas Committee on Sustainable Development has been established and many sectoral initiatives have been developed to integrate environmental considerations more fully into various economic policies and activities. Guidelines on the preparation of local Agenda 21 plans have been issued by the Department of the Environment.

13.16　　　　　　　　Ireland has also adopted measures to honour the UNCED commitment on finance. Ireland is a participant in the EU initiative (amounting to 3 billion ECU, including new and additional funding) towards strengthening assistance to developing countries in the field of sustainable development and increasing funding for Agenda 21.

The European Union

13.17　　　　　　　　The European Union is a leading force for progress at international level in efforts to deal with global environmental problems and to promote the pursuit of sustainable development. Environment policy at the level of the Union both reflects and shapes national environment policies.

13.18　　　　　　　　The EU has developed a comprehensive policy for the protection of the environment. Successful implementation of this policy is increasingly understood to depend on the proper integration of environmental considerations into other policy areas including industry, agriculture, energy, transport and tourism.

13.19　　　　　　　　A high-quality environment, which the EU seeks to achieve, can be a stimulus to innovation and competitiveness within the Union and can promote employment. A strong and visible environmental role can be important in bringing the EU closer to its citizens. The Maastricht Treaty considerably strengthens the capacity of the Union to deal with environmental problems and to promote sustainable development.

13.20 The major developments that have taken place in environment policy at European level during recent years have been –

- the strengthening of the provisions relating to environment policy in the Treaty on European Union;

- the adoption of the Fifth Action Programme on the Environment (Towards Sustainability); and

- the establishment of the European Environment Agency.

13.21 *The Treaty on European Union* which came into effect on 1 November 1993 introduced as a principal objective the promotion of sustainable growth respecting the environment (Art. 2) and required that environmental protection requirements be integrated into the definition and implementation of other Community policies (Art. 13OR(2)).

13.22 The Treaty also provided for the extension of qualified majority voting to practically all environment legislation and enhanced the role of the European Parliament in relation to environment policy.

13.23 The European Community's *Fifth Action Programme* on the Environment, entitled *Towards Sustainability,* has moved Community environment policy away from a reliance on regulatory/control systems towards the achievement of sustainable development by ensuring the integration of environment considerations into other policy areas, focusing in particular on industry, agriculture, energy, transport and tourism.

13.24 The programme is based also on the concept of shared responsibility on the part of all principal actors in society and aims at promoting such sharing through implementation of a broad range of instruments including legislation, market related measures, financial support mechanisms and information/education/training. The Programme is currently undergoing a review.

13.25 A report *"Environment in the European Union"* published by the Agency in November 1995 for purposes of the review of the 5th Action Programme concluded that insufficient progress is being made to reduce pressures on the environment and that there is a need for policy acceleration.

Policy Response

13.26 Ireland enjoys a high quality environment. It is an objective of national policy to maintain and enhance this natural resource for the benefit of all who live in Ireland and for future generations, and as a positive contribution to important economic activities, such as tourism and agriculture, which depend on it.

13.27 Accordingly, Ireland will continue to support the development of environmental policies at EU level. We are also positively committed to enhancing the role of the European Union as a leading force internationally for advancing environmental protection and sustainable development.

13.28 In this context, Ireland recognises that it may be necessary from time to time, in a spirit of international and environmental solidarity, to agree and implement measures for the benefit of the European and global environment which may be of lower priority by reference to solely national considerations.

Trade and the Environment

13.29 In recent years, increasing attention has been given at international level to the inter-relationship between trade and the environment and the need to take account of environmental considerations in the multilateral trading system. Analytical work, in which Ireland has fully participated, has been in progress within the OECD for some years. There has also been considerable discussion within the European Union.

13.30   A *Committee on Trade and Environment* has been established within the World Trade Organisation (WTO), whose central task is to examine whether any changes in the rules of the WTO/GATT multilateral trading system are necessary to take account of environmental concerns. These rules already permit certain measures to be taken to protect the environment — for example measures to protect human, animal or plant life or health or to conserve exhaustible natural resources.

13.31   The central issue for the Committee is whether these grounds are broad enough to encompass action that Governments may be required to take under the terms of international environmental conventions or may wish to take on a unilateral basis in order to protect the global commons. The Committee is due to report its conclusions to the WTO Ministerial Conference to be held in December 1996.

Policy Response

13.32   Ireland will continue to stress the importance of the environmental dimension in international trade — not least because of the importance of a clean environment to our food-related trade and our tourist industry. We believe that environment protection consensus can be of sufficient importance to warrant some restrictions on international trade. But we also recognise that such measures could be used for protectionist purposes and therefore believe that they should be clearly defined on a multilateral basis.

The Marine Environment

13.33   The marine resource is communal and international cooperation is imperative in order to protect and conserve it. This is particularly so in the case of the Irish Sea which is affected by activities carried on in Ireland and the UK and by sea-based operations authorised by the authorities in either country.

13.34 The conservation and protection of the quality of the marine environment, including coast protection, poses a major challenge for all maritime countries and especially for islands such as Ireland. At the same time our marine resource provides economic opportunities in areas such as fisheries, aquaculture and the development of tourism.

Policy Response

13.35 The Irish and UK authorities have sought to promote cooperation on marine matters of mutual interest through the establishment of the *Irish Sea Science Coordination Group*. Recommendations made by the Group provide the basis for a more integrated science programme for this shared resource. They represent an important input to the Government's continuing efforts to protect the quality of the Irish Sea and enhance understanding so as to underpin its sustainable development.

13.36 Ireland is party to a number of international conventions relating to the marine area which have been given effect through domestic legislation. In addition, arrangements are in hand to ratify the *Convention for the Protection of the Marine Environment of the North-East Atlantic (the OSPAR Convention)*, which reinforces environmental protection mechanisms.

13.37 The Convention, inter alia, prohibits the dumping of industrial waste at sea with immediate effect and the disposal of sewage sludge at sea from 31 December 1998, and restricts disposal of materials at sea to dredge spoil and inert material of natural origin. The *Dumping at Sea Bill, 1995*, published in November, 1995, will implement the dumping at sea provisions of the Convention in Ireland.

Global Nuclear Safety

13.38 Accidents at nuclear plants, such as that which occurred at Chernobyl in Ukraine in 1986, have focused public attention on the potential for destruction that unsafe nuclear reactors provide. More recent knowledge about unsafe nuclear reactors in the former Soviet Union and in the countries of central and eastern Europe have led to calls for some reactors to be closed down permanently or, where there is no alternative energy replacement option, for the facilities to be improved and upgraded to current international standards.

13.39 Safety of nuclear power plants is a leading environmental concern of the European public. Concerns about nuclear safety are not confined to countries in which nuclear plants are actually located. They are more widely shared because of the well-known potential of nuclear accidents for significant trans-boundary effects.

13.40 It is vital to ensure that, where nuclear power is chosen as an energy source, the highest standards are applied in order to protect public health and the environment. It is equally important that the concerns of neighbouring countries are fully taken into account in decisions relating to nuclear power installations.

Policy Response

13.41 Ireland's nuclear policy objectives place a heavy emphasis on nuclear safety and radiological protection. Ireland has welcomed, for example, the decision taken by Ukraine to close the Chernobyl nuclear plant in the year 2000. While recognising that certain countries have retained nuclear energy as an option for power generation, Ireland has opposed any expansion of this industry.

13.42 At every opportunity Ireland has conveyed its concern about the risks inherent in nuclear power at European Union level, at the *International Atomic Energy Agency (IAEA)*, at the OECD/NEA and at other international fora.

13.43 Through the European Union's assistance towards the reform of the economic and energy sectors of central and eastern Europe and the former Soviet Union, Ireland continues to insist on the highest levels of safety in, and no expansion of, the nuclear sector.

13.44 Ireland has consistently taken a position in international fora in favour of having environmental, health and safety issues associated with the nuclear industry effectively addressed. It is our view that the International Atomic Energy Agency has a key role to play as the global forum for the promotion of internationally acceptable safety levels in the nuclear industry.

Regional Nuclear Safety

13.45 The Government's policy agreement, *A Government of Renewal,* acknowledges the serious and continuing threat that the operation of Sellafield, ageing nuclear reactors in Europe and on the west coast of Britain, and the increasing traffic on the Irish Sea involving nuclear materials, pose to the health and safety of the Irish public and to Ireland's environment.

Policy Response

13.46 The Government are at present considering a number of options, including international action, to address the threat of pollution that Sellafield and Thorp pose and the risk to the health and safety of the Irish public from these and other nuclear installations.

The Government are also pressing for action at the *International Maritime Organisation* to tighten the code already agreed for the transport of irradiated nuclear fuels, with particular reference to material transported on the Irish Sea.

13.47 The possibility of strengthening the *EURATOM* provisions on nuclear safety in the context of possible Treaty changes arising out of the 1996 Intergovernmental Conference was raised by the Irish member of the IGC Reflection Group. (See Chapter Three: The European Union and the New Europe).

The third report of the Irish Sea Science Co-ordination Group was published by the Departments of the Environment in Dublin and London in June 1995.

Chapter 14

CULTURAL RELATIONS

The Promotion of Irish Culture Abroad

14.1   The international cultural reputation
which Ireland has developed in recent years reflects a country in which the
arts display genuine vitality; where music, literature and film-making are
enjoying considerable success and where there is a genuine appreciation for
the life of the imagination.

This constitutes an important national strength and opens the door to
many opportunities which not only benefit the arts but the country as a
whole. Such opportunities include the possibility for development in the
intellectual/ information industry areas, cultural tourism and the attraction
of business.

14.2   There is a receptiveness to Irish
culture abroad and a store of goodwill which awaits full exploitation. This
is demonstrated by the demand for greater exposure to Irish arts and artists,
and a desire to enter into joint ventures and other forms of cultural

19. Logo of l'imaginaire irlandais, *Irish
contemporary art festival in France.*

exchange with this country.

The Government are committed to a policy which will translate this abundant goodwill, available both at home and abroad, into meaningful interaction designed to benefit Irish artists, the wider cultural community and, indeed, the country as a whole.

14.3 The projection of a positive image of the country abroad is important for practical as well as public relations purposes. The promotion of Irish music, drama, literature and other cultural activities is a valid and cost-effective way of furthering the country's interests. It encourages tourism and assists in convincing potential investors of the desirability of being associated with a country where talent and enterprise are valued and encouraged. With regard to tourism, for example, this is expected to be the world's biggest service industry in the next century and is becoming increasingly competitive. The promotion of a positive cultural image abroad will help retain Ireland's share of this increasingly discerning and sophisticated market.

14.4 These factors are equally applicable to the development of our links with the Irish abroad, including those of Irish descent, who are an important source of tourism and inward investment and who are very effective in promoting the country's wider interests.

14.5 In promoting culture abroad, the Government have four main policy objectives –

- to contribute to international tolerance through the promotion of, and respect for, cultural diversity;

- to present a vibrant, positive and integrated image of the country;

- to develop existing ties with Irish communities abroad, for example, in Britain, the United States, Canada and Australia;

- to contribute to the development of a common cultural heritage within the context of the European Union.

14.6 The Department of Foreign Affairs has responsibility for the promotion of Irish culture abroad. The Department's network of Embassies and Consulates assists in this function, while the Cultural Section at headquarters, through continuous contact with missions abroad, monitors, inter alia, the level of demand in other countries for the various categories of cultural events which can be made available.

Cultural Section works closely with the Arts Council, with foreign Embassies in Dublin and with host organisations abroad regarding travel arrangements, programmes and payment of companies and individual performers, as well as shipping art works for exhibition. The Section also acts as the secretariat for the *Cultural Relations Committee (CRC)*.

14.7 Cultural activities, as with trade, benefit from a diplomatic presence on the ground. The limited extent of Ireland's diplomatic network is a restraining factor in terms of the scope of activities which can realistically be attempted in the promotion of Irish culture abroad.

14.8 At present, the annual allocation for cultural activities abroad amounts to £400,000. While this figure has increased from £213,000 in 1993, it is still a modest amount for the promotion of culture worldwide, particularly compared to the resources devoted to cultural promotion by some of our partners of a similar size in the European Union. The requirement for strict control of the national finances restricts the Government's scope for immediate action, but they nevertheless intend to undertake a review of funding devoted to this area.

14.9 The *Arts Plan 1995–1997*, prepared by An Chomhairle Ealaíon/The Arts Council at the request of the Minister

311

for Arts, Culture and the Gaeltacht, states –

> "The Arts Council believes that in order to develop the arts in Ireland properly and to take account of the necessary international dimension of arts development through all the art forms, an independent agency is needed.
>
> Such an agency would serve the purposes not only of the Arts Council but also those of the Department of Arts, Culture and the Gaeltacht and the Cultural Relations Committee. The question of the relationship of such an agency with An Bord Tráchtala would also arise. The Government endorse this concept of an agency to handle the promotion abroad of all aspects of culture, both heritage and the contemporary arts."

The Department of Foreign Affairs will initiate a debate with the Cultural Relations Committee, the Department of Arts, Culture and the Gaeltacht, An Chomhairle Ealaion/The Arts Council, and An Bord Trachtála about the structuring of such an independent agency.

Bilateral Cultural Relations

Cultural Agreements

14.10   Since the early 1960s Ireland has concluded a number of cultural agreements designed to encourage cooperation and facilitate contacts in the fields of culture, science and education. These agreements also provide for the promotion of an increased knowledge of the culture, especially the language, history, literature and art, of the other country.

14.11   Ireland has signed cultural agreements with twelve countries: Norway (1964), France (1967), Spain (1980), Belgium (1980), Greece (1980), Netherlands (1980), Germany (1983), Italy (1984), China (1985), Finland (1985), Portugal (1990) and the Russian Federation (1991).

14.12   In recent years, successive Governments have sought to encourage cultural contacts with other countries through the conclusion of exchange programmes involving reciprocal visits by cultural experts. The Government intend to continue that policy.

Cultural Relations Committee

14.13   The Cultural Relations Committee (CRC), established in 1949, advises the Minister for Foreign Affairs on the expenditure of funds allocated to the Department of Foreign Affairs for cultural promotion abroad. Under its terms of reference, the Committee is to advise the Minister on how: "to carry out or give financial support to Irish cultural projects of a high artistic standard, with a view to the enhancement of Ireland's image and reputation abroad".

14.14   The CRC is a voluntary, non-statutory body. Its members are appointed by the Minister for Foreign Affairs to serve for two years, although they may be reappointed. Meetings are normally held every two months.

14.15   In recent years, the CRC has broadened its range of activities to include long-term support for programmes of Irish studies in universities abroad. It has also adopted a policy of actively supporting Irish participation in major visual arts events such as the *Biennale* exhibitions in Venice and Sao Paulo.

14.16   The CRC supports the work of the *Ireland Literature Exchange (ILE)* Programme. ILE encourages the translation into other languages of works by Irish writers and provides information to publishers abroad on the publishing sector in Ireland.

14.17   The resurgence of interest in the arts in Ireland in recent years has manifested itself in increased demand for

313

international outlets for cultural activities, with a consequent increase in the CRC's workload. This increase in workload requires a review of the Committee's working methods.

14.18   In future, the CRC will be asked to meet more frequently. This should allow the Committee more time to concentrate on broader policy issues as the number of applications for assistance placed before it at each of its meetings would effectively be reduced. The desirability of the Committee assuming an initiating role, in addition to its current purely advisory one, will be examined, along with a proposal to extend the term of office of the Committee in order to allow for the realisation of new policies which may be adopted during the Committee's term of office.

The creation of formal links between the Department of Foreign Affairs and the Cultural Relations Committee on the one hand, and the Department of Arts, Culture and the Gaeltacht and the Arts Council on the other, as proposed in *The Arts Plan 1995–1997*, will also be explored.

14.19   The CRC will be asked to consider the possibility of extending the proportion of funding allocated to projects in non-English-speaking countries. The Government consider that greater emphasis is needed on promotion in EU and other European countries, particularly those in central and eastern Europe, with which we are currently establishing closer political and trade links. In countries such as Japan, where we have important economic interests, cultural promotion is a very effective way of creating a distinct and favourable image of Ireland.

Multilateral Cultural Cooperation

The European Union

14.20   Ireland is committed to cooperation with other member states of the EU in developing our common cultural heritage. During the drafting of the Treaty on European Union, Ireland proposed the inclusion of a legal base for action in the field of culture. Ireland cooperated with the European Commission in the drafting of the text of a new Title on Culture (Title IX) which it was eventually decided should be inserted in the revised EC Treaty. Article 128 of the EC Treaty now states that: *"the Community shall contribute to the flowering of the cultures of the member states, while respecting their national and regional diversity and at the same time bringing their common cultural heritage to the fore".*

14.21 Ministers of the fifteen member states with responsibility for cultural affairs meet regularly in the Council of Ministers. Ireland is represented at these meetings by the Minister for Arts, Culture and the Gaeltacht. Recently, the Council adopted a programme *"KALEIDOSCOPE"* for a three year duration. This programme comprises five key elements –

- promotion and spread of culture;

- support for events and cultural projects carried out in partnership or through networks;

- training;

- access to culture;

- cooperation with non-member states and international organisations.

14.22 A proposal for a project to assist the translation of literary and dramatic works, known as *"ARIANE"* has yet to achieve the unanimous support required in the Council. Efforts are however being made to ensure that the Commission's own programme in this area can continue in 1996, pending the development of a compromise that would achieve the unanimity required at Council. The Council is currently considering the Commission's proposal for a cultural heritage programme, *"RAPHAEL"*.

14.23   Article 128 recognises the cultural
dimension of the audiovisual sector and the practice has developed of
Ministerial Councils relating to cultural and audiovisual matters being held
concurrently. Recently, the Council adopted a common position on a
second *"MEDIA"* programme to follow on from the first range of incentives
to promote European audiovisual production and from which the Irish
audiovisual sector has derived considerable benefit. Currently, the Council
is considering proposals from the Commission to amend the *Television
Without Frontiers* Directive, adopted in 1989. Amongst the aims of the
Directive is to guarantee that over 50% of television broadcasts in Europe
would be reserved for European audiovisual production.

Council of Europe

14.24   Ireland is a member of the Council of
Europe and officials of the Department of Arts, Culture and the Gaeltacht
attend meetings of the Council for Cultural Cooperation (CDCC) and the
subsidiary Culture Committee, which meets twice yearly. The work of this
Committee includes programmes on –

- review of national cultural policies;

- promoting the cultural dimension of communication;

- training of cultural administrators;

- support for artistic creativity and exchanges;

- books, reading, translation and archives;

- promotion of European cinema.

14.25   The Council of Europe has a
continuing task to promote and broaden freedom of expression and the free
flow of information across frontiers. To this end, its *Steering Committee on
the Mass Media (CDMM)* is studying –

- Democracy and Media;

- Media in a pan-European perspective;

- Media and Conflict;

- Media in the field of intolerance.

UNESCO

14.26   The *United Nations Educational, Scientific and Cultural Organisation, (UNESCO)* is a specialised agency of the United Nations. Ireland became a member state of UNESCO in 1961 and national coordination for all UNESCO related matters is provided by the Department of Education.

Chapter 15

THE IRISH FOREIGN SERVICE

15.1   A range of foreign policy objectives is outlined in the earlier chapters of this White Paper. The Government are conscious that the capacity to achieve these objectives will depend to a significant extent on the calibre and commitment of our foreign service; policy choices therefore cannot be made in isolation from consideration of the future development of the foreign service.

15.2   Irish diplomacy has a well established reputation for professionalism and effectiveness; the Government are determined to build on those strengths, to ensure a foreign service that reflects the vision of the Irish people, advances their interests and articulates their concerns.

Current Structures

15.3   A snapshot of the current service indicates the following –

20. Officers of the Irish Embassy at Aras na hÉireann/Ireland House, Tokyo; from left: Mr Patrick Sammon, First Secretary; HE Mr Declan O'Donovan, Ambassador; Ms Orla Tunney, Second Secretary. Ireland House contains the Embassy Chancery, the offices of the IDA, Bord Tráchtála and Bord Fáilte.

- Total annual running costs of the foreign service, at home and abroad, account for less than half of one per cent of total Government expenditure.

- In the service as a whole, at home and abroad, there are 975 members of staff, 246 of those in the diplomatic grades.

- About 50 per cent of staff serve at Headquarters and the remainder abroad. The structures at Headquarters are set out in the appendices.

- There are 47 overseas resident missions: 38 bilateral Embassies, 4 multilateral missions, 5 Consulates.

- Four of these Embassies and one Consulate operate primarily as Development Cooperation Offices in countries identified as priority countries under the bilateral aid programme.

- The geographical spread is uneven: almost half of our missions are in Western Europe and another 7 are in North America. There are 8 missions in sub-Saharan Africa, 3 in Middle East/North Africa, 5 in Asia, 1 in Australia, 1 in South America and 4 in Eastern Europe. (See list in the appendices.)

- The missions are generally small in size. Over half have only one or two diplomatic officers. Only nine have more than four diplomatic officers.

- Secondary accreditation is widely used: our 38 resident Embassies are accredited on a non-resident basis to 55 other states.

- There are also 58 Honorary Consuls (non-career officers who are paid a modest annual honorarium for their services) in 43 countries throughout the world, who carry out consular and other work on our behalf in their countries of residence.

15.4　　　　　　　　　　In relative terms, the Irish foreign service is of a very modest size. Numbers of diplomatic staff have remained more or less static over the past decade, with resources being stretched to cover new work areas. Among the smaller European Union members with a broadly comparable range of international interests and obligations — such as Belgium, Denmark, Finland, Greece, Portugal, Sweden — all have more than twice as many missions and twice as many diplomatic staff as Ireland.

Strategic Challenges

15.5 As is clear from the earlier chapters, a number of extremely important bilateral relationships — for example with Britain and the US — will remain critical to Irish foreign policy priorities. Building and sustaining the peace process on this island will continue to be the key challenge around which other priorities are ranked. However, in planning the decade ahead, the Government are conscious of wider trends which will shape the development of the foreign service and underpin the choices on resource allocation. Among the most significant are –

i)   *New Emphasis on Multilateralism*
     The ending of the bi-polar world of the Cold War era has meant that issues formerly dealt with on a bilateral or regional basis have emerged squarely onto the international agenda. Issues of large-scale conflict and human rights violation challenge the conscience of the international community and impose responsibilities on all states, large and small, to work towards their resolution. The Government are determined to ensure that Ireland fully meets its responsibilities to make an informed and effective contribution to the multilateral consideration of these issues.

ii) *EU involvement*
     The single most important factor influencing Irish national development is our membership of the European Union. Fundamental national interests are engaged in both the internal development and external projection of the Union; it is imperative that our foreign service continues to maintain a coherent overview of the process.
     The fact that the Union increasingly seeks and is called upon to play a more active and integrated role in international affairs places

increasing burdens on all its members. Because decisions commit all member states, participation in the decision-making process is not discretionary.

As the level of Union activity and the number of working groups increases, Ireland cannot opt out and abdicate particular areas of policy-making to our larger partners. In effect, our Union membership commits us to a level of involvement and activity which would not arise for a small state outside the Union.

iii) *Development Cooperation*
The tragic scale of hunger and poverty in parts of the developing world, and the Government's commitment to very substantial increases in Irish development assistance, means that the effective management of our aid programme will continue to be a priority within the foreign service.

15.6 The Government will ensure that the priorities which underpin the whole of the Programme for Government — in particular the emphasis on employment creation in Ireland — will permeate decision-making in the foreign policy area. Protection of our economic interests and promotion of foreign earnings will therefore remain at the heart of policy formulation.

Future Directions

15.7 In charting future directions for the foreign service, the Government have adopted twin starting-points: first, the foreign service must be adequately resourced to fulfil its responsibilities and secondly, all resources allocated must be utilised to best effect.

15.8 The Government are conscious that a significant additional workload is being created by the growth in international and EU activity and that Irish national interests require that our foreign service be equipped to deal with this. They also recognise the national benefit in having a more developed network of overseas missions and intend to work towards that goal in a selective and incremental way.

15.9 At the same time, conscious of the budgetary constraints that must condition all public expenditure planning for the foreseeable future, the Government will ensure that every opportunity is availed of — for example, through technology development and through cooperation with EU partners — to maximise the cost effectiveness of the service. They are also conscious that human resource management is central to the effectiveness of the foreign service and must form an essential part of planning.

The Mission Network

15.10 Following a review of the mission network in 1994, the Government decided that there were compelling arguments in cost-benefit terms for opening new Embassies in Hungary, the Czech Republic and Malaysia. A combination of bilateral and EU-related considerations meant that a resident Irish diplomatic presence in these countries had become a matter of some urgency; it was therefore decided to proceed with such openings immediately.

15.11 These new Embassies involve a further development of the Ireland House model, with An Bord Tráchtála representatives integrated in the staffing structure from the outset.

15.12 The Government intend to continue to develop ties with strengthening economies and new democracies around the world; where national interests dictate, they will be ready to consolidate these ties through resident diplomatic accreditation. They are conscious that Ireland remains under-represented in regions such as Eastern Europe, South-East Asia, the Middle East, Central and South America — areas where there is considerable foreign earnings potential and which are also developing increasingly close relationships with the European Union.

15.13 The EU dimension is likely to become increasingly important in deciding on the future shape of our mission network. In addition to their normal work of advancing our direct national interests, Embassies now have an important additional function in influencing the relationship between their host country and the European Union; ensuring that the host country's policies towards the European Union are as favourable as possible to Irish interests and that the country is familiar with and responsive to Irish policies across the whole spectrum of activities covered by the European Union.

15.14   This means that while bilateral, political and economic interests will continue to determine priorities in opening new missions, the extent to which countries have substantial and important relationships with the European Union will be a significant factor to be taken into account.

Effective Management of Resources

15.15   The *Strategic Management Initiative,* which is being taken forward on a civil-service-wide basis, is designed to ensure that all Departments adopt a rigorous approach to objective-setting and resource allocation. The Department of Foreign Affairs is participating fully in this exercise and in 1994 prepared a Management Plan covering all areas of the Department's work. The Plan will continue to be refined and adapted to adjust to changing circumstances and progress towards implementation will be carefully monitored.

15.16   As indicated above, the Department has dealt with a very considerable increase in EU and international activity over recent years without any corresponding increase in resources. Apart from redeployment to open new missions, overseas coverage has been extended through extensive use of low-cost non-residential accreditation and expansion of the Honorary Consul network.

15.17   In further value-for-money moves, a Departmental Inspection system has been introduced to improve interaction between headquarters and missions and enhance effectiveness; an internal audit function has been established to test the effectiveness of management controls and procedures. A cross-Divisional Planning Group has also been created to help improve the Department's capacity to anticipate and respond to new developments.

15.18 It is essential that the potential offered by the communications and information-technology revolution be fully exploited. The technological revolution has the capacity to transform many of the traditional tasks of diplomacy: satellite television and electronic mail, for example, have radically changed the manner in which missions carry out their reporting function. The Department of Foreign Affairs is currently implementing a three-year IT plan which will significantly upgrade facilities in advance of our EU Presidency and ensure that up-to-date equipment is in use at headquarters and missions abroad.

15.19 The Government will ensure that the emphasis on value for money within the foreign service is fully maintained. Flexibility and innovation will be strongly encouraged. For example, the scope for economies through co-location of Embassies with our EU partners will be fully explored.

Human Resources Issues

15.20 The Government recognise that the greatest asset of any foreign service is the calibre and commitment of its staff; they note with appreciation the many positive comments on the work of officers at all levels in the Department of Foreign Affairs during the preparatory White Paper seminars.

15.21 Management of an organisation with offices in more than 30 countries is inevitably complex and the diplomatic lifestyle, involving frequent transfers of residence for officers and their families, can give rise to special problems.

15.22 Issues of selection and staff development are under continuous review. Graduate entry procedures to the Department of Foreign Affairs have recently been the subject of a consultancy study and the results of this study are currently being implemented. The aim of the Department is to continue to attract top graduates from a broad cross-section of Irish society, men and women with the ability and flair to project modern Ireland within the international community.

15.23   The training of officers in the foreign service is a matter which attracted considerable comment during the relevant White Paper seminar. Contributors clearly attached importance to ensuring that officers have the all-round skills and language proficiency to carry out all aspects of their brief. The Department of Foreign Affairs is committed to such training and a range of programmes is currently in place although resource constraints have inhibited the development of a more intensive approach and especially the type of in-service and mid-career training which provides on-going stimulus. The Department will conduct a detailed analysis of the training needs of all personnel in the Department and will develop a structured programme for addressing those needs. The Department will also examine the scope for extending opportunities for mid-career training and development.

15.24   With offices in more than thirty countries, officers stationed abroad transfer their residence on average every four years. The Department of Foreign Affairs provides a range of supports to help officers and their families deal with such regular transfers; however, the staff associations — including the Spouses' Association which represents the spouses of diplomatic officers — have highlighted the difficulties faced by families abroad, particularly in relation to the social and educational welfare of their children. The management of the Department recognise these difficulties and will continue to work closely with the staff associations in seeking to put in place support systems that are as effective as possible.

Linkages

15.25   It is recognised that a foreign service
career requires a distinctive formation and specialist skills. Improved
linkages between the foreign service and other sectors would enhance the
effectiveness of the foreign service. The Department will enhance links –

- with the rest of the civil service and semi-state sector, so as to ensure
  that there is coherence and a common sense of purpose in projecting
  Irish interests abroad;

- with the private sector, to establish a cross-fertilisation between the
  respective strengths of industry and diplomacy;

- with relevant academic institutions, to ensure that up-to-date
  research and a sound theoretical base underpin policy formulation;

- with other comparable foreign services so that we can learn from and
  import best practices from other countries.

15.26   Wherever feasible, exchanges and
secondment arrangements will be developed with these sectors; there will
be an emphasis on flexibility to encourage take-up of the schemes both
within the foreign service and the target sectors.

A Dynamic and Flexible Foreign Service

15.27   The policy approach described
throughout this White Paper gives rise to important organisational and
management challenges for the Department. The Government will ensure
that the Department is equipped to provide the dynamic and flexible
response which these challenges demand.

HOUSES OF THE OIREACHTAS

Chapter 16

THE DEMOCRATIC ACCOUNTABILITY OF FOREIGN POLICY

16.1   In its policy agreement, *A Government of Renewal*, the Government have made the achievement of a system of open and inclusive government one of their main priorities. They have pledged to reform the institutions of the State at national and local level to provide service, accountability, transparency and freedom of information and to extend the opportunities for democratic participation by citizens in all aspects of public life.

16.2   This Chapter examines the arrangements already in place for ensuring the democratic accountability of Irish foreign policy and sets out a number of initiatives by which the Government intend to ensure greater transparency in the conduct of foreign policy and the maximum degree of public ownership of that policy.

The President

16.3   The first office of the State defined in the Constitution is that of the President. The Constitution lays down that

21. *Information pack issued by the Oireachtas Public Relations Office.*

the President shall be directly elected by the people and shall take precedence over all other persons in the State.

16.4 While the Constitution does not vest the President with any specific powers in relation to external affairs, the President does hold certain discretionary powers and retains certain duties under the Constitution — for instance, in relation to the signing into law of Bills — which could potentially involve her or him in matters touching on foreign relations. The Taoiseach is required by the Constitution to keep the President generally informed on matters of international policy.

16.5 The Constitution accords the President the right to communicate with the Houses of the Oireachtas by message or address, or to address the nation on any matter of national or public importance. In both cases, the President is required to consult with the Council of State before communicating a message or address and to obtain the approval of the Government to the message or address. This can include matters having external implications, as was the case on 2 February 1995 when President Robinson addressed the Houses of the Oireachtas on the theme of "Cherishing the Irish Diaspora".

16.6 In addition to rights and powers arising under the Constitution, the President also has certain executive powers in the area of foreign relations on the basis of section 3 of the *Republic of Ireland Act, 1948* including the power, acting on the advice of the Government, to accredit diplomatic representatives and to conclude international agreements at Head of State level.

16.7 However, perhaps the most important and public role which the President fills in relation to foreign policy is that of "first citizen" of the State in contacts with other nations and international institutions. In terms of diplomatic protocol, the highest form of contact between nations is that which takes place at Head of State level, through the medium of a state visit. The exchange of state visits is an important means by which nations seek to promote their identity and image, develop their bilateral relations, and deepen political, commercial and cultural contacts.

16.8　　　　　　　　A rolling programme of incoming and outgoing state visits, and other visits involving the President, is drawn up by agreement between the President and the Government, taking into account the balance of Ireland's foreign policy interests. Care is taken to ensure coordination between Presidential visits and those of the Taoiseach, Minister for Foreign Affairs, and other members of the Government.

16.9　　　　　　　　In common with most aspects of diplomatic activity, the frequency of visits at Head of State level has intensified in recent years. In the five years after taking up office on 3 December 1990, President Robinson made 14 state visits and 33 other overseas visits. Over the same period, there were 8 state visits by foreign Heads of State to Ireland.

16.10　　　　　　　The Government will continue to cooperate with the President in drawing up and facilitating a programme of visits at Head of State level which reflects Ireland's foreign policy goals.

The Oireachtas

16.11　　　　　　　The Constitution invests the Oireachtas with the sole and exclusive power of making laws for the State, subject to the provisions of Article 29.4.3 which provides for the application in the State of laws enacted, acts done and measures adopted by the European Union and its constituent Communities.

16.12　　　　　　　The accountability of the Dáil to the people is recognised in the Constitution in a number of ways which have an impact on our foreign relations. For instance, war shall not be declared, nor shall the state participate in any war, save with the assent of Dáil Éireann. Money Bills may be initiated in Dáil Éireann only.

16.13　　　　　　　The Houses of the Oireachtas exercise an important role in relation to foreign policy; in debating and approving treaties and legislation, and in discussing issues of foreign interest and questioning the Government on their foreign policy.

16.14 Every international agreement to which the State becomes a party, other than those of a technical or administrative character, must be laid before the Dáil, and the State cannot be bound by any such agreement involving a charge on public funds unless the terms of that agreement have been approved by the Dáil. No international agreement may become part of domestic law of the State without the approval of the Oireachtas.

16.15 In practice, however, the amount of legislation on matters associated with foreign policy is very small, and the number of treaties coming before the Oireachtas is not great. The most frequent involvement of the Oireachtas arises through the debate of foreign policy issues and the tabling of Parliamentary Questions by members of the Dáil.

16.16 Every year, the Dáil holds a major debate on foreign policy in the context of its examination of the Estimates for funds to be expended on Public Services. Of particular relevance in the conduct of foreign policy is its consideration of the votes for Foreign Affairs and International Cooperation. The Dáil also conducts an annual examination of the outcome of expenditure under these votes, based on a report of the Comptroller and Auditor General.

16.17 Both Houses of the Oireachtas also hold frequent debates on matters of immediate foreign policy interest. Of particular interest as regards EU policy is the Taoiseach's report to the Dáil, following each meeting of the European Council.

16.18 Parliamentary Questions allow the members of the Dáil to enquire into any aspect of foreign policy. The Minister for Foreign Affairs is the recipient of the majority of questions dealing with foreign policy. However, questions relating to aspects of EU and commercial policy are directed to the Minister having responsibility in that particular area, while the Taoiseach answers a considerable number of questions on Northern Ireland.

The Committee System

16.19 The scope of the Committee system within the Oireachtas has extended increasingly into the foreign policy area. For many years, the Public Accounts Committee of the Dáil, has scrutinised the outcome of expenditure on Public Services, including that on Foreign Affairs and International Relations. In 1973, a Joint Committee on the Secondary Legislation of the European Communities, comprising representatives of the Dáil and Seanad, was appointed. This was followed by a Joint Committee on State Sponsored Bodies in 1978 and, for the period 1983–87, by a Joint Committee on Cooperation with Developing Countries.

16.20 In May 1993, an important step was taken with the establishment of a *Joint Committee on Foreign Affairs.* This Joint Committee incorporated the functions of the Joint Committee on the Secondary Legislation of the European Communities but, following on from the Government's commitment in *A Government of Renewal,* a separate Joint Committee on European Affairs was established in March 1995.

16.21 The Joint Committees on Foreign Affairs and European Affairs have significant powers and are important instruments for maintaining the democratic accountability of foreign policy in Ireland. They are made up of a Select Committee of the Dáil[1] and a Select Committee of the Seanad. The Minister for Foreign Affairs, or a Minister or Minister of State nominated in her or his stead, serves as an *ex-officio* member of both Committees for discussion of a Bill or Estimates for Public Services. Members of the European Parliament representing Irish constituencies (including Northern Ireland) and Members of the Irish Delegation to the Parliamentary Assembly of the Council Europe are also entitled to participate in meetings of the Select Committees, although they do not have the right to vote.

16.22   The Joint Committee on Foreign
Affairs is the largest of the Parliamentary Committees, with 31 members
drawn from both the Dáil (21 members) and the Seanad (10 members).
Under the terms of its Orders of Reference it –

—   debates Bills referred to it by the Dáil and Seanad;

—   considers the impact of policy and legislation in respect of the
    Department of Foreign Affairs and reports to both Houses of the
    Oireachtas;

—   considers any aspect of Ireland's international relations as it may
    choose, with the option of reporting its views to both Houses of the
    Oireachtas;

—   discusses reports relevant to the Department of Foreign Affairs
    referred to it by the Dáil and reports to both Houses of the
    Oireachtas;

—   submits an annual report to both Houses of the Oireachtas;

16.23   It has the power to –

—   send for persons and request information, although information may
    be withheld if a member of the Government certifies in writing that
    such information is confidential or that its disclosure would be
    prejudicial to the State's international relations;

—   engage specialist assistance, subject to the consent of the Minister for
    Finance;

—   discuss and draft legislative proposals in relation to Ireland's
    international relations and recommend them to Ministers;

—   print and publish evidence taken before it, together with related
    documents.

16.24   Ministers are obliged, where
practicable, to discuss legislation relating to Ireland's international relations
with the Joint Committee, prior to its approval by Government. Ministers
and Ministers of State are also obliged to appear before the Joint

Committee to discuss matters relating to Ireland's international relations which are relevant to their Departments. They, in turn, may request the opportunity to explain or debate current or proposed policy.

16.25   The Joint Committee examines, on an ongoing basis, the key foreign policy issues of the moment, and is frequently addressed by visiting parliamentary delegations from other countries. The Joint Committee has established three sub-committees, on Northern Ireland, Development Cooperation and the United Nations, to give special attention to policy in these areas. The Joint Committee adopts its positions by majority vote. Its meetings are normally held in public.

16.26   The *Joint Committee on European Affairs* is made up of 17 members, drawn from the Dáil (11 members) and the Seanad (6 members). Its mode of operation is similar to that of the Joint Committee on Foreign Affairs. Its Orders of Reference enable it, inter alia, to examine legislation referred to it by the Dáil and to report back to the Dáil; to consider legislative proposals from the European Commission, acts of the EU institutions and other matters arising from Ireland's membership of the European Union. Its meetings are normally held in public.

16.27   The Joint Committee has examined legislation across a wide range of EU activity and has been monitoring preparation for the 1996 Intergovernmental Conference. The Joint Committee participates in the bi-annual meetings of the Conference of Parliamentary Committees on European Affairs of EU member states (COSAC). The Joint Committee is scheduled to host the meeting of the Conference to be held in the latter half of 1996, during Ireland's Presidency of the European Union.

16.28   Provisions exist under the Orders of Reference of the Joint Committees on Foreign Affairs and European Affairs for the two Committees to liaise and consult with each other, and to hold joint meetings. Two joint meetings were held between March and November 1995.

Representation in International Organisations

16.29   Members of the Dáil and Seanad
represent Ireland in the consultative assemblies of the Council of Europe and
the Organisation for Security and Cooperation in Europe, in which Ireland
has, respectively, four and five seats. In keeping with Ireland's observer status
at the WEU, two members of the Oireachtas attend meetings of the WEU
Assembly as observers.

The Government

16.30   The Constitution makes specific
provision[2] for the role of the Government in relation to foreign affairs. Under
its terms, the Government are responsible to Dáil Éireann for the exercise of
the executive power of the State in, or in connection with, the external
relations of the State.

16.31   The Government have collective
responsibility for the Departments of State administered by the members of
the Government. As pointed out in Chapter Two, a number of Government
Ministers, in addition to the Minister for Foreign Affairs, have responsibility
in the foreign policy area.

16.32   The Taoiseach plays a particularly
important role, both internally, in relation to policy formulation, and
externally, as the highest representative of the Irish Government. This role is
particularly significant in the context of the European Council, which brings
together the Heads of State or Government of the member states of the
European Union at least twice a year. Successive Taoisigh have also played an
important role in the area of Anglo-Irish relations and Northern Ireland.

16.33   The Government shall consist of not
less than seven and not more than fifteen persons, who must be members
of the Dáil or the Seanad. The Taoiseach, the Tánaiste and the Minister for
Finance must be members of the Dáil, while the remaining members may
be members of either House, although no more than two may be members
of the Seanad.[3]

16.34   This means that the Minister, the
Government and Dáil Éireann are each, in their turn, accountable to the
people for the formulation and implementation of Ireland's foreign policy.
However, in certain circumstances, the Government are obliged to consult
the people directly on foreign policy. This occurs when the Government
wish to enter into arrangements with one or more other states which serve
to restrict the Government's freedom to determine matters of foreign
policy, as laid down in the Constitution.

16.35   In   such   circumstances,   the
Government can proceed only when they have obtained the specific
endorsement of the people through a referendum to amend the
Constitution. This has been necessary on three occasions, each time in
relation to Ireland's membership of the European Union[4].

16.36   Notwithstanding this requirement,
Ireland follows the normal pattern in parliamentary democracies of
according responsibility for the day-to-day operation of foreign policy to
the Government. Such practice is predicated on the unpredictability of
external events, the need for a credible external interface capable of
representing the State in international negotiations, and the need to be
able to act swiftly in matters of security. This latter point is reflected in
Article 28.3 of the Constitution which provides that, while the State may
only declare war or enter into a war with the agreement of the Dáil, the
Government may take whatever steps they may deem necessary for the
protection of the State in the event of invasion.

16.37   The sensitivity attaching to
international relations has meant that access to information on
Government policy is, in most countries, more restricted in regard to
foreign policy than it is in respect of other policy areas. The Government
are determined to increase the degree of openness in all areas of
Government policy and will shortly be publishing a Bill on Freedom of
Information. In this Bill, the Government will be seeking to provide for
greater access to official information, including in the foreign policy area,

although it will be necessary to maintain certain minimum safeguards of the type found in even the most open of systems of government.

The Department of Foreign Affairs

16.38 The Minister for Foreign Affairs is responsible for the operation of the Department of Foreign Affairs. The Minister is usually assisted by one or more junior Ministers. The present Minister for Foreign Affairs, the Tánaiste, Mr. Dick Spring TD, is assisted by Ms Joan Burton TD, who is Minister of State at the Department with special responsibility for Overseas Development Aid, and Mr. Gay Mitchell, TD, who is Minister of State for European Affairs[5].

16.39 The Secretary of the Department of Foreign Affairs, who is a career civil servant, is designated under law as the accounting officer for the expenditure of public funds from the votes administered by the Department of Foreign Affairs. He is responsible to Dáil Éireann for the discharge of this responsibility.

16.40 The Department of Foreign Affairs assists the Government, through the Minister, in the formulation and execution of foreign policy. Under our constitutional arrangements, the Department itself is not directly accountable to the people for its work in this area. The Department is responsible to the Minister for Foreign Affairs who acts on the collective authority of the Government. The Government, in turn, are responsible to Dáil Éireann, which is directly elected by the people.

16.41 This does not mean that the Department of Foreign Affairs cannot, under the direction of the Minister, take steps to ensure that it is directly informed of the views of the people, especially of those persons or non-governmental organisations active in particular policy areas, or that it cannot seek to inform the people of Government policy. The Government are determined to ensure a better understanding and sense of public ownership of its foreign policy, and this White Paper sets out a number of initiatives which have been taken, or will be taken, in this regard.

16.42   The *Cultural Relations Committee*, made up of experts and practitioners in the field of arts and culture has been advising Ministers since 1949 on which projects for the promotion of Irish culture abroad are deserving of financial support by the Government.

16.43   The *Irish Aid Advisory Committee* was set up in November 1993 to offer advice to the Government on development cooperation matters, including Ireland's Aid Programme. The Committee, which is made up of 14 members selected on the basis of their expertise in the area of development cooperation, organises an annual public forum to allow for the feeding-in of a wide range of views. The first such forum, which took place in November 1994, served as the first in the series of seminars which preceded the White Paper.

16.44   The Government have also established a *Committee for Development Education*, which brings together a wide range of experts with a mandate to develop policy and provide state support in the area of development education.

16.45   New initiatives set out elsewhere in the White Paper include –

• a commitment to keep the public fully informed of developments in the Intergovernmental Conference considering the amendment of the Treaty on European Union, and on the Irish approach to the issues arising at the Conference (Chapter 3);

• the publication of an annual report on issues at the United Nations and on Ireland's voting pattern on these issues (Chapter 5);

• the establishment of a *Joint Standing Committee on Human Rights*, involving representatives of the Department of Foreign Affairs, the NGO community and academic experts in the human rights field (Chapter 8);

• the establishment of a *Humanitarian Liaison Group*, and the *"Rapid Response Register"* to ensure the fullest possible coordinated response by Government Departments, agencies, and people to humanitarian emergencies (Chapter 9).

16.46　　　　　　　　　　The Minister for Foreign Affairs has also decided, following the success of the public seminars which were organised to prepare this White Paper, to hold similar seminars in the future. These seminars will focus on different aspects of Ireland's foreign policy and, as with the White Paper seminars, they will be fully open to the public.

16.47　　　　　　　　　　None of these initiatives will replace the existing dialogue and exchanges which the Department currently undertakes with a wide range of NGOs.

16.48　　　　　　　　　　As part of the Government's desire to encourage a greater interest in Irish foreign policy, it has been agreed that the Department of Foreign Affairs, in association with the Royal Irish Academy, will publish a series of foreign policy documents of historic interest. It is hoped that this initiative will encourage and assist greater academic interest in the study of Irish foreign policy.

FOOTNOTES

1　Given the primacy of the Dáil in the area of state finances, consideration of the Estimates for Public Services in respect of Foreign Affairs and International Relations is the sole responsibility of the Dáil Select Committee, which is required to report to the Dáil.

2　Articles 29.4.1

3　The provision allowing for members of the Seanad to be appointed as members of the Government, has been availed of on only two occasions. The most recent was the appointment of Senator James Dooge as Minister for Foreign Affairs between October 1981 and March 1982.

4　The Third, Tenth and Eleventh Amendments to the Constitution were passed to enable Ireland to ratify the Treaty of Accession (1972), The Single European Act (1987) and the Treaty on European Union (1992), respectively. The additions to the Constitution agreed in these referenda appear as Article 29.4.3–6.

5　Ms Burton is also Minister of State at the Department of Justice, while Mr Mitchell is also Minister of State at the Department of the Taoiseach.

Appendices

1. Written Submissions received from the Public

Amnesty International — Irish Section
A.P.S.O.
Christian Aid (2 submissions)
Church of Ireland, The General
Synod
Mr. Roger Cole, Glenageary,
Co. Dublin
Concern
Comhlámh
Communist Party of Ireland
Mr. Frank Conlon, Gaillimh
Mr. Johnny Couchman, Carlow
Cuba Solidarity Campaign
Debt and Development Coalition —
Ireland
Development Studies Centre
Dr. Sara Dillon, Faculty of Law,
U.C.D.
E.C.O. — Tibet
The European Bureau for Lesser
Used Languages
European Movement, Irish Council
FEANTSA — European Federation
of National Organisations
Working with the Homeless
Ms Bronagh Finnegan, Dublin 1
GOAL
The Green Party/An Comhaontas
Glas
Greenpeace Ireland Limited
Mr. Seán Guerin, U.C.D., Dublin 4
Mr. Martin Hawkes, Donnybrook,
Dublin
Mr. Michael Heery, Bray,
Co. Wicklow
Institute of European Affairs
Ireland Action for Bosnia-
Hercegovina
Irish Aid Advisory Committee
Irish Business and Employers
Confederation
Irish CND
The Irish Commission for Justice and
Peace

The Irish Council of Churches
Irish Congress of Trade Unions
Irish El Salvador Support Committee
Irish Fair Trade Network
Irish Farmers' Association
Irish Missionary Union
Irish Mozambique Solidarity
Irish National Committee for
UNICEF
Irish Red Cross Society
Irish Refugee Council
Jack Fitzgerald Branch, Dun
Laoghaire Labour Party
Joint Committe on Foreign Affairs
Mr. Peadar Kirby, Dublin 6W
Prof. Edward Moxon-Browne,
University of Limerick
Rev. Séamus Murphy S.J.,
Washington DC
Ms Mary Catherine Murray,
Ballsbridge, Dublin 4
The National Platform
The National Spiritual Assembly of
the Bahá'ís of the Republic of
Ireland
Mr. Caoimhín Ó Donnchú, Cork
Mr. Francis O'Donnell, c/o UNDP,
Ankara, Turkey
Mr. John O'Toole, Sandymount,
Dublin
Mr. Brian Quinn, Clontarf, Dublin
Refugee Trust
Rescue Trust
Royal Irish Academy — National
Committee for the Study of
International Affairs
Security and Neutrality Study Group
Self Help Development International
Tibet Support Group Ireland
Trade Union Campaign for Nuclear
Disarmament
Trócaire
Sr. Mona Tyndall, Missionary Sisters

2. The European Council and the Council of Ministers

The European Council
The European Council consists of the Heads of State or Government of the Member States of the European Union and the President of the Commission. These are assisted by the Ministers for Foreign Affairs of the Member States and a member of the Commission. The European Council meets at least twice yearly and is chaired by the Head of State or Government of the Member State which holds the Presidency of the Council.

The Council of Ministers
The Council of Ministers consists of a representative of each of the fifteen Member States of the Union at Ministerial level. The following chart lists the different formations of the Council of Ministers and the Minister/Ministers who have prime responsibility for representing Ireland at the Council.

The Council of Ministers	Minister For
Agriculture	Agriculture
Budget	Finance
Consumer	Enterprise and Employment
Culture	Arts, Culture and the Gaeltacht
Economic and Finance (ECOFIN)	Finance
Energy	Transport, Energy and Communications
Education	Education
Environment	the Environment
Fisheries	the Marine
General Affairs	Foreign Affairs
Health	Health
Industry	Enterprise and Employment
Internal Market	Tourism and Trade
Justice and Home Affairs[1]	Justice
Labour and Social Affairs	Enterprise and Employment
Research	Enterprise and Employment
Social Affairs	Enterprise and Employment
	Equality and Law Reform
	Social Welfare
Telecommunications	Transport, Energy and Communications
Transport	Transport, Energy and Communications

1 The Minister for Equality and Law Reform is responsible as regards judicial cooperation in civil matters.

3. OFFICIAL DEVELOPMENT ASSISTANCE, 1992 & 1996

MULTILATERAL ASSISTANCE

		1992 Expenditure £000	1996 Estimate £000
EUROPEAN COMMUNITIES			
1	EU Budget (Development Cooperationelements)	10,211	15,000
2 *	EU Development Fund (Lomé)	6,930	6,200
3	Other (Turkey Protocol)	70	
	Sub-Total	**17,211**	**21,200**
UNITED NATIONS & WORLD BANK			
4	International Development Association	3,327	4,429
5	World Bank	1,008	
6	ESAFs (Int. Monetary Fund)	–	500
7	Global Environment Facility	–	425
8	International Finance Corporation	63	80
9	Food Aid Convention	550	620
10 *	International Fund for Agricultural Development	–	300
11	Food and Agriculture Organisation Schemes	70	160
12 *	Voluntary Contributions to UN Development Agencies	800	6,500
13 *	United Nations Industrial Development Organisation	110	180
14	World Food Programme	1	1,000
15	Other	997	1,400
	Sub-Total	**6,926**	**15,594**
	TOTAL MULTILATERAL ASSISTANCE	**24,137**	**36,794**
BILATERAL ASSISTANCE			
15 *	Bilateral Aid Fund	10,877	48,200
16 *	Agency for Personal Service Overseas (APSO)	2,630	10,500
17 *	Emergency Humanitarian Assistance	1,675	5,500
18	Refugees	–	800
	TOTAL BILATERAL ASSISTANCE	**15,182**	**65,000**
ADMINISTRATION			
19	Departmental Administration	1,000	2,000
20	Tax Deductibility	–	2,000
	TOTAL ODA	**40,319**	**105,794**

* **From Vote for International Cooperation**

4. The Department of Foreign Affairs Organisation Chart

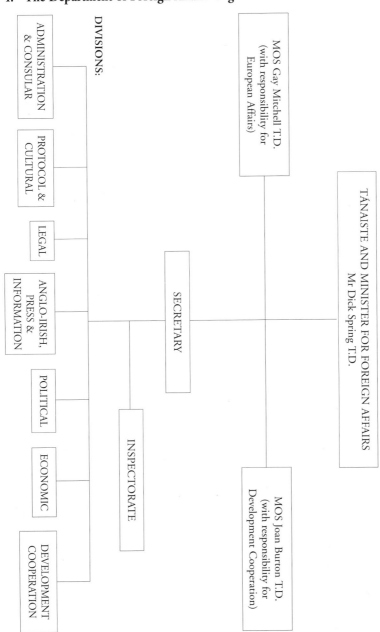

345

5. Ireland's Diplomatic Network

Location of Resident Embassy	Country of Primary Accreditation	Country(ies) of Secondary Accreditation
Buenos Aires	Argentina	Chile Venezuela Uruguay
Canberra	Australia	Indonesia New Zealand
Vienna[1]	Austria	Slovak Republic Slovenia
Brussels[2]	Belgium	–
Ottawa	Canada	–
Beijing	China	Cambodia Philippines
Prague	Czech Republic	Ukraine
Copenhagen	Denmark	Iceland Norway
Cairo	Egypt	Jordan West Bank/Gaza Lebanon Syria Sudan
Addis Ababa	Ethopia	–
Helsinki	Finland	Estonia
Paris[3]	France	–
Bonn	Germany	–
Athens	Greece	Albania Cyprus Israel Romania
Holy See	Holy See	–
Budapest	Hungary	Bulgaria
New Delhi	India	Singapore Bangladesh Sri Lanka
Tehran	Iran	Pakistan
Rome	Italy	Libya Malta San Marino Turkey
Tokyo	Japan	–